Sticky Outcomes!
at the Intersection of Coaching, Neuroscience, & Lasting Change

Praise for *Sticky Outcomes!*

Sticky Outcomes is refreshing. It isn't about learning coaching skills but, instead, about how coaching works. Lyssa deHart provides a crash course in human psychology and highlights the many ways that it is at the heart of coaching. She draws on neuroscience, clinical psychology, communications, and other sources to reveal the inner workings of change. In doing so, *Sticky Outcomes* mirrors the coaching process itself: she invites readers to reflect on and experiment with their practice. deHart provides transcripts of her own coaching as well as refreshingly honest appraisals. She isn't here to wow you with her brilliance but, instead, to model the humility, awareness, and intentionality that lie at the heart of coaching. This book is essential for coaches looking to understand and apply coaching skills.

Dr. Robert Biswas-Diener, author of *Positive Provocation*

I refer to Lyssa deHart's work frequently to add creative and essential dimensions to the coaching skills I use and teach. Her research and transcripts of coaching sessions give depth to *Sticky Outcomes* that make the book a useful guide to refer to frequently on your coaching journey. As deHart says, have the courage to stay present when coaching. Let the thinker you are working with create the dots, connect the dots, and own the dots, and you will be amazed at the insights and wisdom that emerge.

Dr. Marcia Reynolds, MCC, author of the international bestseller *Coach the Person, Not the Problem* and *Breakthrough Coaching*

Sticky Outcomes gets to the heart of what makes change last. Lyssa deHart blends science, compassion, and real coaching experience in a way that feels grounded and encouraging. She shows how psychological safety, partnership, and the ICF Core Competencies all come together to create conversations that truly transform. If you're committed to helping your clients grow in meaningful, lasting ways, this book will resonate deeply.

Valorie Burton, MS, MAPP, MCC, CEO of The Coaching and Positive Psychology (CaPP) Institute and author of *Rules of Resilience: 10 ways Successful People Get Better, Wiser and Stronger*

Sticky Outcomes is a tour de force. Lyssa deHart blends multidisciplinary insight, practical tools, and lived experience to ground readers in coaching's core competencies. Her coach–client dialogues arrive precisely when you want to see her teaching in action, and her "Choice Points" highlight the creative coaching possibilities inherent in every conversation. This book is sure to become a coaching classic—don't miss it.

Carrie Sackett, MS, PCC, author of *Social Therapeutic Coaching: A Practical Guide to Group and Couples Work*

Lyssa deHart masterfully bridges the science and soul of coaching. *Sticky Outcomes* is a love letter to the art of true partnership in coaching. deHart's journey from 'fixing' to facilitating is one every coach must make, and she guides us there with science, stories, and soul. Her focus on client-led direction, metaphor, and vertical development makes this essential reading for anyone committed to coaching that creates lasting change. *Sticky Outcomes* will deepen your practice and remind you why this work matters.

Betsy Salkind, PCC and **Amy Warshawsky, MS, MCC**, co-authors of *Coaching with a Twist: Improv for Coaches*

Lyssa deHart has an uncanny ability to spot the stories people are living inside of and then open the kind of conversation that helps them see the choices they didn't realize were already available to them. In *Sticky Outcomes*, she offers, with the precision of a master coach, a practical way to work with the beliefs that drive our behavior and shows us how transformation happens when the thinker does the thinking. After reading *Sticky Outcomes*, you walk away with a profound understanding of what great coaching requires and a strong sense of your own agency. It's an essential read for coaches, both for its depth and, more importantly, because it reminds us why this work matters in the first place."

Jon Rosemberg, MBA, PCC, author of *A Guide to Thriving*

*Sticky Outcome*s is a fresh and dynamic contribution to our field of coaching! Lyssa deHart's body of work offers a brilliant leap forward in presenting the evolution of consciousness that we are experiencing today in our field of coaching and personal/professional development. You will be empowered by this literary masterpiece.

Fran Fisher, MCC, author of *Calling Forth Greatness*

I just want to say WOW! This is a resource I really wish I had when I started coach training. *Sticky Outcomes* offers a refreshing, grounded approach to professional coaching that goes beyond surface level techniques. Lyssa deHart masterfully integrates neuroscience, emotional intelligence, and decades of practical experience into a comprehensive guide that treats coaching as both art and science.

What sets this book apart is her commitment to partnership over fixing, and her insistence that coaches develop themselves as their primary tool. She demystifies the ICF Core Competencies through real transcripts, relatable examples, and her signature metaphor work, making complex concepts accessible without dumbing them down.

deHart's voice is warm, honest, and occasionally self-deprecating as she shares her own coaching failures alongside successes. Her emphasis on "client-led" coaching, neuroplasticity, and creating psychological safety provides a robust framework for transformational work. It's exactly the book I wish I had when I was studying for my first ICF exam. It's more than a book of information; it's an invitation to grow into the kind of coach who creates lasting change.

Loren Sanders, MBA, PCC, author of *Empathy Is Not a Weakness: And Other Stories from the Edge*

Typical coaching focuses on transactional approaches that address symptoms and taking action for action's sake. In *Sticky Outcomes*, Lyssa deHart takes you beneath the surface to learn how to ask powerful questions that uncover root causes, leading to deeper and sustained insight and transformation for clients. Instead of our tendency as coaches to be "doers," Lyssa helps us learn to be "be-ers" and create more ease, trust, and responsiveness to handle even the toughest coaching conversations.

Using a combination of science, anecdotes, and prose (and of course, metaphors!), deHart provides simple, clear guidance that teaches to the MCC level. Whether you're a new or seasoned coach, you'll be able to immediately apply her concepts and take your coaching to the next level.

David Franklin, MA, MCC, Director of Education for the HeArt of Laser-Focused Coaching

Sticky Outcomes is more than a coaching book. It is a reminder of what actually creates change. Lyssa deHart shows that the real power is not in clever techniques or perfectly crafted questions. It is in presence. Curiosity. Paying deep attention. She uses the word "thinker" in a way that shifts the whole frame. Suddenly the work becomes less about fixing and more about witnessing someone open up in real time. If you want to coach with more depth, more courage, and more humanity, this book will set you up to do so.

Peter Reek, MSc, PCC, author of *Shift: 7 Mindsets for an Inspired Midlife*

Sticky Outcomes is the kind of business book every leader should read. Lyssa deHart combines a great blend of theory, philosophy, science, and actual experience while staying grounded in the very real application of effectively coaching towards transformation. Her writing is humorous and digestible, punctuated by poignant metaphors and real-life examples throughout. She demystifies the balance between the art and science that goes into the practice of coaching with humility, humor, and intentionality. In a nutshell, *Sticky Outcomes* is a must-read for anyone looking to either begin or upgrade their coaching skills.

Marissa Waldman, CEO, Leaderology, developing fearlessly authentic leaders who change the world

Sticky Outcomes!

at the Intersection of Coaching, Neuroscience, & Lasting Change

Lyssa deHart, LICSW, MCC

©2026 Lyssa deHart

All Rights Reserved. No part of this book may be used or reproduced in any manner whatsoever—other than for "fair use" as brief quotations in articles and reviews —without the express written permission of the author.

Published by: Barn Swallow Publishing

Address all inquiries to:
Barn Swallow Publishing
BarnSwallowPub@gmail.com

The author of this book is not dispensing medical advice or prescribing the use of any technique as a form of treatment for mental, emotional, physical or medical problems. The reader is responsible for appropriate medical care with their doctor or therapist. The intent of the author is only to offer information to support getting curious about metaphors and how they show up in the work of coaches and therapists. The information is for you alone. The author and the publisher assume no responsibility for how you use the information.

Library of Congress Control Number - 2026900089

Paperback - 978-1-948317-05-4

eBook - 978-1-948317-06-1

Editor: Kirkus Editing Team
Cover Designer: Lyssa deHart
Interior Book Layout: Lyssa deHart
Author Photo: Lyssa deHart
Cover Image and all Art and Diagrams: Lyssa deHart

Every attempt has been made to source properly all research material and quotes.

First Edition :
10 9 8 7 6 5 4 3 2 1

Printed in the United States of America

Contents

Preface	xi
1. Beyond the Checkboxes	1
2. The Road to Mastery	7
3. Why I Don't Teach to ACC	15
4. Getting Started with Transcript Analysis	19
5. From Client to Thinker	25
6. Coaching Roots	37
7. Coaching as Crafted Partnering	51
8. How We Learn	57
9. Breaking Down the Competencies	77
10. The First Bookend of Every Coaching Conversation	87
11. Shifting from Fixing to Partnering	97
12. The Other Book End	109
13. Safety the Foundation for Courage & Growth	121
14. Presence is a Practice	137
15. Listening Isn't Waiting to Speak	145
16. Coaching Is Both Brain-Based & Meaning-Making	159
17. Awareness Follows Where Questions Lead	177
18. Emotional Intelligence is a Mindset	189
19. Tuning into Metaphors	205
20. The Wild Wild West	219
21. Purposeful Play	235
22. Continuing Your Coach Development	243
A Big Thank You!	249
References	251
About Lyssa	267

For Elsa
You set me on a curious path,
and it has led me to some very
interesting places.
Thank you.

PREFACE

> Give a man a fish and feed him for a day,
> teach a man to fish, and feed him for his life.
>
> —Anne Thackeray Ritchie

Coaching is not about having the perfect questions or being the perfect coach. If anything, the longer I've coached executives, leaders, and ordinary people, the more convinced I am that learning to bring your whole self as a thought partner into the conversation leads to better outcomes and lasting change. I'm also convinced that an obsession with perfect questions, tools, and "getting it right" can get in the way. Perfection kills presence. Prescribed questions tempt you to sound perfect, leaning on formulas for safety. This book is about learning what it takes to show up fully present.

I've done this myself in YouTube videos, and the ones I scripted were wooden. Unless you're acting, leave scripts aside. This doesn't mean we abandon the coaching framework or structure; an effective coach understands the grounded framework that holds the container of a coaching conversation. Leaders aren't looking for you to be perfect. Whether they know it or not, they need you to be fully present and to support them as they explore what's between where they are and where they want to go.

For example, when the president of a corporate division came to our coaching session after being told, with no warning, that a vice president had to be fired by the end of the week, there wasn't a script that could have prepared me for the intensity of that moment. The executive was anxious, overwhelmed, and stuck. My job wasn't to tell them what to do, nor was it to build a step-by-step plan.

Sticky Outcomes!

I was there to listen and be curious on their behalf. My job was to sit with the tension, be with them, and offer the space they needed to slow down and breathe.

They needed one simple question: "Given the circumstances, what's the very first thing you need to focus on right now?"

Then I waited. The calm and the pause gave them the chance to find their own clarity and begin the conversation they needed to have.

In another session, a founder sat stuck, looking at three options: sell one company, grow another, or try to keep both and juggle them as best they could. We could have gone down the rabbit hole of pros and cons. Overwhelmed by the magnitude and implications of each decision point, he just couldn't make a simple decision; there were too many parts.

Instead, I asked, "Do you buy every outfit you try on?"

"No," came the immediate reply.

"When you try an outfit on, what do you do next?"

He responded, "I look in the mirror and then decide if I want to walk around in it."

My response: "What if you tried on each choice like an outfit and walked around in it?"

This perspective took the pressure off the decisions. He didn't have to decide right away; he could try on all the options and see how each felt, not just how each looked on paper. Over time, their decision-making stopped being about fear and became more aligned with what felt comfortable to wear. This approach allowed them to align their decision-making process with their personal values.

And then there was the vice president of sales who prided himself on serving his customers above all else, yet whose team felt unseen and unvalued. I wasn't there to knock his loyalty to his customers.

What I did was ask, "How do you treat your team compared to your customers?"

First there was quiet, then a lightbulb moment: "I treat them

Preface

very differently."

That single insight led to his new leadership goal.

He got excited and said, "I treat my team like I treat my customers."

A way of being that reshaped how this leader showed up for his people and, ultimately, how the team showed up for the organization.

These moments remind me why I wrote this book. *Sticky Outcomes* is about what it takes to be the sort of thought partner people need as they navigate complexity and work toward outcomes that have sticking power.

And while coaching isn't about following rules, you still need to understand the basics. Mozart practiced his scales, and Picasso drew lines until he mastered the fundamentals. Only then could they improvise, innovate, and transform their art. Coaching is no different. The International Coaching Federation (ICF) Core Competencies represent a set of structures. They are the foundation you need in order to develop your own authentic voice as a coach. For the full and official ICF Core Competencies, visit www.coachingfederation.org and search "Core Competencies" to download the current version.

You'll hear me use the word "thinker" instead of "client." I explore Nancy Kline's work in chapter 5, "From Client to Thinker." For now, know that it's the language I use most often to describe the client.

This book isn't about being a perfect coach; it's about real conversations, sometimes messy, sometimes deep, and sometimes filled with "ahas." It's about coaching conversations that invite leaders at every level to pause the noise, hear themselves clearly, and leave not with your answers but with their own insights and actions. That is what it means to get to sticky outcomes.

Why Me?

My path into leadership and confidence coaching wasn't planned. I was a recovering trauma therapist, and after almost twenty years, I was looking for new ways of being with people. I completed my original coach training in 2007–08, which opened up new possibilities for me.

Sticky Outcomes!

The more I worked with leaders, the more I recognized that, at the end of the day, executives, founders, and entrepreneurs are people. And I knew how to work with people. And these people came into coaching to talk about business challenges, yet their humanness always emerged. They brought their fears, doubts, values, blind spots, and their moments of overwhelm and joy.

I know what it is to build something from the ground up. I built my own business from a little shared office in Albuquerque, New Mexico, into something that allows me to work with the world. This gave me a window into the struggles that leaders wrestle with daily: the weight of responsibility, the balancing of priorities, and the sheer determination it takes to keep moving forward when the way isn't clear.

I have never run a division of a multibillion-dollar international company. I didn't need to have that experience to be useful. What I am able to do is put myself in the leader's shoes, getting a felt sense of what they might be wrestling with. Call it emotional intelligence or empathy, and I allowed myself to feel into what they were sharing. This vantage point lets me use what I know, not as expertise to hand them answers, but as experience to inform my curiosity. It shaped the kinds of questions I asked and the degree to which my curiosity supported their awareness.

Coaching, I have come to learn, isn't about being the smartest person in the room or knowing what a leader "should" do. My value was in bringing fresh eyes that opened windows and doors the leader hadn't yet considered.

In a conversation with a colleague in 2017, she said, "People spend 80 percent of their time at work, working or thinking about work. How leaders show up matters. It matters to employees, to the business, to innovation, and it ripples out into everyone's personal life, affecting their health and how they engage with their communities."

As I nodded, she continued, "Lyssa, we aren't coaching just one person; in leadership and organizational coaching, we are impacting a system."

That struck me deeply because it clarified why this work matters. Coaching leaders is about creating healthier systems so that people can thrive. For me, that means supporting positive ripples that extend far beyond the coaching conversation. This was confirmed in an interview I did on *the Coaching Studio* podcast with Professor

Preface

Peter Hawkins (2026), where he made a very important case that we are all part of systems within systems. And to solve the world's issues, we must think about our work from a systemic lens.

In this book, we will look at the ICF Core Competencies not as rules for coaching but as a powerful framework for working with human beings. Along the way, I will invite you to play with the competencies because they give us a clear, grounded, and effective way to partner with people.

What I Wish for You

Whether you are a beginning coach or a seasoned one, my wish is that you expand your ability to understand how to work with human beings. I hold a fundamental belief that coaching is a learned skill. Reflecting on my background as a trauma therapist, I realize how understanding coaching could have enhanced my work in the mental health field. I was a good therapist. I could have been better.

As a mentor once said to me, "Lyssa, if you aren't learning new things that you wish you had known before, you are going in the wrong direction."

I fully resonate with this, and it has led me to adopt a growth mindset that continues to support my personal and professional development. Regardless of background or profession, coaching skills make us better human beings, full stop.

Here is a truth: when you dedicate yourself to helping others grow, you inevitably discover that you, too, must do your own work. Coaching, like many professions, can let you stay in a superficial, problem-solving, transactional place. If you want to cultivate transformation and truly teach others to fish, it calls for self-awareness, courage, and a willingness to do your own work. It asks you to keep looking inward, to build on your self-awareness, and to cultivate the humility that allows you to truly partner with another human being.

> We are not fish mongers, we're fishing & adventure guides.

There is a place of humility, insight, and awareness you will

Sticky Outcomes!

find, one that helps you create the conditions that allow others to do their most important work: standing next to them, but not doing it for them. Ultimately, the purpose of a coaching conversation is to create a safe place for struggle and breakthrough, for the questions that matter, and for the courage needed to make change.

So here is my request of you:

- Step into this work with bravery.
- Commit to your growth.
- Hold up the mirror so your thinkers can see themselves.
- Ask questions that open doors to insights.

I hope you see this book as an invitation to grow into your fullest capacity as a curious thought partner. May you discover, session by session, how to trust yourself, trust the wisdom of the people you coach, and trust the process that creates partnership. Coaching with presence, courage, self-awareness, and compassion contributes to making this world a better place.

Lyssa deHart
Bainbridge Island, WA
January 2026

CHAPTER ONE

BEYOND THE CHECKBOXES

> "The real voyage of discovery consists not in seeking new landscapes, but in having new eyes."
> —Marcel Proust

Whether you're stepping into coaching for the very first time or you're a seasoned leader wanting to bring coaching into your way of leading, this journey begins with a simple truth: coaching is a partnership. And like any meaningful partnership, it rests on trust—trust in your thinker, trust in yourself, and trust in the process itself.

This guide is your first companion on that path. Think of it as both a map that lays out the terrain ahead and a mirror that reflects back to you the kind of coach you have the capacity to become. Inside this book, you'll find the deeper principles that support coaching becoming transformative.

Before we proceed, it's important to clarify that this guide is not about becoming a 'check-the-box' coach. Here, we don't rush to fix or solve. We slow down to listen; instead of leading with answers, we partner with powerful questions. We learn to stay curious, to notice what's alive in the moment, and to trust that awareness itself has the potential to open up new ways to explore and will often lead to answers that we would never have expected.

This book is grounded in the International Coaching Federation (ICF) Core Coaching Competencies, and it's also rooted in something less tangible: the belief that coaching is a relational art. People grow in safe and brave spaces, and your way of being is your most transformational tool. So, while I may discuss the competencies at times, I'm going to share the behaviors and examples of how we are being in our capacity as a coach. These ideas will work for you if you are a parent, a manager, an entrepreneur, a leader, or if you decide to become a professional coach.

You'll Learn How To

- Understand the value of clear agreements
- Create trust and psychological safety
- Maintain presence, even when things get messy
- Listen with your whole self to another human being's whole experience
- Evoke awareness through curiosity and inquiry
- Support sustainable, client-owned growth
- Explore how the brain changes, how the nervous system regulates, and how metaphors can unlock meaning

And, hopefully, learn how to have fun while doing good work.

Before we dive into the heart of coaching, it helps to get your footing. These first practices aren't busywork; they're the structure that will support you as you play, experiment, stretch, and grow. Think of them as tools for your coaching toolbox, the essentials.

Recording Yourself

One of the most useful and humbling practices you'll take on is recording yourself. At first, it might feel uncomfortable, though some people enjoy the sound of their own voice. I personally get annoyed with my questions; they're often better in my memory than they are when I hear them in the recording. Yet listening to our recordings is a form of biofeedback. It grounds us in reality and gives us real data—what was said, what was asked, the energy in the room, tone, timing, and where the questions led the thinker.

Raenotes

Raenotes is one of my favorite tools for looking at transcripts, reflecting on my work, and providing feedback. You'll use it to upload your recordings, markup the transcripts, and notice emerging coaching skills. You'll also start tracking your choice points, the moments where you could have asked one question but went with another. Even when you love your questions, come up with several more options; this is how we develop our ability to get comfortable asking open-ended questions that benefit the human being we're working with. Over time, those little moments of awareness change the way you listen and shape how you partner with your thinkers.

Learning Triads

Another key part of development is coaching in triads. In these small groups, you'll take turns being the coach, the thinker, and the observer. Each role gives you a different view. In the coach seat, you practice. In the thinker seat, you feel what it's like to be coached. When you're in the observer seat, you begin to catch things you might have missed—the shifts in tone, the moments that land, the silence that opens something new.

In *The Artist's Way*, Julia Cameron said, "It's impossible to get better and look good at the same time," so no judgments needed as you play with what is possible.

If you are not in a coaching program that offers triads, find friends who are also working on becoming coaches and form your own development triad. Three people is a minimum, as it gives each person a different coach/thought partner and a different client/thinker. Plus, there is always an observer to share things we might miss when we are in the thick of a coaching conversation.

Reflective Practice Journal

Coaching isn't just about what you do. It's also about who you are. That's why I encourage you to keep a reflective journal. Some people write every day. Others jot a few notes after a session. The format doesn't matter; the habit of capturing your learning is what matters. A journal illuminates insights, tracks hooks, and exposes discomfort, and allows you to play with who you are as a coach. You will most likely capture the moments that surprise you.

Sticky Outcomes!

So, What Is Coaching?

According to Sir John Whitmore, coaching is "Partnering with clients in a thought-provoking and creative process that inspires them to maximize their personal and professional potential" (Whitmore 1992).

Let's break that down:

In partnering, coaching isn't something done to or for someone; it's something done with them. Coaching is about fostering thought-provoking conversations in which we invite awareness; it's not the place to offer ready-made solutions, or even our opinions on what the thinkers should do.

> Maximizing potential = a focus on growth & forward movement

What Coaching Is Not

Many people come to coaching from roles where advising, treating, or managing others has been the norm. It's vital to clearly distinguish coaching from other helping modalities:

Professional Roles: A Framework

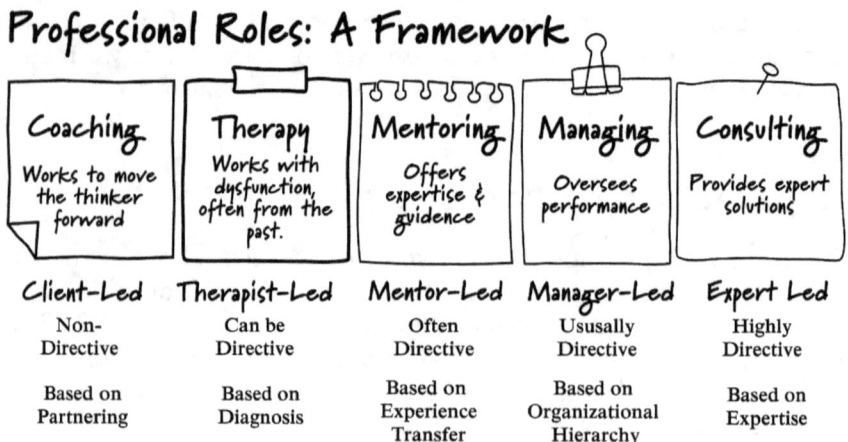

Coaching	Therapy	Mentoring	Managing	Consulting
Works to move the thinker forward	Works with dysfunction, often from the past.	Offers expertise & guidance	Oversees performance	Provides expert solutions
Client-Led	Therapist-Led	Mentor-Led	Manager-Led	Expert Led
Non-Directive	Can be Directive	Often Directive	Ususally Directive	Highly Directive
Based on Partnering	Based on Diagnosis	Based on Experience Transfer	Based on Organizational Hierarchy	Based on Expertise

Coaching may touch on similar content, such as emotions, values, decisions, or relationships, but the approach to these topics is fundamentally different from that of other modalities. This is why clarity matters. As coaches, part of the job is to maintain the distinctions between coaching, consulting, psychotherapy and other support professions.

Coaching the Person, Not the Problem

In her book *Coach the Person, Not the Problem*, Dr. Marcia Reynolds points out that when people come to us, they **almost always** bring what looks like a problem to solve.

- "I need a plan."
- "I don't know how to talk to my boss."
- "I'm overwhelmed by all my priorities."
- "I need next steps for XYZ."

It can feel natural, even helpful, to dive in, offer suggestions, or structure steps. But Reynolds's point is that **the "problem" is rarely the real issue.** And I have found this to be true from my experience as well.

If we stay at the level of the situation or problem, we are coaching symptoms. The deeper work of coaching happens when we listen for the assumptions, beliefs, and stories that give rise to the problem in the first place. As Reynolds writes, the real gift of coaching is not in solving what's on the surface, but in helping people see themselves differently.

This is where coaching distinguishes itself from consulting, advising, or mentoring. Consultants solve problems. Advisers provide expertise. Mentors share knowledge. What coaches do is create a reflective space where the thinker can pause, hear themselves, and surface what is driving their choices, fears, or stuckness. Reynolds calls this reflective inquiry, mirroring back not just the words but also the emotions, shifts, and inconsistencies the thinker may not notice on their own.

A leader comes into coaching convinced they need tips for time management. But what unfolds is not a lack of time management skills, rather a deeper belief, "If I don't do it all myself, it won't get completed perfectly."

Sticky Outcomes!

Once that belief emerges in the conversation, then we can really explore what is impacting the management of time. We might discuss beliefs around delegation, trust, and capacity building that no checklist of productivity hacks could possibly unlock.

Sure, giving advice feels good; we feel helpful. Yet—and this is strong language—***we're stealing another person's opportunity to learn.*** When we give room for the thinker to uncover their drivers of behaviors, actions, and outcomes, they discover for themselves what they need to learn and focus on.

CHAPTER TWO

THE ROAD TO MASTERY

> Mastery is not a function of genius or talent.
> It is a function of time and intense focus
> applied to a particular field of knowledge.
>
> —Robert Greene

If you're going after an International Coaching Federation (ICF) credential, you've probably wondered what really shifts between the credential levels of Associate Certified Coach (ACC), Professional Certified Coach (PCC), and Master Certified Coach (MCC). While the learning hours, coaching hours, and recordings are essential, the challenge can be in developing your mindset and approach to coaching. Ask yourself, what changes as you develop, show up, and create the container of a coaching conversation? My guess is that it's the mindset you carry into your practice.

Carly Anderson, MCC, a coach I admire, inspired me to think about this developmental arc in a new way. Carly uses the analogy of "Helicopter Coaching" in her article of the same title, to describe the shift from skillful to masterful coaching (Anderson 2019). Her words inspired me to craft my own analogy for how coaches grow, using something I am familiar with: **driving.**

Driving School → Road Trip → Embodied Travel → Tada!

Okay, there is a little more to it. Let's take a look.

Driving School

At the ACC level, you are working at a driving school, and you are an instructor. You may even be the best instructor. You've studied the manual, and your focus is on making sure you are applying these ideas correctly in your coaching. Like any good driving instructor, you're sitting beside the thinker with a second steering wheel, blinker, and your own brake, just in case.

Picture this: you ask a question, and when the thinker pauses, you feel that desire to jump in and either ask another question because maybe they didn't understand or explain the question. When they answer, it could feel like they are taking a left turn; in your mind, they need to go right. You gently redirect them back to the stated goal or offer another question to keep things moving. The session feels contained because you're holding the controls, and if needed, you can jump in to keep the conversation on track.

At this stage, you're in practice mode, plain and simple, trying the competencies on, using the structure, staying in the lines. It can feel like you're working hard to be a good coach.

The Road Trip

By the time you reach PCC, the dynamics are changing. Fingers crossed, you are no longer the driving instructor; you have morphed into a passenger. The thinker is fully in control of the steering wheel and the radio, and you are sitting next to them as the thought partner.

Imagine this: the thinker suddenly takes an unexpected turn down a side road you didn't notice. Instead of steering them back to the original path, you get curious about what's happening. You might ask, *"What feels important about this turn?"* What is clear is that you have let go of the wheel; but you're noticing the landscape with them, whether the road feels bumpy or smooth. You hear a rattle, and you are willing to ask these sorts of questions, co-discovering what's important to the thinker and exploring where the road might lead.

At PCC, you're fully present. You're watching, listening, and noticing not only what's being said, but *how* it's being said, and powerful beliefs that are emerging. You might reflect something back or ask a question that helps the thinker choose where to head next. The big shift is partnership. You're not only tuned into what the thinker wants to do, but also who they want to be as they're doing it. You trust their pace and their choices enough to let them lead you through what they believe is important.

Becoming the Vehicle

At the MCC level, there is a huge shift. You're not the driving instructor anymore, sitting there with a second brake and wheel just in case. You're not really the passenger either, pointing out turns or keeping an eye on the map. What starts to happen is that you begin to take the role of the vehicle or vessel that holds the conversation.

Think about it this way. When you head out to your car and get in, you start it, and off you go. The car doesn't tell you where you should drive. If you've got a GPS on, the map may give you a list of turns, but the car itself doesn't argue if you suddenly cut through a neighborhood or decide to take a back road instead. The car goes where you lead, following your direction wherever you decide to go.

That's the kind of partnership that shows up in MCC coaching. The coach becomes the vehicle, simply holding that container of trust and curiosity so the thinker can do the navigating. Sure, you may notice a sign on the side of the road and bring it into awareness with such questions as *"What was that sigh?"* Or *"What have you learned about yourself?"* But this comes from what the thinker is already seeing or saying, not from your own agenda about where they should be going.

Imagine the thinker sitting in silence, thirty seconds, maybe more. You can see the wheels turning, and instead of jumping in the way you might have done earlier in your development, you let them process.

By the time you're coaching at this level, your questions sound different. They are often very simple, coming from deep listening, and they are offered in a way that helps the thinker turn inward to look at what they're learning about themselves, their situation, and the meaning that's emerging for them. They're creating their own dots, connecting those dots, and taking ownership of what emerges.

The important piece here is that the thinker is the one driving.

Fran Fisher, MCC, says "Coaching isn't being *done to them* or *done for them*, it's happening *with* them" (Fisher 2021). And the vehicle that carries them, the curiosity, the presence, the silence, the partnership, that's you.

Sticky Outcomes!

Why This Matters

At each stage, there is value. Yet each level represents a deepening relationship with trust. At ACC, you are learning to trust yourself. At PCC, you are learning to trust the thinker. At MCC, you embody trust in the process itself. This unfolding is the real path of development.

This is also true of the thinker. Not every thinker is ready to be fully autonomous; we may all find ourselves moving between the levels to meet the thinker where they are. But my caution to you is this: don't assume that the thinker needs more guidance. Start by giving less and let them surprise you.

Comparing the Three Levels

Level	Coach Role	Partnering	Directionality	Thinker Experience
ACC	Instructor	Developing	More coach directed	Guided support
PCC	Passenger	Collaborative	Co-created direction	Empowered choice
MCC	The Vehicle	Embodied, fluid, + partnering	Fully client lead	Autonomy + insight

Progression Matters

These levels mark the journey of learning within your development. The movement from unconscious incompetence to unconscious competence.

This progression is reflected in how you practice and develop this craft of coaching through the lens of the competencies. Note the following examples:

→ **Unconscious Competence**
I now know & can do with confidence

→ **Conscious Competence**
I have to think & spend energy to be competent

→ **Conscious Incompetence**
I now know what I don't know

→ **Unconscious Incompetence**
I don't even know what I don't know

o Establish and hold agreements (Competency 3) You get clearer (and more consistent) about partnering on what the thinker wants to accomplish, and what success looks like in the conversation.

o Use silence and presence (Competencies 4 & 5) Silence stops being awkward and becomes space you intentionally create, so the thinker can hear themselves think.

o Evoke awareness without attachment (Competency 7) You can offer an observation, knowledge, or a feeling without needing the thinker to take it, agree with it, or do anything with it at all.

o Celebrate the thinker's ownership of growth (Competency 8) You notice progress and ask about it, in a way that reinforces the thinkers autonomy and momentum.

Credentialing Paths at a Glance

To earn an ICF credential, you'll need a mix of training, practice, and assessment:

Level	Training Hours	Coaching Hours	Mentor Hours	Perform eval	Exam
ACC	60+ hours	100 hrs	10 hrs	1 recorded session	ACC exam
PCC	125+ hours	500 hrs	10 hrs	2 recorded sessions	PCC/MCC exam
MCC	200+ hours	2500 hrs	10 hrs	2 recorded sessions	PCC/MCC exam

Note: Each level can be earned through the **Level 1, 2, 3, or Portfolio paths**, depending on the type of coach education you've completed. Always check with your school and read your paperwork and certificate of completion.

Sticky Outcomes!

Your Toolkit Begins with You...

The foundation of coaching isn't a specific model of coaching, or a specific "coaching tool," or even the latest framework. It's you. *You are the tool.* Who you are, how you show up, and how much you're willing to be in partnership, using what you know to inform your curiosity.

Trust begins in three directions:

O **Trust in the thinker.** Believe that they are whole, resourceful, capable, and creative. They don't need you to fix them; they need you to hold space for them to discover their own answers.

O **Trust in yourself.** You're learning, which means you'll get things "wrong" sometimes. A clumsy question, a missed moment, it all becomes material for growth if you're willing to reflect and keep going.

O **Trust in the process.** Awareness leads to choice, and choice leads to change. Coaching works because insight belongs to the thinker, and this ownership makes it sustainable.

In 2018, I had just gotten my MCC and I already scheduled to give a live coaching "Fishbowl" demonstration. Only now was I coming into the Fishbowl Event as an MCC, not a PCC. I was a little nervous—okay, a lot nervous. They asked for names, then drew my coaching partner's name. We met, then sat down in front of more than 150 eyeballs.

It was the hardest experience of my life. Here I was, a newly minted MCC, and the coaching conversation sounded a lot like it was going in circles:

I asked, "What would you like to coach on today?"

Client, "I don't know, what do you think we should talk about?"

I said, "I don't know, it's your coaching, what would be important for you?"

Client, "I don't know, what do you think?"

It just went on like this for fifteen minutes; my face was hot, and

Road to Mastery

I had a stinky sweat going. It felt like a lifetime with all those eyeballs staring at me.

Someone even asked, "Is this even coaching?"

"No, no, it was not," was my instant thought as my face turned red.

The feedback was fine; this was an example of a coach working really hard to give the client autonomy, blah, blah, blah. That was about all I remembered of the feedback.

When I was preparing to leave at the end of the event, I was chatting with one of the MCC assessors, Fran Fisher, who had given me feedback. I mentioned how hard that experience had been.

Fran said, "It's okay, Lyssa, everybody bombs sometimes..."

"Wait, *What?* I **bombed?**"

I sat with this for days, okay, probably weeks. But it has proven to be one of my best learning moments. I would handle that sort of situation completely differently today:

New me, "What would you like to coach on today?"

Client, "I don't know, what do you think we should talk about?"

New me, "I don't know, it's your coaching, what would be important for you?"

Client, "I don't know, what do you think?"

New me, "Well, there seems to be a pattern of my asking you to name for yourself the focus, and you're asking me what it should be, and I wonder if that pattern shows up anywhere else, and if that might be important to talk about?"

That's how I would handle that situation today. But I wouldn't have gotten there without walking through the fire of that bomb.

CHAPTER THREE

Why I Don't Teach to ACC

> Coaching is unlocking people's potential to maximize their own growth.
>
> —Sir John Whitmore

Many programs are designed to get coaches just far enough to pass the ACC credential. A safe baseline. A starting point. But I don't teach that way, and here's why.

ACC-level coaching is valuable, and it's where most of us begin to learn the craft. But it's also the entry point, or the first mile marker. If our learning stops there, we are only scratching the surface of what coaching can be: a life-changing experience leading to new and, hopefully, important places of discovery.

You didn't pick up this book just to check the boxes. You are reading this because you want to partner in a real way. You want that dopamine hit when the person in front of you lights up on a new insight or profound awareness that matters in how they will move forward in their life. You want to support changes that stick, helping leaders and people thrive in the overwhelming and complex world we find ourselves in. And you want to be an agent for positive change, I can feel it... Okay, that was a lot of projection on my part, but that is what I am deeply hoping is important to you. So, sit with all that, and see if it resonates.

Coaching is Developmental

Learning to become a coach is about so much more than just asking questions. On a personal level, it's about becoming, growing as both a person and a professional. It's often said that we cannot hold the space for things we haven't worked on in ourselves. Our stuff will inevitably show up with our thinkers. If I am uncomfortable with messy emotions, trust me, those messy emotions are going to show up regardless.

If I am strongly opinionated and walk through the world with a lot of certainty about what I believe, I am definitely going to find that other people in the world think in many different ways. And part of our growth and development is in learning to expand ourselves and our comfort with discomfort.

This is why I teach beyond the ACC level. Yes, you'll build a strong foundation there, but then we'll keep going. Past any formulas, past the safety of the "right" questions, jumping into the deeper waters where coaching transforms into partnership and real change. A place where your Thinkers feel seen, heard, and empowered—not managed, directed, or rescued.

Mile Markers, Not Destinations

Credentials are milestones, not finish lines. I sometimes think of myself as an old Toyota truck. I want to be the kind of coach who has 250,000 miles, maybe even 300,000 miles, on me before I'm done. And here's the thing: even at the MCC level, we're only talking about 2,500 hours of coaching and 200 hours of coach training. If you were a car, you wouldn't even get a discount at 2,500 miles; that's basically brand new. So even at MCC, I believe we are still beginners. I have chosen to adopt a beginner's mindset; every day is a school day. And I hope that the idea of a beginner's mindset stays with you for the rest of your life as well.

This is why I believe that your capacity to coach grows with your personal development. You begin to trust yourself. You no longer need to overanalyze every question or chase the "perfect" question. Instead, you shift your focus, keeping your eyes on the partnership.

Coaching isn't about getting to a single mile marker and then parking the car; it's about keeping yourself on the road, mile after mile, growing into the kind of coach who never stops growing and learning. Coaching is a skillset; being a good coach takes dedication to honing your craft.

You're Not Here to Stay Small

You're probably here because you feel the call to make a real impact. I know that for myself, when I was a waitress, I wanted to ask a more important question than, "How would you like that cooked?" That restlessness pushed me toward social work. I wanted to have conversations that mattered, conversations that could change lives. I wanted to be part of the solution and not a part of the problem. I also wanted to do the work that would help me become a better person. One who could leave the people I worked with stronger, braver, and connected to their own wisdom and ultimately more empowered.

That is a growth-level goal. That is the path I hope you feel invited to explore.

While credentials can be valuable, they are not the sole indicator of a coach's growth and capability. It doesn't matter to me if you have an MCC or an ACC. The letters are just markers of time and work. I have seen beautiful coaching at every level of training; I have also seen the opposite. So, the credential isn't the thing I am focused on; your journey and the development of your understanding about how people work, and how to support them—this is what is important.

What you learn and what you know will show up in your capacity to be a thoughtful partner, in your ability to create space where the work is meaningful, and where the outcomes are sticky, so people can live stronger, better lives.

Activity: Your Road Beyond the First Mile Marker

Take a few minutes and capture the following:

1. Picture yourself five years from now as a coach. Don't focus on titles or credentials; focus on how *you show up*.

    o   How do you want to be with people?

    o   What do you want people to say after being with you?

    o   What strength do you have that you can continue to develop?

Sticky Outcomes!

2. Write down three "mile markers" you hope to pass on that journey. These aren't about hours or certificates. What qualities do you want to embody—patience, courage, presence, curiosity, or something else that matters to you?

3. Finally, choose one of those mile markers. Below, write one small step you could begin practicing *this week* that moves you in that direction.

Chapter Four

Getting Started with Transcript Analysis

> We do not learn from experience...
> we learn from reflecting on experience.
>
> —John Dewey

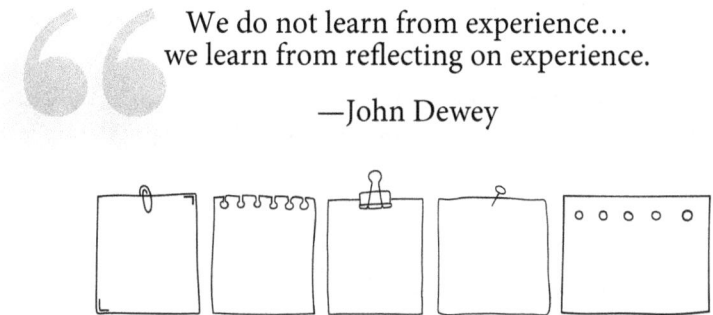

When you first sit down with a transcript, it can feel overwhelming. There are so many words, and really, where are you supposed to focus anyway? How do you listen for the important-sounding parts of what the thinker offered you, and what was your question in response to what they offered?

We don't grow by pretending everything is perfect. Growth comes when we look back with inquisitiveness, with a willingness to notice and get curious about what was really there. Not to judge, but to discover. To ask ourselves: what did my thinker actually say? How did I respond? What else might I have asked?

The practice of transcript analysis is humbling because we all miss things. Over time, I have discovered that this reflective process builds confidence, because once you start reviewing transcripts, you listen differently the next time you're in a live session. It's like weight training for your coaching brain. One lift won't do it. You practice, and with time, you get stronger, steadier, and more flexible when it counts.

Transcript Analysis is the Best Biofeedback

I believe in transcript analysis for one simple reason: our memories lie to us (Doidge 2007). Not on purpose, but they just aren't that reliable. Daniel Schacter, a memory researcher at Harvard, says memory isn't

Sticky Outcomes!

like a hard drive. It's not reproductive, it's reconstructive. More like a living document that gets revised every time we recall it (Schacter 2001). Which is why people are often surprised when a transcript or recording reveals what was actually said, because what we thought we heard, or remembered later, may have been edited, distorted, or even invented by our own brains. When you go back to a recording and a transcript, you get to hear what the thinker actually said, what you actually said, not what you imagined was said. And those two are often very different.

I remember a mentor coaching session years ago. The coach client swore their client never mentioned emotions. They were certain. But the transcript told another story. Right there on the page, clear as day, the client had said how painful the experience was, and the emotions were very visible.

The coach stepped right over the emotions, asking, "So when it comes to your goal today, what's the first thing we want to look at?" When we looked at the transcript, the coach was stunned. They simply hadn't heard it.

This is a very human thing, to remember the parts that sparked our brain. Don't get me started on all the biases our brains have; we will get into those in future chapters. This is what happens when our ears filter out the stuff we aren't listening for, or when we're so focused on our own agenda that we miss something important the thinker just said.

Transcript analysis makes you stop and ask, *Was I really listening? And if I was, what exactly was I listening for? Did the question come from presence, or from the habit of how I tend to listen?* This practice builds awareness. You start noticing: **What did the thinker say? What did I ask back? Was that question in service of them, or was I just checking a box?**

Introducing: Choice Points (CP)

Another piece of transcript work is to investigate what I call choice points. These are not determinations of good or bad; they are simply other questions we might have asked, questions that might have gotten to the heart of what was important to the thinker based on what they had just shared with us.

Getting Started with Transcript Analysis

Here's the thing: you might ask a perfectly great question. You might even love it. For example, "As you shared that, what did you learn about yourself in that moment?" This is a great question; there is nothing wrong with that. But if you stop there, you limit your growth.

Choice points train your brain to come up with two or three other possible questions you could have asked. Not because the first question was bad, but because practice with alternative questions wires your brain for flexibility. You learn to hold multiple ways of responding in your back pocket.

That's the real muscle-building of coaching. It's not about "best" questions. I find that I look at my questions on a scale of usefulness. Some are more useful; some are less so. Yet, by stretching into choice points, you prime your brain to notice and choose the most useful questions in the moment, with your thinker.

For example:

Original Coach Question: "You mentioned feeling a sense of lightness. What would help you keep that feeling as you move forward?"

This is a somewhat leading question. If I want to shift into more client-led questions, then I need to play with how I ask the questions.

Choice Points:

CP: "Are there any specific actions that would support this insight that you're having?"

CP: "What actions would support your insights?"

CP: "You mentioned lightness, what is that telling you?"

Each of these questions will invite the thinker in a slightly different direction. Learning to assess your own questions is a powerful way to learn. Remember, we aren't looking for the "perfect" or "best" questions; we are playing in order to grow.

Activity: Choice Points

Highlight ideas the thinker shares that you might be curious about, and then write up choice points for what your follow-up question might be.

Sticky Outcomes!

Coach: "What is showing up for our coaching conversation today?"

Thinker: "I've recently gotten a promotion and moved to a new department. The work itself feels okay because it's similar to what I've done before, but the big shift is in managing people. I went from leading a team of two to suddenly having about seven direct reports. That feels like a huge stretch.

"What makes it all harder is that I'm younger than most of the team, and sometimes I feel like they don't take me seriously because of my age. Honestly, I've been feeling like an impostor. It's uncomfortable telling people who are older than me what they need to be working on. I'm just trying to make sure I'm communicating well and not shutting down under the pressure of feeling like I don't belong."

Develop three follow-up questions, choice points that might be useful:

CP:

CP:

CP:

This isn't about second-guessing yourself. It's about building your range. Each time you look deeper at what the thinker shared with you, you get another chance to look at the questions you might have asked, or the choice points you could have taken. The more you play, the more you'll catch yourself listening differently in the moment.

Getting Started with Transcript Analysis

Even when you love, and I mean *LOVE*, the question you asked, pause and play with other choices. How else could you have asked? Was there a cleaner, more concise option? Was there a question that could have handed the lead back to the thinker? Or was there a way you could ask with more conscious intention?

That's the gift of this practice, practice, practice. It's not about being perfect. It's about noticing, stretching, and building your coaching muscle so you can show up differently next time.

CHAPTER FIVE

From Client to Thinker

> "The quality of your attention determines the quality of other people's thinking.
> —Nancy Kline

On my podcast, *the Coaching Studio*, I had two interviews with coaches that took place within a month of each other. In both interviews, the guests used the term "thinker," an unfamiliar term to me in the coaching context, which sparked my curiosity. So, down I went into the Google rabbit hole and discovered Nancy Kline's work.

The idea of "thinker" had me questioning the language I was using to describe the human being I was working with. As a therapist, I had used the label of "client" for many years, but this new framework, "thinker," intrigued me.

It wasn't just a mindset shift, but an entire reframing of my perspective of the coaching relationship that resonated with my deeply held belief in humanistic, client-centered coaching. What I called someone mattered because it changed *my* relationship to the work we were doing. If they were the "thinker" and I, the coach, was the "thought partner," then it was clearer to me whose work belonged to whom.

The History of Coaching Language

Back in the day, we called people in therapy "patients," which set up a very specific dynamic. This label came from the medical model when therapy was trying very hard to prove it was more than hocus pocus. So, the nascent field modeled itself on the medical field.

Carl Rogers, of humanistic psychology, helped bring the term "client" into the mainstream with his groundbreaking client-centered therapy in the 1940s. Rogers wanted to move away from the traditional, doctor-patient ideas of relationship, and instead create a more equal partnership. For Rogers, it was about creating collaboration, honoring the individual's desire for a "Good Life" with autonomy and agency in making their own choices. Using the term "client" was a deliberate way to reflect this shift, putting the focus on mutual respect and self-determination (Rogers 2000).

> Agency is the capacity to act, make choices, and influence outcomes while, autonomy is freedom from external control and the ability to self-govern (Dictionary.com 2025).

Yet, as we evolve in the humanistic fields, the term "client," while better than "patient," still carries distinct implications that shape the perceived roles and dynamics within the coaching relationship. If you are at a doctor's office, you are a "patient"; at an attorney's office or a CPA's office, you may be a "client"; in a car showroom, you are probably a "customer." Each of these labels puts you into a different role. In coaching, you will probably hear the person being coached referred to as either a "client" or a "coachee." In each of these professions, the role the professional fills is that of an "expert," supporting, consulting, servicing, and guiding the patient, client, or customer.

Let's Differentiate

In the 1990s, as coaching started to differentiate itself from therapy, its practitioners began looking for a way to describe the "client" in a new, fresh way, and to distinguish that coaching was not therapy or consulting.

The term "coachee" emerged as a way to further distinguish coaching from therapy. Personally, I dislike the term "coachee." The diminutive "-ee" seems a bit patronizing to me. It's giving the "thinker" a nickname; it's sweet, familiar, and friendly, but that is not our role. For me, there is a subtle implication of a one-up, one-down relationship. From Transactional Analysis, it's a bit more parent to child. And while the intent may have been to differentiate, and it does sound playful, it also sounds childish, and it doesn't quite fit the depth of the work, or the idea that the thinker is a whole, capable, resourceful, and creative human being.

So Why Thinker

There are a few reasons, from my perspective, but mostly because coaching is a space for thinking, not just logical or rational thought, but full-bodied, emotionally informed, sensory-rich thinking.

When we call someone a thinker, we move away from the idea that coaching is something being done to them. Instead, we invite a shared space where the person engages in their own best thinking, with the coach as a committed, present partner.

This approach draws from Nancy Kline's Thinking Environments, which rests on a very simple idea: The quality of everything we do depends on the quality of the thinking we do first. And the quality of our thinking depends on how we are treated while we are thinking (Kline 1999).

Kline identified ten components that create the conditions for someone to do their best thinking, including:

> O **Attention:** Listening with respect, interest, and without interruption. This is often difficult to do because we must suspend our excitement, our knowing, our concerns, and our judgments.
>
> O **Equality:** Each person is equal in the thinking process; even within a hierarchical system, people can be invited to share as equals. Each person has something to share. This is about making sure everyone at the table has a chance to share. And, the external processors leave space for the internal processors to share their thoughts.
>
> O **Ease:** Creating a relaxed atmosphere where urgency and pressure dissolve. Silence is not a void; it's spaciousness. There is no pressure to "get somewhere," but rather an ease and flow to the conversation that allows the thinker to

process their thoughts fully.

- **Appreciation:** expressing genuine, specific value for the person's qualities and contributions. We are not pulling out the pom-poms; rather, we are noticing and naming the thinker's insights and wisdom as they emerge. We are also remembering that all of us are more creative when we feel safe, and striking the balance between challenging and appreciating so that people don't feel overwhelmed and shut down.

- **Encouragement:** In Kline's work, this element is about competition. If we are in competition with the thinker, or if the thinker on a team is in competition with a teammate, the focus on the work of exploring ideas is sidelined to the individual striving to be right. Creating a Thinking Environment is fundamental to innovative and collaborative thinking.

- **Feelings:** Strong emotions, especially strong negative emotions, put the kibosh on "good thinking." When these emotions go unspoken, people simmer instead of exploring. This isn't about unloading every grievance or being disrespectful. But it does require us to name feelings, take ownership, and clear the air so that the environment is available for the work to move forward.

- **Information:** Before we make any decision, we need all the data points to be explored. Consider a decision you might have made with only some of the facts you needed. How good did you feel about your decision? When information is limited or incorrect, it creates decisions that lead to those strong negative emotions mentioned above. Another element is around the denial of reality. We need to have a full understanding so that we can see the consequences more fully.

- **Difference:** In this component, we are inviting differences. Suspending our assumptions and biases, so that we can listen. Even in disagreement—actually, most importantly in disagreements—slowing down, suspending our reactions and responses, and choosing curiosity about the difference is what creates the meaningful environment of openness and communication.

- **Incisive Questions:** From a coaching framework, these are the questions we ask that are open, clean, and thinker-led. I would add that these questions are concise as well. We are not limiting the thinker to our particular bias, direction, or assumptions about how they might think or determine anything. This goes hand in hand with partnership and agency.

- **Place:** This is the Thinking Environment, the place that communicates that the thinker, and the energy between them and the coach, matters. This might show up in our pace and tone, in the connectedness and safe environment we establish through our agreements, and our checking in and asking directions. It is the place that says, *Your ideas are important. I am listening.*

Through these components, the coach is not a strategist, fixer, or expert, but a **thought partner**. We are a presence that, through spaciousness and stillness, invites the thinker's own ideas, insights, and awareness to emerge. We become the vessel for their benefit.

Transactional Analysis and the Role We Play

Have you ever found yourself in a conversation, chomping at the bit, ready to share your wisdom or insights? You can see so clearly, from your emotionally detached position, the pathway forward that someone could take. Have you ever been attached to some idea or tool and felt that little jolt as the person disagreed or stepped past your brilliant insight? Thinking to your secret self, *If only they would listen to me, they could move through their situation a bit faster with a better outcome.*

Transactional Analysis (TA) was explored and named by Eric Berne, a psychiatrist in the late 1950s; he made psychoanalytic ideas more accessible by describing three ego states:

> Parent: Critical or Nurturing
>
> Adult: Here-and-now presence; curious, aware, equal partnership
>
> Child: Rebellious, Conforming, or Free

We slide between these states in everyday life. Your boss micromanages you, showing up as the parent. You might snap back as a parent, or maybe you choose to meet them as adult, or you find yourself complying as conforming child—or rebelling as the rebellious child. Different people will respond in different ways to the input coming toward them.

Breaking Down the States

The parent state often reflects our ideas about authority. It stems from our interactions with our actual parents or parental role models and from our teachers, bosses, or anyone in a position of power over us, who shape our experience of this role. This is the voice of authority and typically carries with it a general expectation of hierarchy and obedience.

The child state is the part of ourselves that is a time warp to our childhood. It's where our intuition, creativity, spontaneous drive, and enjoyment live. It's also a position in many cultures that represents less power. Children can rarely control the situations around them in a direct manner. They rarely get to choose anything, from where the family will live to what's for dinner. A conforming child will do as they are told, while a rebellious child may do the opposite. We all tend to fall on a spectrum in how we respond, and this can also depend greatly on how we view the person trying to parent us.

The adult state is where one might hope all adults would live. It is our sense of confidence, personal agency, and autonomy. It also functions as the mediator between our internal child and parent states. It is often the part of us that is able to be calm in the face of other people's upset. A healthy adult state can calm intense emotions because it is proactive and thoughtful in response rather than reactive and demeaning. When you think of people who are your best examples of what an adult can be, they are typically examples of what you, at your best, want to be.

Coaching Model of Transactional Analysis

I have taken the TA framework and changed it a bit for coaching. The translation looks like this:

From Client to Thinker

> **Expert:** the one assumed to know the most
>
> **Equal:** shared power, shared authorship
>
> **Novice:** the one presumed to know the least

In considering Thinking Environments, as coaches, we need to let go of the **expert** role. Let's consider the idea of the thinker as whole, capable, resourceful, and creative. If that is true, does it mean that the thinker is the expert and we, the coach, might just be the novice? At times, we might show up as equals, yet the thinker is always the expert in their life, their situation, and their capacity to do something different. They have to do the work, and they have to be the ones to choose what they will do.

If we, as coaches, bring our expert stance into the session, we tend to decide, educate, explain, and interpret. That can tilt the conversation away from partnership. Again, I am far more interested in what happens when a coach chooses to be the novice to the thinker's expertise.

I do not mean that the coach is a novice in coaching skills; we have a lot of experience, we know many things, and we have much we can share. But should we? We are novices to the thinker's life, their strengths and values, their meaning-making, and their internal landscape. We are traveling in unfamiliar territory, their territory. When we adopt this perspective, we allow ourselves to be more thoughtful and present to what is being shared, so that our questions are more useful to the process of insights that will support the thinker to move forward with agency.

But, Aren't We More than Thinkers?

One of my course participants messaged me recently, pushing back on this concept of the *thinker*.

They shared, "Something I've been reflecting on: Clients aren't just thinking in a session, they are also feeling, creating, playing, being, etc., so I find myself rebelling against using the word 'thinker' instead of 'client.' For some, using the word *thinker* can lead to a bias for thinking, especially if you're a coach who has been told they think too much."

I *loved* this insight because it reminded me of the importance of language and its unintended consequences; what I said and what I meant were understood in a way that I hadn't considered.

My Response

For such a thoughtful inquiry, I felt the need to give a thoughtful response:

"I really appreciate you sharing some of the concerns you brought forward about the 'thinker.' I love that you have been noodling over this.

"So, to your point, thinking can be construed as only in the head. But that is not how the thinking system works. Given the neurons in the gut, heart, and head, our thinking takes place in a holistic system of the body, mind, and energy space. Our brain makes sense and meaning from the information coming into it.

"For some people, the word 'thinker' has a bias, okay, recognize the bias and decide if it still works or if it is time to challenge it. That's all we do when we take an implicit bias and make it explicit, and then decide if we agree with how we have been making choices.

"I 100 percent agree with you that thinking is not a head-only process. Brains are great for aggregating information; they are informed by the environment, touch, taste, smell, emotions, energy, and experiences.

"In this sense, I would invite you to consider expanding your definition of thinking to include all the elements you mentioned—feeling, creating, playing, being—because those are absolutely part of the thinking process.

"For me, coaching isn't just about how a person thinks with their head brain, it's about the whole, messy, somatic, vibrant, creative, brilliant human experience. And yes, while 'thinker' works for me, it doesn't always capture the complexity of who we are working with or the magic happening in a coaching session. That said, I like the languaging of it so much more than "client," and a thousand times more than "coachee."

Critical Thinking

You don't have to go too far to hear something or witness something that makes you wonder: *Where is the critical thinking in that decision?* It seems that it's not a skill people get a lot of support to develop. Yet how can we possibly get a promotion or create our own business without this ability to parse through our choices? To learn to think for oneself is the act of being able to think critically. Not in a negative way; critical thinking here means the objective analysis and evaluation of an issue in order to form a judgment (Dictionary.com 2025).

One way of looking at coaching is that it is all about creating the environment for people to learn how to think for themselves. In an interview with Carol Kauffman, Nancy Kline explains that her life's work centers on one observation: the quality of everything human beings do depends on the quality of the thinking we do first. Coaching, then, should help people think for themselves.

And we create the space by listening in a generative way, not waiting to reply. True attention actually creates better thinking in the other person, allowing them to noodle through all the data points that lead to a clear, objective evaluation of the choices they have in how they want to react, respond, gather more information, or move forward.

I recently purchased a car; I picked it off the internet, and I was really excited about it. I just knew I was going to love it because it was a newer model of a car I already had. I had decided to keep my old car, so what happened was that I basically had two cars of the same model, with one being seven years newer. I soon discovered that I didn't actually like the newer car better. So here I was with two cars, one I was paying for monthly but wasn't driving. In retrospect, I could have used a bit more time thinking this decision through. On the other hand, I learned a lot by getting the car and discovering that it wasn't for me.

I had a big decision to make: sell the car, keep it, or trade it in. I decided to trade it in and get a different car that I would actually use. I did multiple test drives, lots of research, deciding based on the ride, feel, experience of driving, and technology. When I traded one car in and purchased the next one, I felt at peace. I have to say, I love my new car. And while I may have eventually gotten to the best choice another way, no one was going to be able to tell me what to do. I needed the work of gathering information, the experience, and the space to do both. Luckily, without my husband being annoyed with me, this allowed me to get to a place of alignment with my decision. Plus, big bonus, I wasn't paying every month for a car I didn't enjoy driving.

Some things we just can't be told. We have to muddle through the experience to get to that aligned space. *What do I need to do, what are my choices, and what is my best next step?* That is a generative process that coaching can hold for us.

Brains and Belonging

What emerges in Nancy Kline's work is the alignment between science and the human experience. In an interview with Carol Kauffman, Nancy points to Paul Brown's research, which shows that when people experience attention, ease, and appreciation, the limbic system literally opens up, creating connections, what she calls a "rearrangement of the architecture" of a person's thinking and life (Kauffman 2010). This aligns with what positive psychology has been telling us for years: Barbara Fredrickson's broaden-and-build theory and Richard Boyatzis's work on emotional attractors, which he spoke about in our interview, demonstrates that positive states spark creativity, broaden perspective, and help people see possibilities they couldn't access under stress.

And what is striking is how universal this seems to be. Kline shares that even in cultures where hierarchy is the norm, the components of a Thinking Environment still break through. In one example, a Muslim community group applied the ten components of the Thinking Environment and found that when everyone, regardless of gender or role, was treated as an equal thinker, the quality of ideas and solutions changed dramatically. The science suggests that safety and appreciation open the brain; her cross-cultural work shows that those same conditions also open communities (Kauffman 2010).

A Way Forward?

So where does this leave us, coaches who want to partner more fully with our clients? And, if words and labels matter, what are we to choose? As with so much in coaching, it's about context, intention, and choice. Words are tools, and the power of coaching lies in using them intentionally.

For me, "thinker" feels right in many situations because it emphasizes partnership. But it's not a one-size-fits-all solution. Language needs to be flexible, just as we work to be flexible as coaches, to meet each person where they are.

Activity: What Resonates for You?

Take a moment and think about the language you use for the person you're coaching. There isn't a "correct" term, just notice the one that feels right in your bones.

On a piece of paper, jot down the words you've used over time, and then sit with each one for a breath or two. Notice what happens in you when you say them out loud. Notice the subtle shifts in power, tone, and relationship. Notice which word opens you up, and which one quietly nudges you into being the expert.

Ask yourself:

- ? What changes in me when I say "client," "coachee," or "thinker"?
- ? Which word helps me show up as an equal partner?
- ? Which word pulls me into fixing, explaining, or leading?
- ? Which word feels most aligned with how I want to coach?

There's no right answer, just the one that's yours today; always leave yourself room to change.

Chapter Six

Coaching Roots

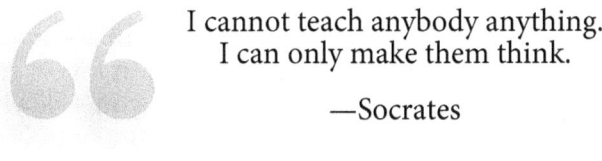

I cannot teach anybody anything.
I can only make them think.

—Socrates

Coaching didn't just appear out of thin air in the 1970s and 1980s. Those decades brought it into business, yes, but the ideas behind coaching go back much further. You can trace these ideas from ancient philosophy, through centuries of thought on learning and human change, and into the late 1800s when they begin to take shape in modern psychology. Coaching drew from those traditions, but it also became its own thing.

That's the part I want to underline. Coaching isn't therapy; it isn't consulting; it isn't mentoring, though it borrows elements from all of these strategies. It grew out of a rich shared history, but it took its own shape. And understanding that history matters, because it hopefully helps us coach with more respect for where we come from and for the art of working with people.

Understanding the roots matters to me. These roots shape how we practice today. They remind us that this work isn't just about tools or checklists. It's about depth and partnership, about purpose, and about turning theory into practice.

I like to picture those roots as four streams we draw from: asking instead of telling, agency and purpose, listening to the whole self, and the way beliefs shape behavior. Each of these streams flows into modern coaching, giving us a foundation we can stand on as we partner with the people in front of us.

Asking Over Telling

The first root dates back to Socrates. He didn't lecture. He didn't hand out five-step formulas for living wisely. He asked questions. Often, they were unsettling ones, questions that required people to pause, reflect, and think for themselves.

That spirit carries into coaching. We know that people rarely transform because someone told them what to do. Transformation comes when they discover their own answers. In more recent times, the counseling method known as Motivational Interviewing reinforced this idea.

Developed in the 1980s to support people in making difficult changes, such as breaking addictions, it showed that change sticks when it arises from a person's own reasons, not from being persuaded.

I think about this every time a leader across from me says, "Just tell me what to do." The temptation is real. Maybe it would make me look smart. But the moment I give in, the conversation shifts from theirs to mine. And there have been plenty of times when any idea I came up with would have been useless for their specific situation. The people we work with are not baby birds for us to feed.

The truth is that if they stop thinking, they stop owning, and they stop having opportunities for discovery. In a literal sense, we have stolen their learning. **We want them to create the dots, connect the dots, and take ownership of the dots.**

● ● ●

Why This Matters for Coaching

Coaching is not about persuasion, and it's not advice dressed up as questions. It's the disciplined practice of curiosity—to ask, reflect, and invite, even when silence stretches, or the path feels unclear. It's the belief that a question that comes from listening is more powerful than any ready answer we could give.

Coaching Applications:

- O Ask open-ended questions that spark reflection
- O Reflect back the thinker's words so they can hear

themselves

- ○ Explore ambivalence without rushing to solutions
- ○ Support autonomy: "What matters most to you about this?"
- ○ Trust the thinker to have their own answers

One of my thinkers shared something that has stayed with me. "I don't actually know what someone else is thinking. And what if the story I'm telling myself about what they want or need is off? What if they're not stuck or resistant? What if they're actually fed up with the hamster wheel they've been running on and are waiting for a moment to get their own clarity?

"When I think about it like that, my shoulders drop. Just be open. Let it be possible that my assumption is just my story and has nothing to do with them. What if everyone is ready for their own insights, if only they're invited in the right way?"

Mic drop.

Agency and Purpose

Agency has always been at the heart of coaching. Back in the 1950s, psychologist Julian Rotter started looking at a simple but powerful question: where do we think control sits in our lives? He called it the locus of control. The two circles shrink or grow depending on where you focus.

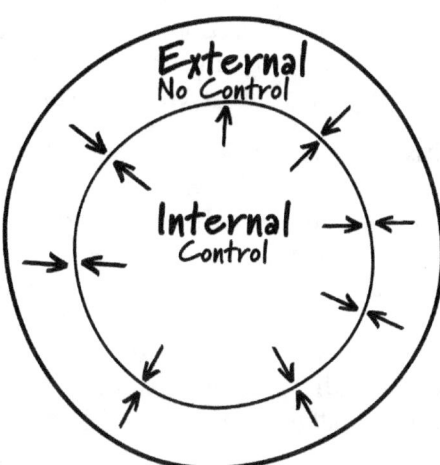

Sticky Outcomes!

Some people have an external locus. Life feels like it is happening to them. They might feel pushed around by circumstance, by other people, by the system, the world, by time, or by all these elements sitting just *beyond their control.*

So, as you look at the donut, you can see that the more you focus on your external locus of control, the bigger you make this circle. And, sadly, this is an indication of fighting against reality.

This external focus is incredibly disempowering. It tends to bring up most of the negative emotions—anger, frustration, helplessness, hopelessness, and fear, which seem to live below all the other negative emotions. I say this because, while you may not feel afraid when you are angry, fear is still the predominant response to threat. We may respond to that threat with anger (fight), running away (flight), helplessness (freeze), or any negative emotion you want to add here.

Typically, this focus is our desire to have the universe conform to us in some way. We may be trying to get people to understand our point of view, be fair, load the dishwasher differently—you name it—but we are often upset because someone out there in the world doesn't understand something we feel strongly about. And it often comes across as bossiness, micromanaging, or control. This applies to the world at large as well. We don't have to look too far to find people losing their minds over disagreements about politics, the economy, the environment, or what is true or real. The external-locus focus feels like hitting your head against a wall. The wall is fine; it's your head that hurts.

Then there are people who have cultivated more of an internal locus of control. They focus where their power is. The belief is that they have control in a few areas. **I have come to sum that up as** *what you say, think, and do.*

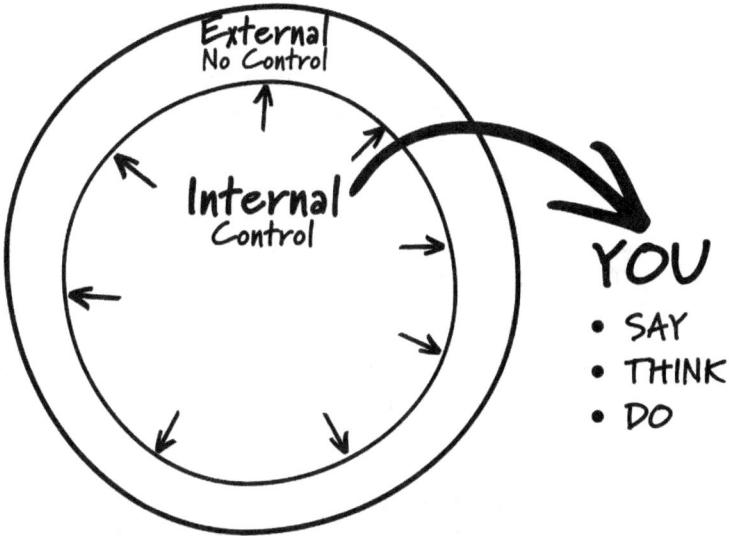

This focus is not easy. But my personal experience—and what I have been told thousands of times through the past thirty years—is that the more we focus where our control is, *the more empowered* we feel.

Thoughts and emotions are connected in that we might start with a thought, "That's not fair!" And it will manifest an emotional response. Or, conversely, we can be sitting at a table and notice our jaw clenching or our head spinning, and a thought will emerge from the physiological experience we are having and the meaning we make from it.

The goal of locus of control is that we are working on expanding the internal circle—where we have power in what we say, think, and do—and making it bigger. Basically, the idea is to move from being a bagel into a bicycle tire, expanding your influence by how you show up and focusing on where your power is.

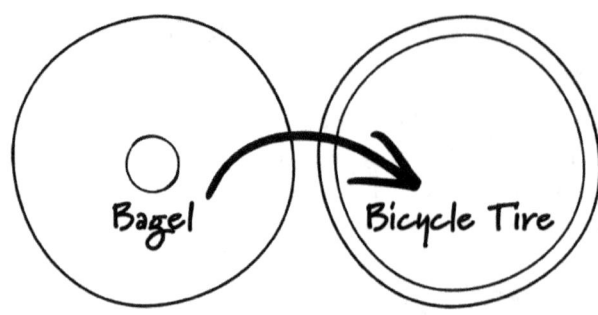

Around the same time as this locus of control idea emerged, Alfred Adler, one of the great voices in early psychology, named something equally profound: that every human being is motivated by the desire to belong, to contribute, and to live with purpose. He called this striving for significance. Adler noticed how often people's struggles could be traced back to outdated beliefs formed in childhood—private logic that may have once kept them safe but no longer served them in adulthood.

Together, these insights shape much of what we recognize as coaching today. Someone may show up saying they want strategies, steps, or a plan. But underneath, the questions are more human: *I can't influence the people or things I care about. I don't feel like I have a voice. Do I really have a say in my life? Do I matter here? Am I choosing my way forward, or just reacting to everyone else's expectations?* And this is often the work that needs to be explored so that people can move toward what they want for their lives.

Real, Not Real

I worked with an executive who felt completely trapped by the board's relentless focus on quarterly numbers. Every conversation came back to outcomes, markets, and governmental decisions—all things they could not control. Rather than have them spend money building yet another plan that was fundamentally based on wishes and fears, I decided to try another route: "When you think about yourself in this role, what impact do you want to have beyond the numbers?"

We sat quietly for a bit, then the leader began to talk, not about deadlines and numbers, but about shaping culture, developing people, and creating a workplace where people wanted to stay. Part of their numbers was also driven by turnover, sick leave, and a lack of innovation.

The belief that began to light them up was that if the focus was on the people and creating value for the consumer, the numbers would follow. The shift in focus from external pressure to internal agency changed the emphasis to who they wanted to be as a leader, so we started talking about the conversations they needed to have, with whom, and how they wanted to show up in those conversations.

The same dynamic shows up around delegation. Leaders say things like, "I can't delegate, it never works." And usually, it's not about stubbornness. It's about the conditions under which they delegate. Are they delegating to the right people? Maybe they don't trust the team they do have. Or they delegate tasks without providing the necessary training or support, resulting in the work being either half-done or done poorly, which just confirms the story: "See, delegation always fails." That cycle keeps them trapped, carrying more than they should.

Here's the irony. Strong leaders know the opposite is true. Delegation isn't a weakness; it's one of the best inoculations against burnout. A global study in 2025 found that leaders who delegate burn out less, even though more than 80 percent of rising leaders admitted they don't feel skilled at it (Development Dimensions International 2025).

And the brain doesn't always make it easier. Neuroscience shows that we're wired to resist letting go of control because of the time needed to adequately train someone and the fear of having to fix mistakes. Letting go sets off the amygdala's alarm bell. Finishing tasks ourselves gives us a dopamine hit. So, no wonder it feels safer to hang on to every element of the project (Oviawe 2015).

But as *MIT Sloan Review* put it, if your team thrives without you micromanaging every detail, that's not a weakness. That's leadership at its best (MIT Sloan Review 2024). When done well, delegation spreads the load, builds trust, and taps into the collective genius of all the brains in the room.

Coaching creates the space where leaders can wrangle with these sorts of questions, and they can be brought into the open not as abstract theories but as lived realities. When a leader begins to see that they are not simply at the mercy of market shifts, organizational politics, or the weight of expectations, that opens up the possibility for them to shift. They rediscover agency. And when that rediscovery is connected, as Adler shared, people start to thrive as their actions are tied to contribution and meaning.

This is why agency and purpose matter in coaching. It's not about denying the realities of external pressure but about helping people see where they do have influence and reconnect with the deeper reasons they choose to act. When leaders reclaim that sense of authorship, they stop simply reacting. They begin leading.

Listening to the Whole Self

Another important element of coaching is found not in philosophy but in the body. Somatic psychology and neuroscience have shown what many of us intuitively know: insight is not only a head activity. It lives in breath, posture, tone, and sensation.

Think about it: when someone says, "I'm fine," but their shoulders are slumped, which is more true? When a leader says they're confident but their voice drops and falters, what do you really trust? The body often tells the truth before the words catch up.

The nervous system is constantly scanning: *Am I safe? Am I under threat?* As coaches, when we are grounded and present, we co-regulate. Our calm becomes their calm. Our curiosity becomes permission for them to explore. When we notice shifts in their breathing, pauses in their story, or metaphors that rise unbidden, we are listening beyond words to the whole human in front of us.

Imagine working with someone who insists they aren't stressed, but as they speak, their foot taps rapidly under the table. This brings to mind a recent session in which the thinker was sharing how discouraged they felt with their whole organization and the utter chaos their team was dealing with. Their hands were waving all over the place.

My response was, "Yeah, I'm hearing it—I waved my hands like theirs—and if you were no longer in this space of discouragement, where would you want to be, maybe jostling over toward?"

The thinker responded with, "I think I was struck by—you know, you're doing this—they waved their hands again—and mimicking me. I'm like, gosh, is that the energy I have? I think I just want to get to this place of serenity or acceptance that the work I do, that my team does, is valuable. And whatever is going to happen will."

The thinker then gave a *huge sigh*.

I asked, "What just happened there with that big sigh?"

And the response was just what we had been talking about: "I know that I have no control over all this nonsense going on. Right. So intellectually, I know it here—pointing at their head—and so the sigh was me asking myself, When are you going to just accept and know that you'll be OK and sort of let go of all the spin that is happening?"

Listening to the whole self means we trust the body as part of the conversation. Sometimes, it's the most honest voice in the room. And a change that's felt in the body becomes integrated and lasting. When the coach is attuned, both to the thinker's cues and their own internal state, they can create safety and access deeper truths.

Coaching Applications:

- Notice and reflect physical shifts: "I noticed you paused; what happened there?"
- Invite the body in: "Where do you notice that in yourself?"
- Manage your own state to model calm and presence.
- Use silence and slowing down to let insights land.

Beliefs Shape Behavior

In the middle of the twentieth century, Albert Ellis and, later, Aaron Beck started pushing psychology in a new direction, which we now call the "cognitive approach." The idea sounds simple and obvious now, but it was a game-changer at the time: thoughts shape feelings, and feelings drive behavior.

If you carry a belief such as "I must be perfect to succeed," the pressure is pretty predictable. As pressure builds, anxiety creeps in. You start to avoid risks. Burnout happens when the stress goes on for too long. But if that original belief shifts to "I can ask for support," the whole chain starts to move in a different direction.

Try on something like *Done is better than perfect*, which is what I told myself every day when writing my first book. Right away, the pressure eases, stress lightens, and there's more room for creativity and resilience to show up. Ellis pointed out that the stories we tell ourselves—what he called "irrational beliefs"—are often what hold us in a pattern of suffering when we don't need to. Coaching takes that understanding forward by asking leaders to listen to their own self-talk and ask, *Is this belief actually serving me?*

At the same time, Carl Rogers was showing us something that underpins nearly every coaching conversation today. He believed all people carry a natural drive toward what he called the "good life," a life of self-growth, openness to different experiences, and a desire for authenticity.

That drive only really flourishes when people are met with empathy, resonance, and what Rogers named "unconditional positive regard." He demonstrated that being deeply heard and accepted could be more transformative than any clever technique. His emphasis on client-led growth lines up directly with modern coaching's commitment to client determination.

We don't need to, or want to, push leaders toward our version of the "good life." Instead, we want to focus on creating a relationship where they can hear themselves, trust themselves, and decide for themselves what thriving means on their own terms. And we can support them to hear themselves so that they can explore what's possible.

Alfred Adler added another piece to the puzzle. He believed people are always striving for belonging and significance. We want to know we matter. We want to feel like we're contributing.

But when that striving gets blocked or twisted, it shows up as discouragement, overcompensation, or even unhealthy competition. I see it in coaching when leaders hold tight to old stories: "If I don't control everything, I'll lose respect," or "My worth is measured only by results."

Adler's work points to something we see again and again. Beneath so many struggles is a basic longing to belong, to feel valued, to live with purpose. Coaching makes room for those needs to be

Coaching Roots

named. And once they're out in the open, people often find themselves ready to shift toward beliefs that are healthier and more empowering.

We don't impose new beliefs; we hold up the mirror. A leader might come in convinced that "delegating means I'll lose control" or "I must handle everything, or it will all fall apart."

But through reflection and curiosity, a leader can start to see the belief for what it really is: a story they are telling themselves. When that happens, they can challenge and replace it with something truer.

For example, consider shifting from the belief *I should be able to do everything myself*, to *Delegating creates capacity and trust*. That one change doesn't just alter someone's leadership style. It reshapes how their team feels about their own work and even how the organization functions. Beliefs shape behavior. And curiosity, combined with presence, makes space for new beliefs to take root.

Coaching Applications

- Explore default thinking: "What's the story you're telling yourself?"
- Check alignment with values: "How does that belief serve you now?"
- Let insight emerge, no need to impose fixes

The Deeper Work

Like an iceberg, we see only a small part of what is going on with another person above the waterline, while the bulk of their identity lives below the surface. And let's be clear, the larger part below the surface is what takes out ships. Yet in coaching, we often focus above the waterline. We talk about, and coach around, the actions and the results. But changing actions without meaningful insight means those actions rarely become new habits or ways of being, so they never develop the stickiness needed for lasting change.

In my humble opinion, the real work of coaching has to at least explore below the waterline, where experiences, stories, values, fears, and long-held beliefs live. Coaching invites people to explore those depths safely, at their own pace, and to develop insights that can create deeper awareness and insight. This deeper exploration and the owned "ahas" are what lead to stickier outcomes.

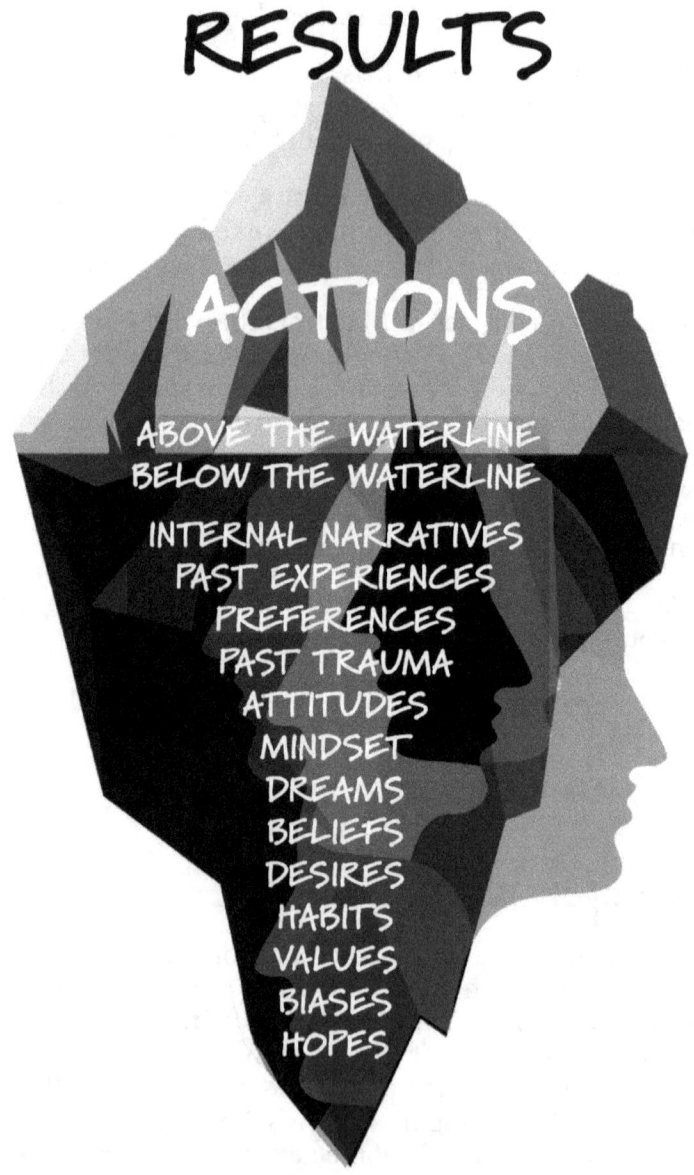

Executives and leaders do not walk into coaching as blank slates. They are not baby birds in need of feeding. They bring the full weight of their history, beliefs, and meaning-making patterns into the room. Some arrive convinced that success means perfection. Or that they can't delegate because it never works. Still others carry the unspoken story that their worth is tied only to results. These beliefs are not simply private struggles; they ripple through entire organizations.

When coaching is grounded in its roots, it offers leaders a rare moment to pause and examine what is happening below the waterline. Questions that honor agency and curiosity shift the focus from external pressures (shareholders, boards, markets) to internal authorship. Leaders begin to see that they have more choice than they imagined, and that thriving is not about adopting someone else's definition of success but about aligning leadership with their own values, purpose, and sense of belonging.

Activity: Attention and Practice

When you're coaching leaders, listen for the stories that might be running the show. Adler called this *private logic,* the beliefs people form early in life or in past workplaces that once made sense but may not serve them now. Hold these up with curiosity, not judgment. Then invite exploration with questions like

- "What about that belief—how does it serve you now?"
- "What story is guiding your choices right now?" Or
- "As you hear yourself sharing that belief, what is important about it in this moment?"

Conversations like these become turning points—not just for the leader's growth but for the way they lead their people and shape their organizations.

When you practice noticing these private-logic beliefs, what do you notice when you ask or invite inquiry and curiosity around them?

CHAPTER SEVEN

Coaching as Crafted Partnering

> When someone really hears you without passing judgment on you, without trying to take responsibility for you, without trying to mold you, it feels damn good.
>
> —Carl Rogers

I often tell people, "I am a short-term solution to your long-term life." Our role is not to give direction but to offer curiosity, presence, and partnering. When coaches move beyond doing to and for people, something shifts. We begin to embody qualities that shape the space beneath the surface of the conversation. This is what I call the Rule of 8: the invisible architecture of master-level coaching. These eight qualities are ways of being that work together moment by moment as we have coaching conversations.

The Rule of 8

The Rule of 8 is a way of thinking and partnering in a coaching conversation. These are the eight qualities that, over time, become the "foundation" of mastery. These are often invisible, but you can feel them when they're there.

Dynamic Partnership:

Mastery begins with cocreating clarity. As we develop mastery, alignment isn't set once and left behind; it is revisited naturally as the session unfolds, noticing shifts and naming them in the moment. Alignment creates momentum; partnership sustains trust.

What this sounds like in practice:

- "What feels most important to bring into the open right now?"
- "How are we doing on moving toward XYZ?"
- "Would it serve to check if we're still on track with what you wanted today?"

Autonomy & Shared Leadership:

Coaching works when thinkers feel ownership. We offer invitations; we are not in the job of handing out instructions. We communicate, "This space is yours." By giving thinkers full choice in how to engage and by partnering fully, they discover that coaching is not something done to them but a process they own. Every move is an invitation into shared leadership. The coach needs to resist the urge to influence and instead learn to lean into curiosity so the thinker fully owns their direction.

What this sounds like in practice:

- "Given that insight, what is emerging now?"
- "What do you need right now?"
- "What is the question that needs to be asked here?"

Ease and Regulation:

Ease is a nervous system skill. It steadies the energy so both coach and thinker can stay open to learning. Ease is the spaciousness. It is not passivity; it is a conscious slowing down that signals safety. It's also the ease with which the coach demonstrates being present in the conversation. Ease says, "We're not in a hurry. Take your time." This is about your own regulation, tone, and energy—the elements you bring into your presence and how you are being with another human being.

When missing, coaching can feel rushed or performative. When present, it regulates the nervous system of both people and makes space for insight to emerge.

What this sounds like in practice:

Hold intentional pauses, slow speech, and allow the thinker's words to settle before moving forward. This is how we demonstrate that we are comfortable and present in the conversation.

Intentional Silence & Reflective Space:

Silence is not emptiness; it is potency. At the mastery level, coaches intentionally hold stillness with reverence, trusting that something meaningful may be ready to emerge. Silence says, "Let's honor what is emerging." Spaciousness signals, "There's no rush." Both create conditions where deeper and more profound truths can surface.

What this sounds like in practice:

Sitting in quiet after a thinker's insight, offering only presence and letting them choose when to speak again. Think zipper emoji. Give yourself a count of three to five before you ask your next question. It's the slowing down of the conversation.

Attunement & Customization:

Attunement listens for resonance in the thinker's language and mirrors it back in their own words. A masterful coach hears beyond words. They notice shifts in tone, pace, or energy and reflect them back in a way that resonates with the thinker's experience. This builds safety and trust. Without it, conversations risk staying flat, missing what's truly alive in the moment.

What this sounds like in practice:

- "Your voice slowed down just now. What are you noticing?"
- "I heard the 'ahhhh.' What is in the 'ahhhh'?"
- "The energy in your voice shifted. What just happened?"

Inquiry for Self-Generated Awareness:

Insight does not come from answers we give but from questions that invite discovery. These are clean, open, resonant questions—ones that help the thinker hear themselves differently. They may challenge the thinker to explore contrasts or to view themselves or their situation from different perspectives.

Think of one succinct, open-ended question at a time, rooted in the thinker's language and what they have offered. Or an observation with an invitation to the thinker to explore.

What this sounds like in practice:

- "You shared motivation feels tingly. What are you discovering as you say that?"
- "What's the insight in the way you just phrased that?"
- "You shared two beliefs that seem opposite. What, if anything, are you noticing?"

Empowerment, Integration, and Ownership:

At the end of a session, empowerment means the thinker leaves with insights they own, not a coach's checklist. Integration ensures those insights become sustainable shifts in identity and practice. This is fundamentally what we experience as partnering, as the thinker decides how new awareness becomes owned and lived behavior.

What this sounds like in practice:

- "What feels ready to change because of this?"
- "How might you live from this awareness?"
- "What might you want to take into other areas of your life?"

Depth, Embodiment, and Systems Awareness:

Depth explores meaning, identity, and the systems that shape the thinker's experience. Masterful coaching is not satisfied with surface-level problem-solving; it stays with meaning, identity, and values long enough for change to take root. Depth asks, "What are you coming to know about yourself through this?" Embodiment follows, inviting the thinker to carry that awareness into their way of being.

What this sounds like in practice:

- "What are you coming to know about yourself that you want to carry forward?"
- "How will you honor your agreement with yourself?"
- "What value do you hold that can support you?"

Coaching as Partnering

From my perspective, the Rule of 8 is a way of thinking and partnering in the coaching conversation. As you develop toward your own mastery, these qualities become second nature. On the learning journey, it's the movement toward unconscious competency.

Relationship as the Foundation of Coaching

Underneath all the qualities in the Rule of 8 is relationship—not in the abstract but in the living, breathing way two humans meet and intersect. Neuroscience keeps reminding us of something most of us already know in our bones: we become ourselves through relationships.

Daniel Siegel writes about how our brains are shaped by the connections we form with others and the world around us. When someone feels seen and heard, their brain literally integrates experience differently. Their sense of self is stronger, and they are able to see and hear others. Interestingly, their capacity to see new options also expands (Siegel 1999, 2010).

This is why how we show up matters as much as our questions. Our tone, pacing, willingness to sit in silence, and attunement to small shifts are all ways of communicating that we are fully here now. And when that message is experienced by the thinker, the conditions for learning, growth, and change begin to open up.

The Rule of 8 is how we create a relational field that supports new awareness. The architecture works because it is firmly set on this foundation: the coach and thinker together, shaping a space where the brain and the whole self can reorganize toward dreams.

Directionality: Purposeful Partnership

If the Rule of 8 is the architecture, directionality is the compass. It is the way coaches ensure conversations remain oriented toward what matters to the thinker. Where does the thinker want to go in this conversation? That's what we hold onto. If something new shows up, we don't plow ahead with an assumption; we pause, ask, and shift the focus to the new outcome.

Together, the coach and the thinker sketch out what the

outcome looks like and what success means in this moment, thereby supporting the thinker to determine the indicators of a successful outcome. And we circle back to what they named. We check in as we go: "Does this still feel like the direction you want to follow?"

When directionality is working, the conversation doesn't get stuck in fear or resistance. Those moments become openings—places to explore in a way that supports growth. It ensures coaching is always about moving toward, not staying stuck in, what the thinker most wants.

When coaching is rooted in partnership, the experience changes. Thinkers don't just take in insights; they start to own them. Remember those dots? We want the thinker to create, connect, and own them. And when they own them, the learning sticks. It becomes part of who they are, not just something they heard in a session.

• • •

Activity: What Will You Play with First?

As you consider these elements for your own coaching, ask yourself.

- What is drawing you in as one thing you want to pay attention to in your work?
- How will you stay intentional about this choice in your coaching conversations?
- Where else in your communication might this element support you?
- What dots are you connecting?

CHAPTER EIGHT

How We Learn

> The essence of developmental coaching is to meet people where they are and invite them to grow into the next stage of their meaning-making.
>
> —Tatiana Bachkirova

Vertical development in coaching is about how an individual evolves in the way they make meaning of their experiences. It's not just what they know (horizontal development) but also how they learn, think, and understand. Developmental theorists such as Robert Kegan (1982, 1994), Jane Loevinger (1976), and Susanne Cook-Greuter (2005) have all shown that growth is about shifts in thinking, not just shifts in our skills. Building on this, Tatiana Bachkirova and colleagues (2020) brought these ideas to the field of coaching, showing how vertical development shapes the way we partner with the people we work with.

This distinction is important because coaching is about developing more than skills and models. When people talk about development in coaching, the first thing that usually comes to mind is adding new skills, models, frameworks, or some cool new techniques. That's what these theorists call horizontal development. But there's another layer of growth that often marks the difference between a good coach and one who is developing mastery. That's vertical development.

If horizontal growth is adding more tools to your toolbox, vertical growth is upgrading the whole toolbox—the one you keep eyeballing at the hardware store, the big shiny one. It's not only what you know but also how you make use of what you know. Vertical growth shifts how you see your tools. In a conversation with Jille Bartolome, MCC, she used the example of taking everything you know, putting it in a box, and then using what's in the box to bring curiosity and inform how you ask questions—not using the tool itself but, in my words, *using what you know to inform your curiosity* (Bartolome 2025).

Consider it this way: a coach who's focused on horizontal development has lots of tools and uses them. They can measure success and keep the conversation on track. But it's not an invitation to let the conversation deviate or get messy. That's never on the agenda, and there may not be a tool for that.

In one of my webinars, the thinker got into emotions. We had begun discussing writing a book, but through the conversation, it became less about having the time on the calendar to write and more about what was keeping them from writing. This wasn't where we started. And one of the observing coaches stated this was not a place they would have felt comfortable exploring, because to them it felt like therapy. But it wasn't therapy; we were very focused on the deeper goal of discovering what was in the way of using the time that had been set aside for writing.

So, a coach who's grown vertically doesn't just use the strategies or exercises to create a list or block time on a calendar—they become the tool. This is a vastly different way of being. They learn to sit with the messy, the paradoxical, the polarities, the discomfort. They can hold ambiguity, stay curious, and create a space where the thinker's meaning-making is allowed to be laid out on the table and explored.

A Cognitive-Developmental Approach

When I read Tatiana Bachkirova's article on cognitive-developmental approaches to coaching (Bachkirova 2020), it put words to something I had sensed in my own practice. I knew that to differentiate coaching from advising, mentoring, and counseling, it couldn't just be about adding tools; it had to be richer than that. Ultimately, coaching is about how people grow, how they develop themselves, and how they evolve the way they make meaning of their experiences. This might be the shift from seeing the world as happening to them to seeing where they have control.

Bachkirova and her colleagues take this developmental lens and bring it to coaching. Their point is simple: it's not enough to know what someone is struggling with. What matters is how they're making sense of that struggle. This is how coaching serves the thinker, helping them evolve their understanding of themselves and the situations they find themselves in.

This matters because while two leaders can show up with the exact same issue, say, struggling with delegation, the coaching conversations can go in very different directions depending on the coach and on the thinker's capacity to self-reflect. One might see delegation as a threat to their competence. Another might believe that no one can do what they do, so they continue to hold on to doing it all. Yet another might notice the bigger picture and frame delegation as a way to build collective strength by training people and then trusting them to follow through.

If we treat all of these leaders the same, we need to look at ourselves. Do we have the capacity to show up differently with each person we work with, to meet them where they are, without limiting them? We know coaching isn't about fixing problems; it's about finding solutions that align fully with, and are owned by, the thinker. It's about meeting people in how they make meaning right now and then gently stretching them toward more complex and adaptive ways of seeing themselves and their world.

Evidence from Practice

Research by Tatiana Bachkirova and Peter Jackson gives us a peek into how this shows up in real coaching conversations; the surface goals that organizations contract for nearly always give way to deeper work on identity and meaning (Bachkirova et al. 2025). They had asked a really simple question: what do leaders really end up talking about in coaching sessions?

Then they put some solid research data behind what so many of us notice anecdotally. On the surface, the answer is about organizationally determined leadership elements, the things most companies send leaders to be coached about: delegation, strategic thinking, communication, performance management, decision-making, upward progression, succession planning, and change management. The typical elements of leadership, if you will.

Bachkirova and Jackson looked at nearly a hundred actual coaching cases and sorted them into forty buckets of conversation topics. A pattern stood out. Leaders might show up asking for help with delegation or communication skills, but the longer the coaching engagement went on, the more the conversations shifted. Again and again, the surface topics gave way to questions of identity, purpose, and who they were becoming.

Coaching often migrated from "How do I delegate better?" Toward questions like "What makes it so hard for me to let go?" Or from "I need to make better decisions" toward "What does it mean about me if I fail?" This wasn't anecdotal evidence; it was rigorously researched. The project was approved and supported by a Harnisch Grant from the Institute of Coaching through Harvard and represented one of the most detailed maps of actual coaching content we've seen.

The analysis didn't just rely on the coach's recollection; the researchers charted the flow of actual conversations so you could literally see how leaders started on one subject and gradually moved into deeper territory. The results were consistent: coaching that began with organizationally determined goals and leadership skills nearly always ended up in the territory of self-concept, values, confidence, and meaning-making (Bachkirova et al. 2025).

Leaders Bring Their Whole Humanity

The research had me thinking about Bronnie Ware's work as a palliative care nurse. Over years of listening to patients reflect on their lives, she noticed the same themes coming up again and again. She called them "the top five regrets of the dying." What people cared about in their final days were meaningful things: they wished they had been true to themselves, worked less, been more open about telling people they loved them, done a better job at staying connected with friends, and allowed themselves more happiness.

Why bring this up here? Because what shows up in Ware's work is not so different from what shows up in coaching rooms or the research that we are looking at. And because leaders are human beings first, the pressure to push toward quarterly targets is real, yet when we inevitably come to how we have lived our lives, rarely do people regret not pushing harder on work. They instead deeply regret not aligning with what mattered most to them as human beings. Coaching creates that rare space where they can explore those bigger questions before it's too late.

How We Learn

Why does this matter for us as coaches? Because it confirms what the theories above—and, honestly, what many coaches know to be true: the real work of coaching executives and leaders isn't about surface-level conversations. Organizations may contract for what they consider ROI-related skills, but human beings bring their whole selves into the coaching space. And when we create that safe space and listen deeply enough, what emerges is not a technical gap that we can fix with blocking out time on a calendar or learning to breathe—although those can be useful—but rather those nuanced themes that connect people to their lives and the lives they want to live.

Think about it. A vice president may say they need help with "strategic communication." Below the surface, what they may actually be wrestling with might be the fear of holding it all together or not feeling safe to discuss their concerns about market changes. A founder may ask for "time management strategies," but the deeper conversation might be about boundaries, self-worth, or the pressure to prove they are good enough and make their parents proud.

These aren't skill gaps. These are fundamental, human, below-the-waterline concerns that drive people to act in ways that move them away from their stated goals. These are deeper, competing commitments that impact the assumptions that shape how leaders lead. This is why developing yourself as a coach matters, but learning to dance in the nuanced, messy spaces with other people is imperative. If you stay only at the sanctioned, organizationally approved goal, you may help the leader demonstrate a skill. But you'll miss the deeper concerns that interfere with real transformation. You'll miss the chance to help them see the patterns that drive their choices, to reflect on the assumptions that keep them stuck, and to reconnect with values that can guide them forward.

And let's be clear: if you think advising someone on these leadership competencies is going to create sticky outcomes, you're kidding yourself…

Advice may feel useful in the moment, but it rarely leads to learning that lasts. For coaches who want to work in organizations, this research is both a challenge and an invitation. From my perspective, the challenge is that you cannot stop at performance goals or surface-level skills and still call it transformational coaching. On season four of *the Coaching Studio*, guest Richard Boyatzis and I discussed getting past the simple goal. He stated that SMART goals limit us; you have to get to the deeper purpose (deHart 2024).

The invitation is to trust that if you create a psychologically safe space, leaders will bring their deeper selves. They will, often unconsciously at first, invite you into the terrain of meaning, identity, and purpose. And that's where real change happens.

So, if you are coaching in organizations, don't be surprised when the sanctioned competency dissolves into something more personal. In fact, expect it. Honor it. Hold space for it. Because that migration, from the external to the internal, from the superficial to the authentic, is not a detour. It is the very heart of coaching.

How People Grow: Three Broad Stages

Here's what matters: the same event can land very differently depending on the lens someone is using. Take a failed project. For one person, it might feel like they're collapsing, as if it's proof they're not good enough. For another, it's a chance to learn. And for someone further along, it could spark a bigger question about patterns in the system itself.

This is where the ego-state model provides a useful bridge. It distills complex developmental research into three broad orientations that coaches can recognize in practice. Here is how Tatiana Bachkirova and her colleagues describe these stages in ways that translate beautifully into any form of working with people:

Unformed Ego: "Others define me."

At this stage, people lean heavily on external validation. They need psychological safety, empathy, and unconditional regard. Person-centered coaching is often the most effective approach here because it helps build the foundation of self-trust.

Formed Ego: "I define myself."

Here, individuals begin authoring their own story. They're ready for deeper challenge, inquiry, and exploration. They no longer just want affirmation; they crave growth. Coaches may need to stretch beyond basic validation and invite more ownership and accountability.

Reformed Ego: "I'm part of a system."

At this level, people see themselves as interconnected, reflective, and capable of holding complexity. They're not only interested in their own growth but in how their growth influences the systems they lead and live within. The coach's presence, depth, and ability to hold systemic awareness become critical.

Why this Matters for Coaches

Coaching mastery isn't about having the cleverest model or the sharpest question. It's about cultivating a way of *being with people*. When you've done your own vertical development work, you show up differently:

- You can hold paradox and ambiguity without rushing to resolve them.

- You support your thinkers in moving from reactive states to reflective and proactive states.

- You listen with curiosity that is unhooked from your own agenda.

- You invite ownership, helping thinkers trust themselves.

- You recognize where your thinker is in their own developmental journey and partner with them accordingly.

Put simply, for coaches, vertical development is the shift from doing coaching to *being a coach*. It's not just about competencies; it's about how you're being in the conversation.

Pulling It All Together

In a coaching conversation, vertical development isn't abstract theory; it shows up in the way you listen and respond. Often, three capacities work together:

1. Distinguish the important from the interesting. Stay focused on what matters most to the thinker, not what hooks your curiosity.

2. Listen at multiple levels. Move beneath surface details into the deeper waters of values, beliefs, and emotions.

3. **Recognize competing commitments.** When a thinker feels stuck, look for the internal conflicts that may be holding them in place, and invite exploration with compassion.

When these come together, coaching moves from problem-solving to transformation. You support your thinker not just in finding answers but in expanding how they see themselves and their world. That's where real, sustainable change begins.

Coaching Demo: Mindset Shift

In the following coaching demonstration, which I call *Mindset Shift*, we can see vertical development in action as it unfolds in a single coaching session. The thinker arrived confused by their own behaviors: I have noticed a trend lately; I am becoming very solution-focused in lots of areas of my life. This is what we might call an unformed-ego stance—uncertain, externally defined, and in need of a safe place to explore. Through the conversation, pay attention to the movement from the unconscious external motivators toward the internal insights and awareness.

Coach: "What is showing up for you that you'd like to noodle through today in our conversation?"

Thinker: "I've noticed a trend lately. I am noticing that I'm becoming very solution-focused in lots of areas of my life. I don't know when I became so like, here's the fix versus what's the conversation.

"I'm not sure when that became a predominant way of operating in the world, but it's something I'm noticing, something I don't like. I would like to talk through how I change that mindset some more to where I'm more in that coaching mindset for myself, not just for my clients."

Coach: "Mhm. What is it when you're in that coaching mindset that is different?"

Thinker: "That's a good question. I think when I'm in the coaching mindset, it's more curious. I spend more time exploring, looking at the why, not necessarily the what. Those are the big ones."

Coach: "And as you're reflecting back on what you just shared, is there a piece of that that is important to name and explore?"

Thinker: "Well, I think when I'm in a coaching mindset, a couple things came to mind as I was saying that. One, I slow down, I take the time to be curious. I think beyond the problem that's right in front of me to the broader context. I make fewer mistakes overall because I've thought through things instead of just, boom, here's the answer, let's move on to the next thing. I think through the implications of that answer as well as, here's the answer, but what are the implications around that particular answer? Is there another answer?"

Coach: "Broader context. [Mhm] Thoughtfulness [Mhm] Thinking through the implications. Who are you being when you are in that space, in that mindset?"

Thinker: "I think I'm being more authentically me. In that space, that's where I feel I'm my best self, because it's not just the problem. I'm not just focused on here's X, or you need to do Z.

"The bigger question is how did this come up to start with, why do we think this is a problem, is this a problem? It's more that exploration. And honestly, that's where I do my best work."

Coach: "So we're moving toward your best self today in this conversation, if I'm hearing you correctly. Is that accurate?"

Thinker: "It is, it is, it is the best version of myself. Yeah."

Coach: "Are there any particular indicators of you when you're in your best self? You may have already named some of them, but are there things you can anchor on, like I'm at my best when I see this?"

Sticky Outcomes!

Thinker: "I'm at my best when I slow down and pull back to see the big picture. And when I'm being curious, it's that curiosity piece that really leads to everything else.

"This is the problem… where did it come from, how did it start, what's been tried before? Instead of that, I get busy—like we all do—and the busier I get, the more I slip into fix-it mode. *Fix it, fix it, fix it. I'm presented with a problem and, okay, boom, here's the fix,* let's move on to the next one. And it never fails that because I didn't take the time to fully explore the question at the start, three more things come up behind it."

Coach: "While you're taking that drink of water, if I'm hearing you correctly, it's that move from the fix-it mode to being in that thoughtful, curious, open [Yes], really curious mindset that is important to explore, and you know you're there because you're being more curious and willing to start asking questions [Yes]. How would you like to begin exploring between the fix-it mode and the fully curious?"

Thinker: "I guess trying to, I'm not exactly sure when I moved out of that curious mode and into this fix-it mode, but I'm really curious about why. I don't know if it's important for me to know the when, but understanding why I keep going back into that fix-it mode I think would help me prevent it in the future."

Coach: "Yeah, that's a really important question, the why? [Mhm.] How do we need to explore to find that?"

Thinker: "Well, that's a good question. How do we need to explore? For some reason I keep thinking that if I determine when that started, that would help me identify the why. And when I said that, I thought, well, it's when I transitioned roles."

Coach: "Interesting. [Yeah.] So what just happened?"

Thinker: "Well, I went from a role where I was very confident that I'd been doing this work for many, many years. I felt knowledgeable and competent, so when people would bring something to me, I felt competent enough to slow down, take my time, ask the questions so I could fully understand the problem before we came to a solution together.

"And for some reason in my new role, I feel like I'm supposed to have the answers. People come to me and they need things now, and I feel like I'm supposed to have the answers, but that's not realistic. There's no way I could have the answers this early on in the position."

As the session deepened, her state began to shift. As we skip to the middle, we can see the change. Through grounding questions, she began to claim her own awareness and access her own insights. Here we see the move into a formed-ego stance: self-authorship, reclaiming inner authority, and naming an experience that starts to answer the *when* and the *why* she has been in the fixer mindset.

Coach: "What's the awareness?"

Thinker: "The awareness is I'm putting a lot of pressure on myself to be an expert in a job I literally just started. Mhm. When I'm not feeling confident, I'm not feeling confident, and that makes me want to just fix the problem. Fix the problem. They're coming to me, they need it, it's my job to fix it."

Coach: "So what is, because that sounds like a lot of pressure. Fix it, fix it, you must fix it [Mhm]. What's driving that, do you think?"

Thinker: "When I first took on the role, the person who was previously in it had already left. I contacted them to ask a question—just a quick, 'Hey, I know you don't work here anymore, but can I run something by you?'

"Their response was, 'That's your job, figure it out.'

"I was like… okay.

Sticky Outcomes!

"I think it stems from that. Seriously, 'That's your job, figure it out.' It landed as, 'It's on me.' I got the message loud and clear that I was supposed to already know.

"Hindsight, now that I've said it out loud... how on earth would I have known that? 'That's your job, figure it out.' I was trying to figure it out by contacting her and asking. I think that's exactly why this pattern shows up—because I've been told, 'This is your job, figure it out.'"

As the conversation continues, she is touching on something larger still: how she begins the return journey to that curious-learner mindset, the one that isn't trying to fix everything but can acknowledge the unrealistic expectation that was placed on her and that she adopted. That expectation is also what pulled her out of curiosity.

Coach: "How do you start to move over to that learner's mindset?"

Thinker: "Oooh, darn. That is the question, isn't it? How do I move from this need to respond and have the answers into a learner's mindset?"

Coach: "I asked you first."

Thinker: "Naming it. Yeah."

Coach: "Naming it."

Thinker: "Yeah, I don't think I even realized that's what I was doing until we started talking about it. That is a lot of pressure. I would never put that kind of pressure on someone else, but I'm totally okay putting that kind of pressure on myself. So the first thing is realizing this is a completely unreasonable expectation that I've placed on myself. For whatever reason, however it came about, I'm putting this expectation on myself now, and it's unrealistic. I think that helps me shift my mindset a little. I'm not exactly sure how to fully step into that, but it does help me shift my mindset."

How We Learn

Coach: "What shifted?"

Thinker: "I'm trying to think. I kind of went into fix-it mode right then. I was like, so now I know what the problem is, what I need to do to fix it. I literally just did that in my own brain. Oh, that's what it is, let's fix it. And then I'm like, calm down, you're still exploring how to even think about it. We can't even move into fix it yet. But I'm really in that mode now, fix it, fix it, fix it. I don't remember the last time I said, what's the conversation versus what's the fix?"

Coach: "What just happened there, where you caught yourself?"

Thinker: "Mhm. I think I recognized the absurdity of it as I was thinking it. I literally just caught myself going, wow, you just did it again. You literally just went into fix-it mode."

Coach: "How do you do more of that?"

Thinker: "Mhm. How do I? I don't know the answer to that. I'm not even 100% sure how I noticed it in that moment, other than the fact that you are talking about it."

Coach: "Would that be important to explore a bit more deeply how you noticed it?"

Thinker: "I think that would be important. How did I catch that in the moment? I don't know if it's because I'm actively sitting here talking to you about it or because my mind is so focused on it at this moment, but I did, in the moment, catch myself saying, hmm, why are you doing that to yourself?"

Coach: "Your whole body moved as you did that?"

Thinker: "It was a step back. Literally just take a step back and look at the broader context here. Why are you so focused on the fix? And that's what brought me here to start with. Why am I so focused on the fix? It is an unreasonable expectation for me to have the answers for everything at this early stage of the game. But this particular one wasn't even about me learning my job, it was about me fixing my mindset right now. I see it spreading to other areas of my life as well, where I go into that fix-it mode, just fix it, fix it, fix it. So maybe that is something we should explore?"

Coach: "I heard you say *take a step back*. [Mhm.] What allows you to take that step back?"

Thinker: "In that moment, it was your pause. You didn't immediately follow up with a question. You weren't moving me through it too quickly, allowing that space for my brain to process it for a moment. I think I don't allow myself time to process. I'm just so go, go, go, go, go from one thing to the next. I'm not giving myself time."

Coach: "Would time be useful here?"

Thinker: "I think that I've heard the phrase *power of the pause*. There is so much power in that for every aspect. It's not just at work, but home stuff, life stuff in general. When I just thought, oh, this is my problem, what do I need to fix it, that pause allowed me to stop for a minute and say, wait a minute, you just had the realization, let's explore that a little more before. Because I don't know how to fix it, because you don't know exactly what it is yet. You can't just keep slapping band aids on it.

"For some reason this whole analogy of Alaska getting lots of holes in our pavement came to mind. They fill them with that really dark black stuff, and they fill the pothole and then it comes out, and they fill it some more, and then it comes out, and they fill it some more. It's just this layer on layer on layer, more layers on it. It's never fully fixed until they repave the road. So I'm filling these potholes over and over again when I really need to slow down, come up with a plan, repave, do an actual repair versus a quick fix."

How We Learn

What happened in this moment is a shift into what developmental theorists call the reformed-ego stance. Earlier in the session, the thinker was operating from an unformed-ego place, externally referenced, pressured to perform, and shaped by expectations that weren't her own. As she gained insight, she stepped into a more formed-ego stance, reclaiming authorship of her experience.

Here, though, when she interrupted her own patterned response, named the absurdity of the fixer loop, felt the somatic shift, and connected it to a larger pattern in her life, she moved into the reformed-ego space. This is where awareness becomes self-transforming. She wasn't just noticing the problem; she was observing herself noticing the problem. She was repaving the road rather than filling potholes. That meta-awareness is the hallmark of vertical development, the moment when identity and agency reorganize around something more grounded, more conscious, and more choiceful.

> Coach: "You mentioned earlier that this is trickling into other places in your life. How does this awareness impact other places in your life as well?"
>
> Thinker: "I get so focused on the what's the answer? Then it just kind of becomes the norm for me to just respond, respond, respond versus taking the time, relax, calm down. You know, being that curious person when I'm being my best self. Um, and I've just kind of, it's become a habit, I've let it become a habit. Um, and noticing that's really important because it's not, that's not who I want to be."
>
> Coach: "And from these insights and awarenesses you're developing today, what do you think is most important in those insights?"
>
> Thinker: "There's so many in the moment running through my head. I think for now the biggest, the most important for me is giving myself some grace so that I can slow down, just slow down. It's okay not to have the answer right now. You don't have to respond to everything right now. Even if someone else thinks it's an emergency, that doesn't mean I have to think it's an emergency. So just giving myself the ability to say, you

know, following, being more curious, just giving myself the grace to be more curious and to slow down.

"It's really hard going into a new job when you've been in something so long that you're feeling really, really confident, and to go into something you're just like, oh. So just naming that. It's hard and it's okay. It's okay. It's supposed to be. If it was easy, everybody would do it, right?"

Coach: "What do you have in your mind as something that you'd be willing to play with to allow that pause to emerge in that curiosity?"

Thinker: "That's a really good question. I think one big step I can take is some type of visual reminder that it's okay to pause. Just pause, just pause. That will allow me time to step back and look at the whole picture instead of just respond, respond, respond, fix, fix, fix. Just pause, think about it, think through it. Things always go better when I take the time to do it right the first time."

Coach: "Is there anything that will support you in getting this visual that you need in order to remind yourself?"

Thinker: "One of the places I feel most centered and most focused is when I'm at the barn with my horse. So I think maybe, uh, I mean, as simple as putting a picture of my horse like right where I can see it at work so that I can remind myself. I mean, I could even do it as a screensaver. Just pause for a moment, just, you know, take a second, remind myself that, you know, you don't have to fix it in this moment. Let's be more curious about what's happening."

Coach: "How are we doing in moving towards that more open, curious mindset that you were wanting to explore today?"

Thinker: "Well, I think for me personally, acknowledging how I've, you know, why. The why of what, the when doesn't really matter, but the why really mattered in my mind to figure out what happened there. Naming that is really important. But also naming that I'm the one putting this pressure on myself, no one else is, is so important."

Coach: "Yeah, so hugely, hugely, insightful."

Thinker: "Yeah. I'm the only one that can stop putting that pressure on myself.'

Coach: "Which really begs a good question. What supports you to stop putting that pressure on yourself?"

Thinker: "Realizing I was doing it to start with. That's the first thing. And then I think being humble, I am in a new position. I don't have all the answers. And honestly just thanking people for their patience while I'm navigating the learning."

That's what needed to happen: the thinker reconnected to their own wisdom through that access point, right there. As coaches, I hope this session serves as a reminder: our role is not to drag a leader to the next developmental stage, but to meet them where they are. When we create the conditions of safety, presence, and curiosity, vertical movement often happens organically. A thinker who begins in a state of reactivity can, within a single conversation, discover self-authorship and even glimpses of systemic awareness. Our responsibility is to notice these shifts, trust them, and support the thinker in making meaning of their own growth.

Activity: Three Ways of Meaning-Making

You've just read about vertical development and the three ego orientations. This next step is for you to explore through your own system, not just understand it in your head. You don't need anything fancy. Just think of a moment from your own life.

1. Start with something real

Think about a recent situation where you felt slightly stressed, uncomfortable, or unsure. Nothing huge, just a moment that stuck with you. Maybe you froze in a meeting. Maybe you didn't set a boundary when you meant to set one. Maybe you spiraled in self-doubt for a minute.

Write one observation about that situation that is interesting to you at this moment.

2. The unformed ego voice

Now stay with that same situation and answer these questions from the most externally driven parts of you—the parts that look to others for cues, approval, and safety. There are no wrong answers, just your willingness to explore.

- ? What felt at risk?
- ? Whose opinion mattered the most?
- ? What were you hoping people would think of you?
- ? What were you afraid this meant about you?

Don't edit as you write. As much as you can, let yourself freewrite with no judgment. This is the stance Bachkirova describes as "others define me," deeply tied to belonging and safety.

3. The formed ego voice

Okay, let's shift gears. Looking at the same situation, explore it from another ego state.

This time, speak from the part of you that stands on your own two feet—the part that has its own values, has its own compass, and is not particularly concerned about what others will think of you.

- ? What did you believe was happening?
- ? Which of your values were in play?
- ? What choices did you make or avoid?
- ? What do you want to learn here?

Notice what shifted for you. Did your thinking or actions become more aligned with how you would want to show up in this situation? This is the place where you are starting to define yourself and bring your actions, intentions, and thinking into alignment.

4. The reformed ego voice

Our final gear shift. Look at the same situation from a wider perspective—the broader systemic viewpoint. Invite the part of you that can hold complexity and see patterns instead of just blame or shame into this same situation.

- ? What was happening in the larger system?
- ? What tensions or competing needs were present?
- ? What patterns do you see now that you didn't see then?
- ? How might your growth touch other people, not just you?

This is the "I'm part of a larger system" part of you that is able to see the bigger picture. It includes the other people, the situation from multiple perspectives, and an awareness of how you want to show up and be in integrity with yourself. This opens the opportunity for greater alignment.

5. Look at the three ways of being.

Now pause and read what you wrote in each voice. Ask yourself:

- ? Which voice felt the most familiar?
- ? Which one stretched me?
- ? How did the story shift as my sense of self and meaning-making shifted?
- ? What does this teach me about the way I interpret my own experiences?

You might notice how quickly you can move between these stances. You might also see places where you tend to get hooked, stuck, or very curious. That's the point—what are you learning about yourself?

Chapter Nine

Breaking Down the Competencies

> It takes about ten years to make a mature dancer. It doesn't matter how much talent you have. The discipline is in the practice.
>
> —Martha Graham

When I first learned about the coaching competencies, I was skeptical. I had a pretty strong therapy bias and, in a deeply humble way, thought, "This is totally silly, I already know all this stuff." Fast-forward about eight years after that original training, I had decided to shut down my private practice, we were moving, and I needed to reinvent myself. Coaching seemed interesting, and I didn't feel like I was throwing the baby out with the bathwater, so I took a harder look at it as a career direction. All of the sudden, the lights switched on in my head, and I started to see how competencies came alive. The competencies made sense as a container for a coaching conversation in a way that made it safe to explore and kept me from tripping into the therapy space. In the next eleven years, I have come to see how nuanced and thoughtful the competencies are and how they keep me firmly on the path of partnership.

It really is like learning to dance. At first, you're counting the steps, trying not to trip, worried about doing it "right." Over time, the steps stop being something you think about and become something you feel. The music sets the rhythm, your body follows, and what was unconscious incompetence works its way toward unconscious competence. I have definitely danced between conscious and unconscious competence on this coaching journey. The competencies are clunky at first, but with time and practice, they stop being a checklist and start becoming a way of moving smoothly in the dance with another human being.

Sticky Outcomes!

The ICF Competencies, when viewed through the PCC Markers, sometimes referred to as the PCC Minimum Skills Required (MSR), offer more than an assessment tool; they illustrate the behaviors that define effective coaching. Each marker points to the behaviors a coach demonstrates during a coaching conversation. One question may meet multiple markers, or it may meet none. For the full and official ICF PCC Markers/MSRs, visit the International Coaching Federation's website at www.coachingfederation.org and search "PCC Markers" to download the current version.

By working with both the Competencies and the PCC MSRs, you begin to see what embodied coaching looks, sounds and feels like. As you listen to a coaching session, pay attention to learning to identify the moments where competencies are demonstrated and partnership is demonstrated, and also notice where it is missing. This is a critical skill and will support your ability to choose your questions, knowing for whom and for why you are asking them. You can spot the difference between asking questions from a place of curiosity versus asking them to steer the thinker in a particular direction.

The following chapters will introduce you to the ICF Core Competencies through the lens of the MSRs. Together, they form both a compass and a measuring stick, not just for credentialing but for growth as a coach who is willing and ready to go beyond "good enough."

Staying in the Role of Coach

We have already discussed a lot about the role of coaching. Still, one of the most common challenges for coaches is knowing where coaching ends and another discipline begins. The MSRs act as bumper guards on the conversation to keep coaches in the coaching lane.

In 2014 when I had completely closed my private therapy practice and was shifting gears into full time coaching. In 2015, I recorded myself in a coaching conversation for a job interview. I have done a lot of assessments since this time, and I can say, it's a really common coaching conversation with a *LOT* of room for growth. This example demonstrated beautifully *what you don't want to do*, how I stayed focused on the problem and that I just missed the important work to be done.

Breaking Down the Competencies

For starters, I spoke equal to or even a little more than the thinker, I had no sense that silence was even necessary. It was strange too, because in therapy, I didn't talk as much as I found myself talking in coaching. My invented meaning-making says, I was in a very real state of discomfort shifting into coaching. I was working very hard on being a perfect coach and making sure I didn't accidentally slip into therapy. Apparently that discomfort came with me talking a lot.

In hindsight, I didn't need to get rid of my therapy style; I needed to shift my focus instead. Therapy is often the movement from dysfunctional to functional, and I see coaching as the movement from functional to thriving. But at the time of this coaching conversation, I still had some ground to cover before I was coaching transformationally. What follows is an example of transactional coaching.

Coaching Demo: 2015

Coach: "Excellent. Well, thank you again. In light of that, did you decide what area you wanted to do some coaching around?"

Thinker: "I'd like to discuss starting a business, which I've become very excited about and have been immersed in lately. And there are a couple of areas that feel like stumbling blocks to me, which I would like to work through. And I was hoping to discuss those with you."

Coach: "Okay, let me ask you a few questions before we get into starting your business. Can you share a little bit about your business?"

I was immediately in the weeds. I was dancing the box step and missing the opportunity to tango. I missed the opportunity to explore the thinker's amazing metaphor of **stumbling blocks**; instead, I took the wheel, steering the conversation quite directly into a discussion around the details of her business. Again, I was trying not to be a therapist, so I was keeping it superficial.

While coaching isn't therapy, it's also not superficial. I see that in lots of new coaches. We are all working so hard to stay in our coaching

Sticky Outcomes!

lane that we keep the thinker focused on the surface, explaining details that have little to nothing to do with the conversation that they want or need to have.

> Thinker: "Yeah, my business is going to be architectural and real estate photography. With my art background, I wanted to do something that has a creative element and gets me out of the house so that I can, um, just interact with the world a little more than I'm doing right now. Sort of where I want to go with the business. Right now, I'm in a place where I'm practicing photography as much as I can, and I'm working toward making my images more professional. And one of the stumbling blocks I'm running into is thinking about taking the next step, because the part where I put together the website and the part where I get the business license and sort of learn the equipment and the technology around it comes super easy to me, and I find that really exciting. I get very nervous about marketing myself, but this is not the kind of business that's going to market itself either. I have to be out there making that part happen, and it's not comfortable for me to do that. So, I guess that's the primary thing I wanted to bring up in this conversation today."

> Coach: "Okay, so then let me ask you a couple of questions, if that's okay with you? By the end of the session, it seems to me that the area you want to focus on is around marketing, and there's some fear coming up around it. Is that what I'm hearing you say?"

Not only have I steered the thinker to the surface (marketing) and the Negative Emotional Attractor (NEA/fear), but I also created a long pre-amble, amble, and post-amble question.

CP: "Thank you for sharing your experience so fully. As you reflect, what is most important to you at this time?"

CP: "I am hearing the discomfort. How would you like to be approaching these things instead?"

Either of these sorts of questions would have gotten the conversation back on track. But, alas, my conversation stays stuck in

Breaking Down the Competencies

the superficial and tactical.

> Coach: "Okay. And by the end of the 30 minutes, what do you hope to walk away with? What would be your goal at the end of the session?"
>
> Thinker: "I'd love to say my goal is to become a great marketer, but realistically, I think I just need to work on some strategies."
>
> Coach: "All right. And do you have a sense of where you want to? Before we start working on strategies for where your marketing might go, do you have a clear sense of what you want your marketing to achieve?"
>
> Thinker: "Um, I don't know. Yes and no. I believe my marketing strategy should focus on interacting with people on a one-on-one basis or in a group setting, where I can introduce myself to those who might need my services. I find that in-person interactions are more powerful, but email is also effective."
>
> Coach: "So, what I'm hearing you say is that for you, the current vision of marketing is more one-on-one or through email."
>
> Thinker: "Yes."
>
> Coach: "Okay. And have you done any research at this point around marketing?"

It's literally painful to see how I handled this conversation. I used every opportunity to direct the thinker back to the problem, and I missed every opportunity to get to the heart of the matter.

> Coach: "So, let me read back what I've heard you say. And it's not everything you've just said, but what I'm hearing you say is that when you know you're feeling confident, you feel like you easily interact with strangers, you feel comfortable doing what you're doing, you look forward to it, and you can leap hurdles."

Sticky Outcomes!

Thinker: "Yes."

I'm over-summarizing here, and because I don't ask a question, the thinker is left with several single-word responses: "Yes." Nothing much is being learned on their part, even though I'm talking a lot. I finally say *leap hurdles*, which isn't her language, *stumbling blocks*, but mine, and again, I have a golden opportunity to dig in a bit deeper… sadly, I start leading the thinker toward an activity. Going back to vertical development, I'm 100 percent in a horizontal position right now.

Coach: "So, if you were to say that as a goal, what might that sound like to you? Like something that feels really empowered as a goal. And I'll give you an example. It might sound something like, 'I easily leap hurdles as I'm comfortably interacting with strangers as I market my business.' And I'm not saying that's the thing to do, but something like that, what resonates for you as a direction you want to go with the marketing for your architectural photography business?"

I am working hard here to provide value, but this is a great example of how my enthusiasm and **coach-led** coaching have led to the thinkers' agency and potential learning being stolen from them. I am not doing this intentionally, but geez, I am still doing it. I am totally leading this conversation, to the point that I am offering examples of what she might say to herself. *Sigh…*

And here is the thing, the thinker said at the end that they appreciated the session. They walked away with some actions; it was a totally adequate session. I passed my ACC with a call very similar to this one. But it wasn't a transformational conversation; I was clearly in the unconscious incompetence phase of my development.

How the Competencies Create the Container of a Coaching Conversation

Think of the coaching conversation as a container. Competencies 1 and 2: Ethics and Coaching Mindset, shape the integrity of the container. But Competencies 3–8 form the structure that holds the

Breaking Down the Competencies

container of a coaching conversation together, ensuring it stays thinker-led from start to finish.

Competency 3 (Establishes and Maintains Agreements) keeps the session clear. We are partnering to understand what the thinker wants to accomplish and how they will know that they have accomplished what they set out to do in the conversation. We discover what is important about what they are bringing to coaching, and we partner with the thinker to decide what they believe needs to be addressed to achieve what they want to achieve.

Competency 4 (Cultivates Trust and Safety) ensures that the thinker's insights and work in the coaching is acknowledged and respected. Showing support and empathy for their experience. While inviting their expression of feelings, perceptions, concerns, beliefs, and suggestions. Making this truly thinker-led.

Competency 5 (Maintains Presence) keeps the coach focused and present. We are acting in response to the whole person and what they want to accomplish. Supporting the thinker to choose what happens in the session. Demonstrating curiosity in order to learn more about the thinker. And, allowing for silence, pause, and reflection.

Competency 6 (Listens Actively) tunes your ear not only to the words, but also to meaning, emotion, as well as what's said and unsaid. Questions are customized to what the thinker is sharing. We are exploring the words that are being used, the emotions that are emerging, and we are noticing energy shifts and other non-verbal cues. Summarizing the through line, not every word, and giving lots of space for the thinker to finish their thoughts and words.

Competency 7 (Evokes Awareness) this is where many coaches want to live. It's about asking powerful questions about how the thinker is thinking, their values, beliefs and values. We are also exploring ways that move the thinker beyond the current situation, into expanded ways of thinking or feeling about themselves and their situation. We are asking questions that support exploration toward the outcome. We might share what we are observing or noticing and inviting the thinker to explore or make meaning. We are asking clean, concise, and primarily open-ended questions. And, allowing the thinker to do most of the talking.

Competency 8 (Facilitates Client Growth) ensures that the thinker leaves the session with their own insights, actions, and understanding of what might get in their way and ideas on how to hold themselves accountable. The eights may be sprinkled throughout a coaching conversation. What have you just learned about yourself? How does this awareness you just shared illuminate your situation? How are we doing in our exploration toward your goal? Where do we need to explore next? This is also where we are celebrating their capacity to think for themselves, "That sounded like a powerful insight, what are you noticing?"

Together, these competencies create a dynamic, co-created structure, solid enough to hold the whole conversation with depth, and enough flexibility to follow where the thinker leads us. The competencies are the framework that allows you to remain a coach while honoring the boundaries of what coaching is and is not.

Learning with the Competencies

The Competencies set a framework for you to learn, so that you can ultimately embody them as a way of showing up in coaching conversations. As we discussed earlier, I believe strongly in recording as much of your coaching as you can. When you listen back to your own coaching and track where the competencies show up... Or where they're missing, you begin to hear yourself differently.

When I first learned about the coaching competencies, I was skeptical. I had a pretty strong therapy bias and, in a deeply humble way, thought, *This is totally silly, I already know all this stuff.*

Fast forward to about eight years after that original training. I had decided to shut down my private practice, we were moving, and I needed to reinvent myself. Coaching seemed interesting, and I didn't feel like I was throwing the baby out with the bathwater, so I took a harder look at it as a career direction. All of the sudden, the lights switched on in my head, and I started to see how competencies came alive. The competencies made sense as a container of a coaching conversation in a way that made it safe to explore and kept me from tripping into the therapy space. In the following eleven years, I have come to see how nuanced and thoughtful the competencies are and

Breaking Down the Competencies

how they keep me firmly on the path of partnership.

It really is like learning to dance. At first, you're counting the steps, trying not to trip, worried about doing it "right." Over time, the steps stop being something you think about and become something you feel. The music sets the rhythm, your body follows, and what was unconscious incompetence works its way toward unconscious competence. I have definitely danced between conscious and unconscious competence on this coaching journey. The competencies are clunky at first. But with time and practice, they stop being a checklist and start becoming a way of moving smoothly in the dance with another human being.

The ICF Competencies, when viewed through the PCC Markers, serve as more than just an assessment tool; they illustrate the behaviors that define effective coaching. Each marker indicates the behaviors a coach demonstrates during a coaching conversation. One question might meet multiple markers, or it could meet none.

By working with both the Competencies and the PCC Markers, you begin to see what embodied coaching sounds and feels like. As you listen to a coaching session, learn to identify the moments where competencies are demonstrated, where partnership is demonstrated, and also notice where it's missing. This is a critical skill and will support your ability to choose your questions, knowing for whom you are asking them, and why. You can spot the difference between asking questions from a place of curiosity versus asking them to steer the thinker in a particular direction.

Maybe you notice how often you talk versus use silence. As in my case, from 2015, maybe you talk 51% of the time to the thinkers 49%... **Sigh**. Or you begin to see how quickly you slide into problem-solving or focus on the interesting details that aren't all that important, instead of staying curious. These are gold moments for growth. Use the markers not as a scorecard but as a learning tool.

The competencies and markers help you move past the clunky box step of early coaching and into something closer to a flowing dance. Not a performance, but a real tango, fully alive, responsive, and co-created with the thinker.

CHAPTER TEN

The First Bookend of Every Coaching Conversation

> Airplanes are off course about 90% of the time. But because we have the end in mind, the pilot can just nudge the plane back on course.
>
> —Stephen R. Covey

If there's one drum I keep beating when I'm coaching, mentoring, or listening to coaching calls at all the levels—ACC, PCC, and MCC—it's this: agreement setting, agreement setting, agreement setting. Without it, you will never have a fully client-led coaching session. You might have a nice conversation, but you're not really coaching. A thorough agreement for the coaching conversation keeps us from wandering in circles in a field somewhere, talking pleasantly while poking around in the dark, hoping to find what's important.

In the context of a coaching conversation, agreement setting serves as one bookend, represented by Competency 3, while Competency 8, which facilitates growth, anchors learning and creates actions and accountability, serves as the other bookend, ensuring a full container across all the competencies. The goal at the start is to prime the thinker's brain for what they want to discuss, why it matters, where they want to go, and how they want to get there.

Agreement setting is the first step in giving the thinker the wheel. The thinker knows the terrain; we, as the coach, are along for the ride.

What the Competencies Point Toward

Here's how Competency 3, Agreement Setting, breaks down. It is demonstrated by four markers. They're not a sequence you have to march through. But if they're missing, you're not really partnering. And if you're not partnering, chances are you're not coaching.

- Coach partners with the client to identify or reconfirm what the client wants to accomplish in this session.

- Coach partners with the client to define or reconfirm measure(s) of success for what the client wants to accomplish in this session.

- Coach inquires about or explores what is important or meaningful to the client about what they want to accomplish in this session.

- Coach partners with the client to define what the client believes they need to address to achieve what they want to accomplish in this session.

Again, these don't need to be completed in order. Depending on the conversation you're having, you might ask questions that evoke awareness. But do make sure you come back and have agreed upon clarity between you and the thinker, for where they want to go, how they will know when they arrive, why it's important, and how they want to navigate between where they are now and where they want to be by the end of the conversation.

Let's explore through the perspective of a transcript of an actual coaching conversation.

Coach: "What's showing up that's important today?"

Thinker: "I've just moved into a new role managing seven direct reports. I'm younger than most of them, and I sometimes feel like they don't take me seriously. Honestly, I feel like an impostor."

From here, the coach might ask:

- "Given what you just shared, what is rising to the surface as important for our conversation today?"

- "What makes this important to you right now?"

- "I heard impostor, what feels different when you don't feel like an impostor?"

The First Bookend of Every Coaching Conversation

A thorough agreement for the coaching conversation keeps us from wandering in circles in a field somewhere, talking pleasantly while poking around, hoping to find what's important.

These questions allow the thinker to name what matters and what success will look like… perhaps they would be calmer, more confident, and able to show up fully at work.

The coach might ask, "If you were handling this better and feeling confident, what would be the indicators of that?"

Now we're priming both the thinker and the coach's brain for the direction and outcomes while keeping the focus on the thinker's meaning-making; it's not about telling stories about all the mean old people on the team. While interesting, I am sure, that is not important. The impostor syndrome and the desire to feel confident is where we need to point our radar.

> Thinker: "When I'm more confident, I'm calmer, not stressed all the time. I don't wake up with a headache, dreading work."
>
> Coach: "So, by the end of our conversation, you'd like to feel more confident and calmer, ready to go to work?"
>
> Thinker: "Yes, that's it."

Then we can move to greater partnering when we ask, "What's the first thing that would be important to explore as we navigate to confident calm?"

That's the client-led invitation. You tell me where we need to start and how you want to explore between where you are and where you want to go.

Think of agreements like getting directions in a new town. You don't just want the destination. You want the turns, maybe how many stop signs or traffic lights, and a few landmarks always help. "Go through the stop sign, look for the big red barn, and then hang a right."

Agreements help both the thinker and the coach know where they're going and how they'll know when they've arrived.

Sticky Outcomes!

The Neuroscience of Priming and Directionality

Understanding priming and directionality can further illuminate the importance of agreement setting in coaching. Agreement setting works because the agreement primes both the thinker's and the coach's brains. Priming is when focusing on one thing causes the brain to notice it everywhere, like when you're shopping for a car and that model suddenly appears everywhere you go. Agreements cue the brain: pay attention here; this matters.

A 2025 study in *Current Biology* showed that the hippocampus isn't only storing memories but also generating predictions that prime the brain to recognize and respond more quickly when familiar information appears (Wokke et al. 2025). That's exactly what agreement setting does. When we ask, "What do you want to accomplish today?" Or "How will you know this has been useful?" We help the thinker's brain predict what to notice. Instead of chasing every detail, their system is primed to catch insights and actions that line up with the outcome they named.

There's also semantic priming. A 2025 *Cerebral Cortex* study found that when we hear a word or concept, the brain automatically activates related meanings before we're conscious of it (Zhou et al. 2025). That's why the "why does this matter?" Part is so important. When a thinker says, "I want to feel more confident leading my team," their brain isn't holding confidence in isolation. It's pulling in connected networks, memories, feelings, and motivations that give the word its richness. Asking about importance ties the session to meaning, which boosts stickiness.

The brain is filtering an overwhelming amount of input all the time (Felleman et al. 1991; Grady et al. 1998). Agreements cut through the noise, *saying pay attention here*, which leads to:

- **Clarity and focus:** the mind is cued to notice what's relevant

- **Efficiency:** instead of chasing every thread, you track what leads to the desired outcome

- **Motivation:** anticipating a meaningful outcome activates dopamine, which fuels persistence and learning (Schultz 1997)

The First Bookend of Every Coaching Conversation

- **Safety:** having a sense of direction and what to expect reduces stress and opens access to creativity and problem-solving

Boyatzis and Jack point to this as well. When coaching begins with vision, purpose, and desired future state, it activates the Positive Emotional Attractor (PEA), tied to openness, creativity, and growth (Boyatzis et al. 2014; Boyatzis et al. 2018). Jumping straight to 'fixing' triggers the NEA, narrowing attention and resistance. Start with purpose, not problems. Agreements orient the brain toward what the thinker most wants: safety, momentum, and meaning, all rolled together.

Follow the Leader

Research has shown that the person receiving a question will tend to follow the direction the coach sets, often without either person realizing it. In frame-by-frame studies of real conversations, Janet Bavelas, Sarah Healing, and their colleagues at the University of Victoria found that thinkers respond in line with the coach or therapist's previous turn 90 to 97 percent of the time. As we construct our questions, we create presuppositions. For example, *What are you feeling about being new at the job?* Points the thinker in a very specific direction. Questions are not neutral; they always carry a presupposition. The structure of the conversation itself gives the coach or therapist disproportionate directional power.

As the questioner, we need to be aware of where we are presupposing or leading the thinker. In my conversation with Dr. Haesun Moon, she described her Dialogic Orientation Quadrant (see image below), which includes Q1: Preferred Future, Q2: Resourceful Past, Q3: Troubled Past, and Q4: Dreaded Future. The more we focus on the Troubled Past or the Dreaded Future, the more the thinker will stay in those quadrants. We absolutely need to acknowledge these elements, and we also need to explore and discover the future the thinker wants. Otherwise, the conversation can spiral into darker places that are difficult to get out of.

This is what Haesun Moon emphasized in our conversation. If a thinker lingers in the "Troubled Past" or "Dreaded Future" quadrants of the Dialogic Orientation Quadrant, it is rarely because they are stuck on their own. More often, we unintentionally guided them there. Moon reminds us that no question is neutral, and microanalysis

Sticky Outcomes!
Dialogic Orientation Quadrant

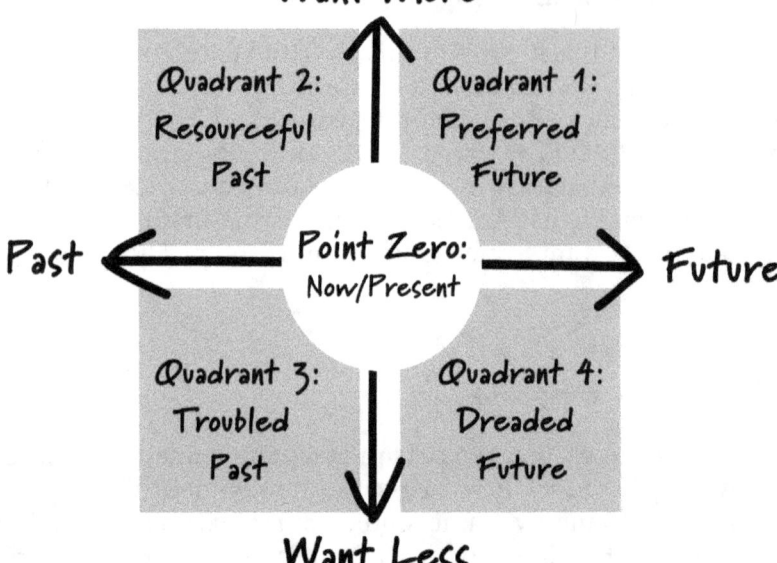

backs her up. Our questions do not just evoke awareness; they shape what the thinker notices and tells us about. What we listen for grows (deHart 2026).

Two Levels of Agreement Setting

There are really two levels of Agreement setting. We need both:

> O Engagement agreement: the container for the relationship, confidentiality, roles, scope, and structure.

> O Session agreement: the here-and-now focus, what matters today, why it matters now, and what would make this meaningful.

The engagement level frames the whole coaching journey. The session level keeps each conversation anchored to the thinker's current needs. Both are essential.

In the session, agreements aren't a one-time step at the beginning. If during the conversation it seems we took a left instead of a right at the big red barn, then we may need to recontract. *It seems we may be talking about something different than calm confidence, or*

The First Bookend of Every Coaching Conversation

is this connected for you? At this point, the thinker might make the connection or decide to either go back to the original outcome or shift to a new outcome. Each conversation is a new chance to partner on gaining that clarity.

Masterful coaches weave agreements throughout conversations. A simple *Does this still feel important?* Or *Is this the road you want to keep following?* Allows the coach to check in, and also makes sure that the agreement on where the conversation is going still applies. And if it doesn't, the coach can determine what else needs to be explored to move the conversation in the direction the thinker desires.

Getting Below the Plan

I had an executive come in, and the first thing they said was, "I need a plan, I just need steps to handle this situation."

On the surface, that sounded clear enough. They needed a plan. But if I had just run with it, the whole session would have skimmed along the surface. As we talked more, it became obvious the steps weren't really the issue. They already knew what to do. The real struggle was the overwhelm and the stress spiral that made it hard to take action or follow through.

If I had fallen for the hook and chosen to focus only on "making a plan," we would have missed the more important conversation. Below are some questions to keep the conversation from staying on the surface:

- "What's important about a plan right now?"
- "How do you show up differently when you have a plan?"
- "If having a plan would bring you equilibrium, what are the indicators of equilibrium?"
- "Where should we begin today?"

Those questions shifted the conversation from fixing to exploring the relationship to the problem. From there, the thinker developed their own insights. By the time we closed in Competency 8 (Facilitating Client Growth), the plan emerged, but now it came from their clarity and awareness.

Sticky Outcomes!

Once More with Feeling!

So here's where I land: agreement setting isn't optional. It isn't a checklist. It's coaching. It is how you and your thinker decide together where you're going, why it matters, how you'll know you're getting there, and where to start.

Agreement setting is not just the first bookend of every coaching conversation. It is also the compass that keeps you on track as you move through the session.

So let me bang that drum one more time: agreement setting, agreement setting, agreement setting. It is both the anchor and the compass of client-led coaching. Without it, you are just having a conversation. With it, you are truly coaching.

Activity: Getting to Agreement

For your next three coaching conversations, practice setting a clean, shared agreement before anything else happens. Keep it simple. Find your own words for these questions so they feel and sound like you. At the very start of each session, ask four things. The first three can be in any order, and the fourth comes before you begin asking evocative questions. Here are some examples, but remember to play and wordsmith your own ways of asking for these elements of agreement setting.

1. Partnering to identify or reconfirm the session focus

These help the thinker name what they want for *this* conversation.

- "Where would you like to focus today?"
- "What feels most important to explore in the time we have?"
- "You mentioned a few threads. Which one feels like the right starting point right now?"
- "What would make this conversation useful for you today?"

2. Partnering to define or reconfirm measures of success

These invite the thinker to describe how they will know the

The First Bookend of Every Coaching Conversation

conversation worked.

- "How will you know this session moved something forward for you?"
- "What would be different by the end of today's conversation?"
- "If we wrapped in 30 minutes and you thought, 'That was worth it,' what happened?"
- "What signs would tell you we're heading in the right direction?"

3. Exploring what is meaningful or important about the goal

These uncover personal significance, value, or meaning.

- "What about this focus matters to you right now?"
- "Why is this the thing you want to spend time on today?"
- "What's at stake for you in exploring this?"
- "When you imagine getting clarity on this, what does it open up?"

4. Partnering to define what they believe they need to address

These help the thinker identify the terrain they want to work through.

- "What do you think you need to look at to get where you want to go today?"
- "What feels like the real work inside this topic?"
- "What do you sense is underneath this that's worth exploring?"
- "What do you want to understand better about yourself or the situation?"

Write the thinker's responses in a few words. During the session, glance back at those notes once or twice. If the conversation drifts, check in, for example: *How are we doing at getting to X?* Or *What else needs to be explored for X?*

Sticky Outcomes!

5. After each session, take one minute to jot down:

- ? What part of the agreement was clearest?
- ? Where did I lose the thread of what was important to the thinker?
- ? When did I start asking questions to try to figure out the goal or outcome the thinker wanted?
- ? What is different when the agreement is clear to both the thinker and the coach?
- ? What would I try differently next time?

This activity trains your brain to orient early, stay oriented, and coach from the thinker's meaning instead of the story details. It is deliberate practice, one nudge at a time, the same way a pilot keeps the plane on course.

CHAPTER ELEVEN

Shifting from Fixing to Partnering

> The greatest good you can do for another
> is not just to share your riches,
> but to reveal to them their own.
>
> —Benjamin Disraeli

One of the most important shifts you will make as you become a coach is learning to move from fixing to partnering. This change is not a matter of refining techniques or having a bigger toolbox; it is a fundamental reorientation of your mindset.

Fixing is seductive, it feels good to help solve issues and to be useful. Many of us became coaches because we care about people, and the instinct to fix is rooted in our genuine goodwill. But in coaching, fixing comes at a cost. It puts the focus on the coach rather than on the thinker. I have said it steals their learning, but I think it also takes away their agency. And it pulls us away from the heart of coaching, which is our thought partnership.

Partnership is the co-creative space where the thinker discovers their own insights and makes their own choices and meaning. And it is rooted in the core belief that every thinker is whole, capable, resourceful, and creative. In coaching it is not about the brilliance of the coach's solutions, but about the brilliance of the thinker's self-discovery. You do not need to work so hard; the answers do not belong to you.

Through the years this has been a less-than-smooth transition for me. I love to solve puzzles, I enjoy being helpful, and I love to share what I know. Yet, when I think about my personal evolution, all the important things I have really learned and applied in my life, each has come through trial and error, trying things on and thinking through how they worked or did not.

I like to use the analogy of going on holiday. If I come to visit you and share all my holiday photos, you may not remember them much past dinner, and you certainly will not have the somatic and lived experience of them that I have. The feeling, say, of jumping out of the airplane is mine; you may remember that I did it, but you do not have that surreal feeling of leaving the plane.

Giving advice and helping people by giving them solutions is like trying to explain your experience through photos and stories—we might enjoy the photos and stories, but they are not ours because we didn't live it.

The "Fixing" Trap: Why It Persists

First and foremost, the fixing trap persists because it feels good. We feel useful, we are saving people time, and hopefully disappointment. Yet fixing undermines the core of coaching, which is about empowering the thinker and supporting their growth. The truth is, we can never fully know what another person needs or is capable of, and so our solutions often come with a bit of hubris.

Fixing:

> Shifts the focus to the coach's perspective about what needs fixing, reducing the thinker's agency.

> Creates a hierarchical dynamic (I am the expert, you're the novice) that moves us away from partnership.

> Is typically focused on above-the-waterline actions & results instead of on more sustainable transformation.

This tendency is reinforced by cultural norms that celebrate expertise and problem-solving. Pretty much every culture has a

Shifting from Fixing to Partnering

sense that there are wise people, and we should learn from them. Yet coaching isn't about being the expert, its value lies in supporting the thinker's ability to think, decide for themselves, and make conscious choices.

What is often called the "fixer mentality" has parallels in psychology. It's not a diagnosis, but it shows up in places like the rescuer role in Karpman's Drama Triangle, the co-dependent patterns described in systems theory and research, and Wolfgang Schmidbauer's idea of helper syndrome, from his book *The Helping Syndrome: When Being Good Is Not Enough*. The common thread is this: fixing often gives the helper a sense of worth.

The hook for each of us is that it feels good in the short term. It's efficient, and you get a lot of praise for being the "go-to" person, the one who always steps up and saves the day. You might make yourself endlessly available, driven by needs for security, value, or simply because you are nice and genuinely want to help. But these patterns, while rewarding at first, will often lead to burnout and unhealthy dynamics in the long run. Plus, what I am capable of, for good or bad, doesn't really tell me anything about what *you* are capable of. I might be brave about ABC but scared of XYZ. It might be the opposite for you. So do I hold unrealistic expectations of the thinker, expecting them to be like me and capable of everything I am capable of, or do I limit them to my solutions based on what I am capable of accomplishing?

Bertrand Russell, in his Nobel Prize speech, noted four desires that can quietly feed this mentality: acquisitiveness, rivalry, vanity, and love of power. Fixers may unconsciously seek achievement (acquisitiveness), compare themselves with others (rivalry), chase validation (vanity), or influence outcomes (power). These drivers usually run beneath the surface, but they can keep us saddling up that white horse to rush in and rescue.

It's sort of a hard list to sit with. When I think about my own hooks, I can see how easily I can get pulled into chasing validation. I have had times in my life where I didn't feel validated. So this is something I try to pay attention to, because I don't need validation when coaching someone. Sure, when I cook an amazing meal, bring it on, but not in a coaching session.

Many of us enjoy being that helping person. Recognizing the pull to jump in is not about negative self-judgment; it's about self-awareness. Seeing our underlying motivation can help us, as coaches, reflect on what hooks us and give us a choice to move toward a healthier, more empowering coaching practice. One where we put the horse back in its stall, join the thinker in the car, slide into the passenger seat, and keep our hands off the wheel. Or better yet, we become the vehicle for change, while the thinker drives their own learning through lived experience.

From Fixing to Partnering: Mindset Shift

Transitioning to a partnering approach in coaching begins with a fundamental belief: the thinker is whole, capable, resourceful, and creative. That is a belief I hold for each person I work with, even when they don't yet hold it for themselves. As Fran Fisher, MCC, emphasizes, coaching involves "being with" the thinker rather than "doing to or for" them. This means:

- **Holding Presence:** Noticing their words, emotions, and energy.

- **Creating Spaciousness:** Using silence and pauses to allow reflection and insight.

- **Fostering Collaboration:** Inviting the thinker to create the direction and focus.

How Partnering Shows Up

- **Thinker-Centered Mindset:** The thinker is the expert in their own life. Your role is to hold space for exploration, not to solve.

- **Adaptability:** Coaching is dynamic. Stay flexible and let the thinker's evolving priorities guide you.

- **Silence and Spaciousness:** Neuroscience shows curiosity and insight thrive when the brain feels safe and unhurried. Silence is not empty; it's an invitation.

- **Curiosity as Reward:** Clean, open questions stimulate the brain's reward system and help insight stick.

- **Mutual Trust:** Coaching is strongest when it feels like a partnership, not a transaction.

Shifting from Fixing to Partnering

O **Integration:** Invite the thinker to connect their insights to the bigger picture of their life and goals.

Coaching Demo: Very Full Plate

It would have been easy to slip into fixing when the thinker began with this:

> Thinker: "Well, lately, I have been in a space of, like, hurry up and wait for a lot of different things. And now kind of, like, a lot of things, they are converging all at the same time. I'm finding myself in the space where I have too much on my plate... I am just trying to sort it all out. And I feel like I've been really mindful of what I'm saying yes and no to. And now I'm like, I was so mindful about saying yes. I'm just feeling so overwhelmed right now."

At this point, many coaches would be tempted to go to a direct, solution-oriented question: Okay, *I am hearing you need to sort it out, what does sort it out mean to you?* That would be a choice point. But notice where it points: straight to problem-solving. Straight into the weeds. The risk is that we would help the thinker sort out all these things. Or we could have latched onto overwhelmed and potentially started with a whole series of *What does overwhelm feel like?* Or *How do you stop being overwhelmed?* Leading to the thinker potentially getting more overwhelmed.

Instead, the coach leaned into the metaphor, partnering with what the thinker had already given: the plate. The coach used it as a safe, nondirective entry point for deeper exploration.

> Coach: "I'm really hearing the overwhelmed. And I'm curious. As you look at this full plate, given that we're going to be talking for about 15 to 20 minutes, what would you like to do with this plate by the end of our conversation?"

This is a different kind of invitation. It acknowledges the overwhelm, honors the container the thinker already offered, and hands back agency. The thinker's response signals the deeper work:

> Thinker: "I think now I really need to say no to things. I was so mindful about saying yes, and right now I'm just feeling overwhelmed. I don't know what to do, and it's really stressing me out. I think it would be helpful to at least clarify one or two things I could say no to today."

Now the goal of the session has emerged. The plate isn't just about tasks; it's about boundaries, discernment, and integrity. What the thinker needs to *say no* to, versus weighing the pros and cons of each decision.

> Coach: "So, clarifying a couple of things that you could maybe *say no* to. As you're looking at that plate, where would you like to begin exploring those things?"

Here we see both agreement setting and a move away from fixing. The coach doesn't prescribe which things to remove from the plate. Instead, they ask the thinker to explore what they see, what choices matter most, and what saying no means in the larger story of how they want to live and lead.

Inter-fluence

Inter-fluence is Haesun Moon's way of describing how two people shape each other's thinking in real time during a conversation. Instead of imagining the coach as the one who "influences" and the thinker as the one who receives that influence, Moon shows that meaning is created between the participants, turn by turn. Moon explains that in real conversations, each person's words and actions naturally shape what the other person says next, and that shared meaning builds as the conversation unfolds (Moon 2022).

Inter-fluence means we're not talking at someone, we're always talking with them. Even if we don't realize it, every question we ask shapes our interactions, and it becomes an invitation to the next part of the conversation. What the thinker says in return then shapes our next question. It's like improv, each of us taking turns and playing with

Shifting from Fixing to Partnering

what was offered. This way of considering our coaching conversations helps us understand the dynamic: the coach isn't fixing or working too hard, and the thinker isn't passively receiving the coach's wisdom but sharing their own. They are building meaning together, moment by moment, through language, attention, and shared understanding.

When we think of coaching as inter-fluence rather than influence, it changes how we ask questions, how we partner, the ears we use to listen, and how we understand our role. We are not responsible for fixing anything. We become more aware that our language steers the conversation, and we also stay humble to the fact that the thinker is shaping us right back.

Coaching Demo: On the Right Path

Another thinker arrived with a different surface-level problem:

> Thinker: "Yeah, the thing that's showing up today has been something that I've kind of coming back to over the last six months or so, which is this kind of nagging sense of discontentment related to my job.
>
> "I've been thinking about this. My grandpa, when I was a teenager, would frequently tell me, 'You know, Ryan, there's no need to be in a big hurry when you're heading down the wrong path.'
>
> "And so, I'm just wondering, am I on the right path?
>
> "Because at times it feels like, holy smokes, I am. And it feels great, um, in so many ways. And then again, at times, I just don't know that there's something different pulling me or there's something sort of pulling me off the current path, that won't seem to go away. And I don't know if I should let it go away or make it go away, or if it's something that I should address. Do I need to pursue it, I guess."

This is the kind of invitation that almost begs for fixing.

The coach could easily respond with analysis, pros and cons, or even advice. But notice the hook: six months of a nagging sense of discontentment, I don't know if I should let it go, make it go away, or if it's something to pursue. If the coach takes that bait, the session will shift into consulting.

If the coach asks, *Should we look at the pros and cons of your choices?* You already know where that question will lead, straight into solving a problem. At this point in the book, I hope you choose a different choice point.

Instead, the coach invited exploration:

Coach: "Is there a significance or importance about this being either pulled toward, or forward, or off the path or, you know, like your grandpa said?"

This small question began to hone in on what was important. The conversation no longer revolved around the pros and cons of a decision. It opened into a deeper inquiry about values, motivation, and the life the thinker actually wanted. What was pulling them?

As the session unfolded, the thinker revealed that what they were really wrestling with wasn't the opportunity itself but the need to noodle through the decision and find the one that aligned with their life.

Thinker: "I've been saying yes to things because they look good, or because I don't want to disappoint people. But when I think about what I actually want… I'm not sure these choices fit."

Here again, the coach resisted the urge to decide for the thinker. They didn't say, *Well then, don't take it,* or *You should hold out for something better.* They stayed in curiosity:

Coach: "What kind of life do you want this decision to support?"

This question reframed the deeper inquiry. The *decision* wasn't about the opportunity in front of him; it was about designing a life that aligned with who he wants to be.

What These Conversations Show Us

In both transcripts, the temptation to fix was strong. It would have been easy to:

- Sort the plate for the thinker.
- Weigh the pros and cons of the opportunity.
- Offer solutions that look pretty and efficient.

Yet, fixing robs the thinker of agency. The real work of coaching happens when we resist the hook, lean into curiosity, and partner with the thinker's meaning-making.

In *Very Full Plate*, the plate became a container for exploring boundaries and integrity.

In *On the Right Path*, the "decision" became a doorway into values, purpose, and long-term vision.

Neither conversation ended with the coach handing over answers. They ended with the thinker owning their own insights, insights that will sustain their growth far longer than any advice ever could or would. They had the opportunity to think critically as they worked through the choices in front of them.

Fixing feels fast, but it's often shallow. And while partnering can feel slower, it's often far more transformational.

Your role as a coach is not to clear someone's plate or decide their path. It's to create the environment where they can look at their own plate, their own path, and say with clarity, *This is what matters most to me.*

Practical Shifts

Here are a few ways to practice shifting from fixing to partnering:

- Language: Replace *Let's look at this* with *What feels most important to explore today?*

- Whole Person Awareness: Invite the body and values into the conversation: *What are you noticing as you say that?*

- Metaphors: Lean into the thinker's imagery: *What would you like to do with this plate?*

- Compassionate Detachment: Offer observations without attachment: *I noticed your tone shifted just now, what, if anything, does that mean to you?*

- Celebrate Autonomy: Acknowledge courage and insight as the thinker names them, reinforcing their agency: *I appreciate that insight, what is it telling you?*

Skills to Artistry

At first, shifting from fixing to partnering takes discipline. You may have to bite your tongue, resist the urge to advise, and trust the silence. But over time, these practices become part of who you are as a coach, the learning journey in motion.

Artistry emerges when skills integrate into presence. Partnering stops being something you "do" and becomes the way you show up. And yet, even at MCC, this is not an endpoint. We continue to unlearn old habits, notice when fixing creeps back in, and recommit ourselves to partnership.

Mentor coaching, transcript analysis, and supervision are invaluable here. Reviewing recordings helps you spot subtle moments when you slipped back into fixing, leading, or solving the thinker's problem. External feedback shines a light on your blind spots. Self-reflection builds awareness. Together, these practices deepen your capacity to stay in true partnership.

We Are Not Here to Fix People

Why understanding this matters in organizational coaching:

Shifting from Fixing to Partnering

Executives are surrounded by people who fix. Their teams fix problems, consultants fix strategies, boards fix accountability, and stakeholders fixate on outcomes. Leaders are often rewarded for being decisive problem-solvers, so it's natural that they expect coaching to operate in the same mode: *Tell me what to do.*

But when coaches step into fixing, they reinforce the very dynamic that keeps leaders reactive and disempowered. The true gift of executive coaching is creating that rare space where the leader is not told, advised, or judged, but instead invited to think, reflect, and choose with agency. Partnership shifts the leader from seeking solutions outside themselves to generating wisdom from within.

This competency supports leaders in:

O Reclaiming Agency: Leaders rediscover that they have the capacity to think clearly without being handed the "right" answer.

O Breaking the Fixing Cycle: They learn that sustainable leadership growth comes not from someone solving for them, but from building confidence in their own insight and decision-making.

O Modeling Partnership: Experiencing this style of engagement often influences how they lead their own teams, shifting from directive to collaborative.

O Building Resilience: Instead of relying on external experts, leaders strengthen their own reflective practices, which helps them navigate complexity with more clarity and calm.

I often have said, "I am a short-term solution to your long-term life. It is not for me to decide for you. It's my job to support you in trusting yourself and your capacity to make your own decisions."

Shifting from fixing to partnering is not a one-and-done skill. It's a practice. You'll catch yourself wanting to fix, sometimes more often than you'd like. That's human. The work is in noticing it, pausing, and choosing to partner instead, handing the work back to the thinker where it belongs. We know that's where the dots get connected, learning sticks, and transformation lasts.

● ● ●

CHAPTER TWELVE

THE OTHER BOOK END

> People believe what they hear themselves say.
> —Miller & Rollnick

Coaching isn't just about awareness. It's about forwarding actions and exploring what happens next, once we have insights and awareness. When I first started coaching, Competency 8 was the hardest one for me. I'd get to the end of a session and suddenly feel like I'd turned into a parent: *What did you learn? What are you going to do? How will you hold yourself accountable?* It felt forced. It felt like I was doing something to my thinker instead of with them. And that's exactly the opposite of what this competency is about.

I was lucky enough to have a really good mentor coach during my early coaching development. I told her that I hated this final competency because, as mentioned above, I felt like I was acting like a parent, giving the thinker a checklist of things I wanted them to do, or pay attention to between sessions.

My mentor asked me a really interesting question, "What do your clients think about these questions?"

I didn't think about this competency much past I didn't like the questions. I hadn't yet made the connection that its real purpose was to anchor the learning, invite insight, and ask about actions, all of which I knew to be beneficial. I am not sure why; it just wasn't how I tended to close a therapy session. In therapy, I did ask people what they were taking away and what they would play with between sessions, but we didn't go much beyond that, which is funny, since in teaching and training, I knew you tell people what they are going to learn, then teach them, then ask them what they learned. It was basic learning theory.

After her question, my response was, "I don't know?"

She said, "Why don't you ask them?"

So I did. Funny enough, what I discovered was that, to a person, my thinkers loved sharing their insights. They loved the recap and the questions I disliked actually helped them clarify their awareness, define their next steps, and gain a sense of ownership.

I've said it many times, I know, but we want the thinker to create the dots, connect the dots, and own the dots. And in many ways, that's what Competency 8 does. It is the ownership of the dots. And why would I take that away from anybody?

Just as Competency 3 sets the stage at the beginning of a session, Competency 8 closes the loop. It's the other bookend, the place where insights get anchored, where awareness turns into something sticky, hopefully sticky enough to carry beyond the coaching conversation.

Insight Without Action Is Just an Idea

The brain loves repetition. When we name something, give it attention, and circle back to it, the brain's wiring gets stronger. Reflection turns a fleeting thought into a hard-wired groove in the brain. This is why anchoring matters. Agreement at the start of a session primes the brain to pay attention. Anchoring at the end strengthens and extends those neural pathways so the insight doesn't vanish when the Zoom call ends.

Boyatzis and Jack (2018) showed that when people articulate their own vision, it lights up the PEA, the system that fuels creativity, memory, and motivation. Norman Doidge (2007) reminds us that neuroplasticity depends on focused attention and repetition. Gupta and colleagues (2021) found that growth is deepest when awareness links to meaningful application.

Motivational Interviewing points to the same. Miller and Rollnick (2013) showed that when people voice their own reasons for change, what they called "change talk," they are far more likely to

the Other Book End

follow through. It's not a voice from outside, it's the echo of their own words that strengthens commitment.

Anchoring takes that one spark of awareness and stretches it: *If this is true here, where else does it show up?* That's how an insight becomes something sticky enough to shift how a person lives, leads, and relates.

What This Competency is Really About

Competency 8 is about supporting the thinker to connect the dots, not only within the session, but across their wider life and leadership. Anchoring means supporting them to pause, notice, and expand:

- "What just shifted for me?"
- "Where else in my life might this awareness apply?"
- "What action moves me forward from these insights?"
- "How will I hold myself accountable?"

When we hold that space, we're inviting the thinker to move from the microcosm of one moment into the macrocosm of their mindsets, patterns, and choices. And it's those mindsets, patterns, and choices that keep people spiraling or stuck. It's seeing how the same awareness might show up in different ways, given new circumstances. Maybe it shows up in the way they relate to people. Maybe it slips into daily choices without them even noticing. These little sparks of insight are the kind of awareness that leads to real change.

Going back to the locus of control, the only real power any of us has is over our internal locus, what we say, what we think, what we do. Because bad things will still happen. Difficult things, annoying things, and annoying people all show up daily. Budgets get blown, mistakes get made, the world stays messy and complex. That doesn't change. What can change is where the thinker puts their focus. The more they return to what they can actually control, their responses and their choices, the more influence they gain over how they experience the world. From the thousands of people I have worked with, the majority find that this internal locus of control, while not easy, is ultimately empowering.

And this is why agency matters. It's why the capacity to hear our own wisdom and explore our own insights is so important. Anchoring helps because it asks questions that move the thinker forward. That inherent knowledge, that we can choose our response to whatever shows up, gives us a way to apply a personal insight to the bigger picture of our lives.

Anchoring learning is also about respecting the thinker's own process. I think of it as critical thinking, accessing the whole system—our beliefs, our values, our sense of who we want to be as human beings. How we want to show up. Real growth doesn't happen because somebody tells you what to do or hands you a list of actions. It happens when the thinker decides what matters to them and how they want to carry that forward.

When a thinker names their insights, designs their own actions and strategies, and defines what accountability looks like for themselves—naming the strengths or values that will support them—they strengthen their ownership.

Agency is the capacity to act, make choices, and influence outcomes, while autonomy is freedom from external control and the ability to self-govern (Dictionary.com, 2025). Agency means the thinker recognizes, *This is mine. I chose it.* Autonomy is ownership that ensures the steps forward align with their values and context. Together, agency and autonomy transform insights and learning into empowered action. And—this is important—it's not just good practice. Respecting the thinker's responsibility for their own choices is a core ethical commitment of professional coaching.

Sprinkling the 8's

I was talking with Clare Norman, MCC, and she shared an idea of sprinkling the eights throughout the coaching sessions. It was one of those "aha" moments. I don't have to wait until the end of the coaching conversation to celebrate, or support the anchoring of insight, or explore where something might get derailed.

While I don't think there is anything wrong with using the last 5-10 minutes to support the thinker in anchoring their learning, it certainly can make the end of a coaching session sound like a checklist.

I now integrate Facilitating Client Growth into the entire session.

the Other Book End

And, while it is the second bookend to a coaching conversation, it isn't just a bookend at the end; it's the anchoring of insights and learning throughout the session.

Every time a thinker has an "aha," we might ask:

- "What are you learning about yourself right now?"
- "How might this insight ripple into other areas of your life?"
- "What feels possible now that didn't before?"

Each question anchors the moment. Each one moves the insight from idea to integration. By the time we reach the "official" end, the thinker has already practiced owning their learning, applying it, and celebrating it along the way. We are hearing all the trees falling, and so is the thinker.

How This Plays Out in Organizational Coaching

Agency and autonomy are especially important when working with leaders, CEOs, directors, managers, and basically everyone in the organization, because all of these individuals are constantly being told what to do, how to perform, or what others expect from them. Their days are filled with external demands, competing priorities, and the weight of responsibility for others.

Coaching provides one of the rare places where they are not managed, advised, or evaluated. Instead, they are invited to think for themselves. Research on Self-Determination Theory (Deci et al. 1985, 2000) shows that autonomy is one of three core psychological needs (along with competence and relatedness) required for intrinsic motivation and sustainable performance.

Paul Brown has spent much of his career looking at how the brain lights up in leadership. His focus is on the limbic system, and it's especially relevant here because leaders are constantly operating in high-stakes, emotionally charged environments. Brown points out that when leaders experience attention, ease, equality, and appreciation, the limbic system opens and reorganizes. He calls this reorganization a "rearrangement of the architecture" of the brain, which allows leaders to access clearer thinking, steadier emotional regulation, and more creative choices (Brown 2015).

In coaching, this means that creating those conditions is fundamental in supporting leaders to think beyond survival mode and into what is possible. This has a direct correlation with the Positive Emotional Attractors, working toward what brings about motivation and a direction that is about possibility and purpose (Boyatzis 2024).

When leaders experience agency and autonomy in coaching, when their learning, actions, and commitments are self-directed, they engage not out of compliance, but out of genuine ownership and alignment. And while this dynamic is especially visible in organizational contexts, it is just as true for any individual: real transformation only lasts when the thinker experiences ownership of their learning and their next steps.

What Does Growth Look Like in Practice?

Throughout a session, we might pause to explore progress toward what the thinker wanted from the conversation: *Where are you now, compared to where you hoped to be when we started?* In this way, they can see where they are, reorient themselves as needed, or keep moving forward.

Or we might ask them to name what they've learned about themselves, *the who*, and about the situation, *the what*. Sometimes those two are intertwined, sometimes they're separate. Either way, when the thinker names it, they own it.

From there, we can get curious about how that awareness carries forward: *How might this shift show up in other places in your world?*

Designing actions, reflection, or accountability doesn't need to sound like homework. I hate getting homework, and giving it, so I never give homework. However, people leave sessions with me with actions, self-determined actions. And it can be as simple as: *What would help this stick?* Or *From that insight, what might you want to play with between now and next session?* Those questions keep ownership where it belongs, with the thinker.

And don't forget the celebration. Too often, we slide past progress

the Other Book End

because there's more work to do. But pausing to acknowledge growth, however small, strengthens the neural pathways that make growth last.

Even how we close the session is part of this competency. We don't slap on a pretty bow in a perfect summary and wave goodbye. We ask: *How do you want to complete today's conversation?* In this way, even how we end the session belongs to the thinker.

Coaches, with practice, become comfortable not rushing through these moments.

Pause near the end (or throughout) to ask:

- "What are you learning about yourself?"
- "What does that awareness tell you?"
- "What feels possible now?"

Partner with the thinker to explore:

- "How might this awareness translate into future decisions or actions?"
- "What support or accountability might make follow-through more successful?"
- "How might you want to close today to feel complete?"

Here, presence and curiosity remain essential. The coach doesn't summarize the thinker's learning. They invite the thinker to speak it, name it, and own it, **dot, dot, dot.**

● ● ●

Coaching Demo: Getting Support

In this coaching demonstration notice the flow of the conversation.

Thinker: "So, one of the things I've been noticing is that I have all these projects and I start them, but then I get distracted, and I don't finish them. And then I feel bad about not finishing them."

Sticky Outcomes!

Coach: "So, you're seeing a pattern of starting and not finishing. What's important to you about noticing this right now?"

Here, the coach isn't jumping into problem-solving. They're helping the thinker connect today's awareness to why it matters in this moment. That's the beginning of anchoring, tying the conversation to what the thinker wants right now, not what the coach thinks should be important.

Thinker: "I think it's just I don't want to keep living in that cycle. I want to feel like I can finish what I start. There is a sense of accomplishment I get when I complete things. And I typically do finish things. So, I am not sure what is going on right now."

Coach: "What is different from when you typically finish things?"

Notice how the focus shifts from "the problem" to "the person." We are drawing out what the thinker is discovering about themselves in relation to the situation. They have *typically finished things*, but right now they are in a cycle of not finishing things. It's important we hear this.

Thinker: "I am in the middle of a new project, it has a lot of moving parts and I am a little worried. When I started, I got excited about the new ideas, but now I am noticing that I am having trouble with the follow through."

Coach: "What are you hearing that is important?"

Thinker: "I think it's the new project and the pressure I have to complete it. My mind is sort of blanking out."

Coach: "Given this insight, what do you need?"

Thinker: "I need to get help. I think I bit off more than I can chew all on my own. I really need more support to get it over the line."

Coach: "As you say that, what actions might support this insight?"

The coach asks the thinker to formulate actions for themselves based on their insights. This is where sticky actions emerge. When actions arise from the thinker's own awareness, they hold more meaning, and people are far more likely to follow through. I don't need to give homework or lay out an action plan if I link the awareness to what they want to do.

I was talking with Jonathan Passmore, and he cited research showing that thinker-generated actions are essential. Coach-led homework often created resistance, pressure, or a power imbalance. Client-led activities, or tasks shaped collaboratively, generated higher engagement, more ownership, and a sense of agency. In short, the more the thinker chose the action, the more likely they were to actually do it and learn something from it. People do need to leave a session with actions, but those actions need to be self-determined (Passmore et al. 2023). That fits my experience too, giving homework is usually a waste of time. Assigned actions don't create agency or authorship, but the actions people design for themselves almost always do.

Thinker: "I think I want to sit with this, I need to think about the right people to call. Probably some journaling as well about what exactly I need help with, that is always useful for me. It helps get more clarity. But it's also that I need to know what I need help with, so I can decide on the best people to help me."

Coach: "Where else might this insight be useful?"

This is the move from micro to macro. The thinker named an insight, and the coach invites them to explore where else it might apply. That's how awareness grows from one project to a broader way of living.

Thinker: "Yeah... I think it shows up in several projects I am working on. Not just this project. I need to reevaluate how I am managing some other projects as well and see if I need more help. I get into a head space of trying to do it all."

Sticky Outcomes!

Coach: "That sounds like an important awareness. How might you support yourself when you get into that head space, so you can see where you need more help?"

Here, the coach resists the urge to assign homework. Instead, they acknowledge the "important connection" and invite the thinker to design support that feels natural to them. Ownership deepens when the thinker generates their own strategies.

Thinker: "Maybe slowing down when I notice myself not completing things. That's a big blinking sign… Also, I need to be asking myself if I have the bandwidth for another project. I need to complete one before I start twelve more."

Coach: "Yeah, that's one of those forever truths. What is the best way for you to pay attention to the big blinking sign?"

Thinker: "Well, pulling back a bit when I notice things aren't getting done and not beating myself up. Take a beat, then focus on one important thing."

Coach: "What do you want to acknowledge about yourself in this moment?"

Thinker: "I already know how to do this. I'm also glad I brought this to coaching today. I was going to ignore it… I showed up for myself and my situation. I feel really good about this."

Celebration matters, and we do this by acknowledging the deep truths, the pearls, the wisdom, and the thinker's important insights. Another way to celebrate the thinker is to ask what they want to acknowledge about themselves, which gives them the opportunity to name what they appreciate about themselves. We have so few opportunities to do this in other areas of our lives, and it's powerful to hear ourselves say what we know to be true. In this, we help the thinker reinforce the neural pathways of capability and progress.

Celebration is not the coach handing out gold stars or shaking their pom poms; it's the thinker recognizing their own growth.

Bringing It All Together

When we invite people to name their learning, connect it to the bigger picture, design their own supports, and celebrate their progress, we're doing more than closing a session. It's amazing how just hearing themselves allows them to practice the muscle of self-ownership. And the more they practice, the more it shows up outside the session. They start catching their own insights as they have them. They pause long enough to name what is important. They begin carrying those discoveries forward into the rest of their lives.

Without this competency, coaching might not get to action or forwarding to the next place. With it, insights are acknowledged and named, actions designed, and the work sticks. The thinker leaves with something they can trust, something they know is theirs.

CHAPTER THIRTEEN

SAFETY THE FOUNDATION FOR COURAGE & GROWTH

> Psychological safety is not about being nice. It's about giving candid feedback, openly admitting mistakes, and learning together.
>
> —Amy Edmondson, Ph.D.

Amy Edmondson, a professor at Harvard Business School, first noticed the importance of psychological safety when studying hospital teams. To her surprise, the highest-performing teams reported making the most mistakes. It was not that they were careless; it was that they felt safe enough to admit errors, talk about them openly, and prevent them from happening again. In her book *The Fearless Organization* (2019), she argues that organizations thrive only when people can raise concerns, ask questions, and experiment without fear of punishment or reprisals.

For coaches, this concept translates directly into the coaching space. A coaching conversation cannot go deep if the thinker feels they must guard themselves, curate how they sound, or protect themselves from judgment. Trust and psychological safety are not "nice-to-have," they are the conditions that allow the nervous system to move from vigilance to openness. Without safety, people stay in the perceived safe zone at the surface, offering only pretty versions of themselves. With psychological safety, people discover that they can be honest, even be challenged and in turn challenging, as well as be able to explore what will lead them to grow.

Edmondson challenges leaders to cultivate psychological safety inside their organizations. What she found is that leaders who only hear what they want to hear risk surrounding themselves with people who don't want to rock the boat. History is full of costly examples of when a culture of agreement leads to disaster. Edmondson uses NASA's

Sticky Outcomes!

Columbia shuttle disaster in 2003 as a cautionary tale. When all the data came in on causes, what was discovered, in part, was a culture in which engineers felt they could not speak up without reprisal. Their silence proved fatal. Fearful environments might create the illusion of order; no one is sticking their head up, because no one wants to be the daisy that gets its head chopped off. In these environments, people suppress the very information leaders most need: perspectives on risk, innovative ways to solve problems, and truths about what is really happening in the larger system.

For leaders, psychological safety serves dual purposes. First, it is about the culture they are creating, which is fundamentally tied to their ego and courage. And second, it is tied to how safe they feel to discuss their ego and courage with themselves, let alone another person.

Strong leadership means being strong enough to hear dissenting voices, to invite hard truths, and to be willing to hear multiple perspectives so that decisions come from a position of greater information rather than curated reassurance.

In the coaching space, leaders get to practice considering dissenting perspectives, exploring their blind spots, assumptions, or the impact they are having on morale and organizational culture. Coaching offers them a mirror and allows them to experiment in a safe space. The goal is that awareness supports how they show up as leaders.

An example of culture shift is demonstrated by Microsoft's move from CEO Steve Ballmer, whose leadership style has been described as high-pressure, forceful, and direct, to Satya Nadella, whose leadership style has been described as growth-oriented and rooted in transformation. He had a clear vision of creating radical change. Nadella set about shifting the organization from "I know everything" to a culture of experimentation and collaboration (Marcos 2025). Under Nadella, Microsoft revised its mission statement to "empower every person and every organization on the planet to achieve more."

To support the changes, the organization began developing a coaching mindset, creating greater safety for people to ask for and get support without concerns of punishment. As these cultural changes were evolving, I worked on a project that trained Microsoft employees to become coaches. It was interesting to see how the movement was evolving, from needing to give answers toward asking questions. I

Safety the Foundation for Courage & Growth

think it started with Michael Bungay Stanier's book *The Coaching Habit* (2016), as managers began learning to ask questions. Initially, it was a bit formulaic, but it was a beginning. When I started working with them, I could see they were in the messy middle. Yet there was safety for these managers to play with changing long habits of telling. As Michael put it, they needed to manage their "advice monster." They still had deadlines, objectives, and goals, but managers were at least starting to play with partnering with their peers and direct reports.

In 2025, while presenting to the coaching team at Microsoft, I learned that their internal coaches, in partnership with the digital coaching platform EZRA, set a Guinness World Record in 2025 for "the most people to complete a business coaching program in one year." Panos Malakoudis showed me the award; it was really exciting. The record was achieved after 4,816 Microsoft employees engaged in coaching sessions within a year. If people hadn't felt safe enough to take up the offer to be coached, Microsoft would not be celebrating its 2025 World Record.

If we want to partner with leaders on their most pressing challenges, we must create spaces for people to learn, play, and grow. To try on new ways of being, see what works, understand that changes don't happen overnight, and be courageous enough not to give up with the first or one-hundredth pushback.

What this means is that we model what a safe container looks like:

- Checking in explicitly and asking permission before offering observations

- Holding space without judgment when leaders admit fear, doubt, or failure

- Trusting that their candor, not our expertise, is the raw material for change

In many ways, psychological safety is the bridge between coaching and leadership. Coaches cultivate safety so leaders can explore their leadership style and vision. Leaders cultivate safety so their organizations can thrive in a complex world. In both cases, courage is required: the courage to stop insulating ourselves from reality, take feedback, and create a vision that allows the entire organization to thrive.

How Trust and Safety Emerge

From a coaching perspective, trust and safety aren't about being nice, nodding often, or speaking in a calm tone to the thinker. They're about intentionally creating the conditions where the thinker can fully show up, bringing what they carry, in all its complexity, with the courage to explore what matters most.

A safe, attuned relational space is what allows a coaching conversation to move beyond surface goals into meaningful insight, emotional honesty, and lasting change. This doesn't happen by accident; it is built through presence, permission, transparency, and partnership.

From a brain-based perspective, safety is essential for creativity, visioning, and self-reflection. If the nervous system is activated into fight, flight, freeze, or fawn, the prefrontal cortex, the part of the brain needed for reflection and choice, goes offline. Coaches cultivate safety by co-regulating through consistent trustworthiness, attuned presence, and deep respect.

Shame, Vulnerability, Trauma, and Well-Being

When we talk about psychological safety, it's tempting to only think about what happens out there, in teams, organizations, or systems. But safety also has an inside dimension. It shows up in the way individuals wrestle with shame, the fear of disconnection, and their own capacity for vulnerability.

Brené Brown's research has popularized these ideas. She reminds us that shame isn't about what we did, it's the story that who we are is not enough. Guilt might say, *I made a mistake*. Shame says, *I am the mistake*. And here's the thing: shame thrives in silence. It grows when we hide the parts of ourselves we most need to bring into the light (Brown 2012).

Scott Peck, in *The Road Less Traveled*, takes a similar tack. He names the courage it takes to step into truth, even when that truth feels risky or painful. Peck sees growth as a spiritual discipline, an honest facing of reality, which includes the shadows we'd rather ignore. Shame is often one of those shadows. Left unnamed, it quietly sits in the background, a voice that tells people what they can and cannot say, who they can and cannot be. John Bradshaw, in *Healing the Shame That Binds You*, calls shame the "soul-murderer." He describes how shame binds people, holding them captive in cycles of perfectionism, hiding, or harsh self-criticism (Bradshaw 1988). From his perspective, healing begins with naming shame for what it is and reconnecting with a sense of inherent worth.

If shame is running the show, there is no real space of safety. A coaching conversation might look calm on the outside, but if the thinker is battling an internal voice that says, *Don't let them see this, it will prove you're not enough,* then safety is only surface-deep. And the work will suffer.

This is where vulnerability matters. Brown reminds us that vulnerability is not weakness; it's the birthplace of courage and connection (Brown 2012). Vulnerability is what allows someone to risk saying, "I don't know, I feel like an imposter," or "I'm afraid I'll fail." In a safe space, those confessions don't spiral into shame; they become doorways into growth.

Now add a trauma-informed lens. If we are to assume anything about the people across from us, let's assume everyone has a trauma history. Some of it is obvious. Most of it is invisible. That awareness invites us to tread lightly. Because if the easiest thing we can do is accidentally re-traumatize someone, then our responsibility is to be careful with assumptions, assertions, and even the tone of our curiosity (van der Kolk 2014).

Most people walk around carrying negative narratives anyway. This is another reason why Richard Boyatzis and Anthony Jack's work on Positive Emotional Attractors matters so much. A brain on shame or negativity closes down to self-protect (Boyatzis et al. 2018). A brain oriented toward dreams, hopes, and purpose opens up. Carol Kauffman, Ph.D., said, "In therapy, we are following the trail of tears; in coaching, we are following the trail of dreams" (Kauffman 2025). That trail of dreams inoculates the coaching session against shame, not 100 percent, but probably over 90 percent. When the thinker names the direction, sets their own markers of success, and chooses where to begin, the conversation belongs to them. That ownership is what makes the session safe. Open-ended questions lead to safety. Clean, simple questions allow people to choose where they want to explore, and this is a huge part of feeling safe. People do not share what they do not yet feel safe to say, if given the choice. Giving them the choice allows the conversation to grow safely.

It is so easy to trigger shame in others. I'll never forget a conversation years ago with a thinker who came into my office really upset. As he was talking, he got angrier with every word. I sat there quietly, just listening.

Suddenly, he jabbed his finger at me and said, "You're judging me!"

The truth was, I wasn't; I was simply listening. But his self-judgment was so loud that even my silence felt like a trigger.

All I could say was, "I'm not sure that is my judgment you're noticing."

It took some more conversation, but I shared that my intent had been to listen, and that I was sorry that the impact had been him feeling judged. He calmed, and we were able to continue forward.

That moment stuck with me. It showed me that safety isn't only about what I do, it's also about what the thinker carries. Trauma shapes how people perceive every glance, pause, and even silence (van der Kolk 2014). And while our job isn't to fix their history, it's to be steady enough, attuned enough, and humble enough not to make it worse. I also believe, in hindsight, that if the conversation had started with a solid agreement—directionality, if you will—about what he wanted from the conversation, he might never have wandered into the space I allowed him to. But given we didn't have a clear agreement, we were far out in a negative field, poking at the wrong things.

What Trust and Safety Actually Mean in Coaching

In ICF terms, this is Competency 4, Cultivates Trust and Safety. You can hear it in the markers: acknowledging the thinker's talents, showing empathy and support, honoring their feelings and beliefs, and inviting them to respond to our contributions (ICF 2020). We're not ticking off a checklist; we're building the conditions that let safety create space for growth.

For the thinker: say what you mean without being rushed; sit with emotion without being fixed; change your mind mid-session;

Safety the Foundation for Courage & Growth

test assumptions without shame (Brown 2012; Bradshaw 1988).

For the coach: stay present without performing; ask permission before you offer your opinions; honor the thinker's pace; get an agreement or, at the very least, a direction of the dream.

Coaching Demo: From Powering Through to Ease

In this demo, *From Powering Through to Ease* with a young entrepreneur, you can see the normal dynamic emerge clearly. The doubts sound familiar: *Why me? I don't have enough experience. What if I can't deliver?*

These are the everyday worries of anyone stepping into a bigger role or stretching past their comfort zone. And just like in a hospital unit or a boardroom, the presence or absence of psychological safety determines whether those concerns get pushed down and hidden or brought into the open where they can be explored, reframed, and transformed.

> Thinker: "I've been struggling with impostor syndrome. I'm stepping into a related but new space. Before, I was doing personal branding and consultancy, digging deep with people, helping them learn what it feels like to market and do business with the masks off.
>
> "Now I'm moving into business ethics, which I'm still developing. Ideas are coming, and things flow as I talk about it and do interviews for my book, but since leaving government work in 2017 or 2018, I haven't had those massive years of experience to lean on.
>
> "By the time I left, I had about ten years in the intelligence community through military service and federal contracting. It feels like I've been pivoting a lot. That was fine when my offers were all related to marketing, because I could lump that experience together. But business ethics feels different. I keep thinking there must be someone out there with more years of experience in coaching or consulting who's

about to do the same thing. And then the question hits me: Why me?"

The thinker starts by naming vulnerable fears: *impostor syndrome. I don't have years of experience. Why me?* They're unconsciously testing the waters. These statements show vulnerability because saying them out loud risks inviting judgment. What makes it possible here is the presence of safety, the sense that they can share unpolished thoughts without being shut down or corrected. And if the coach reacts with judgment, advice, or even quick reassurance ("No, you're great at this!"), the thinker's nervous system registers risk, because the moment unintentionally dismisses the real vulnerability. It's misinterpreted as caretaking or platitudes instead of curiosity. Through this, they learn whether it is or isn't safe to open up fully.

> Coach: "So, it sounds like the narrative running in your head is, 'Why me?' I don't have years of experience. What would be different at the end of our conversation if we really explored that narrative?'"

"*I'm hearing a lot of 'I'm not'...*" This reflection doesn't challenge or contradict. It mirrors the narrative back, which tells the thinker their words are being heard and taken seriously. That, in turn, deepens the sense of safety. Instead of retreating, the thinker leans in further: "*Most of the time I just power through … but when I don't feel strong, the doubts win.*" That's an even riskier admission, but it surfaces because they trust the coach and the container.

> Thinker: "Most of the time, I just power through things. But that only works in the moments where you feel like you have the energy. I don't know if you pay attention to or put any stock in the Enneagram, but I'm a type three. So, I'm supposed to achieve and be good at things. And so it's hard, you know?"

> Coach: "I love the phrase 'I'm supposed to.' That's an interesting story. If I'm hearing you, it sounds like you're moving from powering through toward wanting more ease. Is that right?"

Safety the Foundation for Courage & Growth

Thinker: "Yes."

At that moment, the safety deepened. The thinker had risked sharing not just their doubts but also the identity pressure beneath the surface, the belief that they should always be achieving. They didn't tense up to defend against judgment. They felt curiosity instead. And in that small shift, the conversation began moving forward. Suddenly, it was possible to picture something else, maybe even ease. Maybe powering through wasn't the only way forward.

Coach: "So, as we look at this container of powering through to ease, where is the place to begin the conversation? What is it that you need to draw on that would allow more ease? I don't know. Maybe go with either of those two questions, if one of them resonates more for you?"

This is a long question, and while today I would ask something more concise, it still gives power to the thinker.

- **Priming vs. Imposing**: Naming ease could have tipped into being directive. But because I immediately asked *Is that right?* I returned the power to her. That follow-up shifted the balance from leading to partnering.

- **Safety in transparency**: The thinker didn't have to accept my framing. By checking with her, I gave explicit permission to disagree, redirect, or refine. That's what kept the safety intact; she wasn't boxed in.

- **Ownership of direction**: When she said yes, it wasn't just agreement with me. It was her choice that ease was, in fact, the frame that mattered. The safety of being asked allowed her to own that direction rather than comply with it.

- **Deepening through co-design**: That's what made it possible for my next question—*Where's the best place to begin?*—to go even deeper. Once she had confirmed that ease was important, she could decide how to explore it.

By asking "Where's the best place to begin?" I wasn't giving her the path forward; I was handing her the choice of how to shape the exploration. That question is itself an act of partnering. It tells the

Sticky Outcomes!

thinker: *You're in charge of this process, not me. Your decisions set the direction.*

And that's what happened here. Because she could decide where to begin, whether with what blocks ease or with what supports it, or something else, she kept deepening, moving past surface doubts into the identity-level pressures and possibilities that were waiting underneath.

> Thinker: "I don't expect things to be easy, but I'd like them to feel more easeful. I think I just made that word up. What I mean is, I want the wall I'm climbing to feel a little shorter. Right now, it's like going for a run: if you're not feeling 100 percent, it's easier to say, 'I'll just do a short run,' than to feel like you have to do five miles every time. That's what it feels like—I always have to do the five-mile run. And it doesn't feel okay to be inexperienced."

Here's where safety shows up. The thinker is experimenting with language—*easeful*—and testing a metaphor in the moment. They're letting something unfinished and a little awkward come into the space. That risk only happens when they trust their words won't be dismissed or corrected. Psychological safety makes it possible to try out half-formed language and still feel accepted. This is the kind of meaning-making David Drake, Ph.D., points to in narrative coaching. When a thinker plays with language and metaphor in real time, they are literally rewriting their story (Drake 2018).

> Coach: "I'm wondering, what would make it feel okay to be easeful?"

This question does lead a little, because I introduced *easeful* back into the frame. But the check is still present: *What would make it feel okay for you?* That keeps the ownership on the thinker. It's not me deciding ease is the goal; it's me asking if ease is something they want to pursue. Safety allows a leading question to stay invitational instead of prescriptive.

> Thinker: "What would make it feel okay? I think maybe feeling confident in taking some type of action so I

> can generate actual results, consequences, benefits, something tangible. What I'm stepping into is a largely unexplored space. There's no real road map. I don't know anyone else who has built a business around this. People talk about it, but I haven't seen an actual offer. I don't want to say I'm stuck, because I am taking some action, but the business side has been stalled. Maybe that's the rub, I haven't even put out something small, like a workshop, to test."

Notice how the safety holds. The thinker moves from metaphor into a very real admission: fear of being stalled, of not putting anything out. Without safety, this would likely have been glossed over, reframed as "I'm just strategizing."

Instead, they can name their stuckness and test the idea of trying something small.

> Coach: "Interesting… as you say that, how does it relate back to just taking a short run versus committing to a five-mile run every day?"

This is where the metaphor starts to do the work. By staying inside the thinker's imagery, I signal that their framing is valid. I don't replace it with my own metaphor. That deepens the psychological safety. It shows I'm listening to how they make meaning and am willing to travel inside it with them.

> Thinker: "It's taken me some time, but I think I've developed the pillars my offer will revolve around, as well as a lot of my content. That took time to bubble to the surface, and I didn't want to rush it. But building the offer, even just the skeleton… that's the five-mile run. That's the big thing."

By this point, the thinker has fully claimed the metaphor. It's no longer just an analogy; it's a way of organizing their experience. Safety makes metaphors possible; they emerge because the person feels free to experiment with language and imagery without fear of being misunderstood.

Sticky Outcomes!

Coach: "So, what does the short run look like?"

Again, the invitation stays inside the thinker's frame. Safety here isn't passive; it represents active trust-building. By asking this, I signal that the thinker is the one who gets to decide what counts as a short run. The safety keeps them in the driver's seat of their own discovery.

Thinker: "Maybe just coming up with an idea that reflects part of what's been bubbling to the surface for me. Something smaller, like research or even a workshop, to test the waters. I've got people I can talk to, and I've done interviews, so I already have some of the language.

"That feels shorter and lighter. It's a new topic, yes, but I've done workshops before and gotten great feedback. That would let me tap into something I know I'm good at and feel confident about."

Coach: "There's a shift happening as you're talking, look at that smile."

Thinker: "Yes. I'm good at workshops. That's something I know I can do, and I've had lots of positive feedback. People appreciated that my workshops weren't about selling, they were small, specific, and personal. My first one had ten people, and after that I capped them at five to keep them intimate. So yes, it's a new topic, but I know how to create a good environment. That's something I trust in myself."

The container of the conversation, the trust and safety, the notion of allowing them to lead the direction of the conversation, all of this allowed the thinker to pivot from "I'm not" to "I already know how to do this, and that's something I trust in myself." They literally relaxed into possibility, and this is where the brain becomes creative.

Safety the Foundation for Courage & Growth

Psychological Safety

At the heart of psychological safety are these questions: *Is it safe enough here to reveal myself? Safe enough to admit doubts, to test half-baked language,* to say *I don't know without fear of being shut down or corrected?*

If coaching were a stool, the three legs would be safety, presence, and curiosity. Safety is crucial because it lets a thinker bring forward the unpolished parts of themselves, the "I'm not enough" stories (Drake 2018), the metaphors that carry meaning, the fears they don't want anyone else to hear. Without a safe place to explore, they stay on the surface. With it, they take the risk and open up.

This competency shows up when we

- Reflect back a thinker's words instead of rushing to fix or reassure

- Hold their metaphors as valid containers for meaning, even if they sound clumsy

- Ask permission before exploring, so the direction belongs to them

- Let them test stories out loud and discover the shift for themselves

- Let them lead us through their internal landscape

For leaders, the lens widens; they have a lot of eyes on them. Yet if they can develop the sort of courage that allows them to be curious about what's showing up, then the indicators of psychological safety, curiosity, and exploration become the model for safety in organizations. If a leader can experience being fully heard in the coaching space, they're more likely to turn around and listen to their teams.

The coaching conversation becomes both a mirror and a model. Leaders feel what safety is for them. And if we're lucky, they take that experience back with them and begin creating more of it in their organizations.

Why this Matters

Psychological safety isn't something you can tell someone you are giving them. It shows up in the way we partner, often quietly being present to their process. Safety is observed when someone starts doing the deeper work of thinking through what might be lurking below the waterline. It appears the moment they test the waters with, "I'm not sure I belong here," and they are met with curiosity. That response allows them to keep practicing courage as they name what's really going on for them.

In the coaching conversation above, that safety is what let the thinker move from "I'm not" to "I already know how to do this." In organizations, this is what makes the difference between silence that costs lives and the safety of being willing to stick our heads up and say something.

Especially in the world we find ourselves in, creating the space for people to be real is crucial. We, and the people we work with, have to practice courage so that we can all stand strong and face our fears.

And maybe that's the point. Safety is what gives people enough courage to do their work, grow, and share themselves with the world in meaningful ways.

Activity: What Let's You Know You're Safe?

1. Remember a real moment of safety

Think of a specific conversation where you felt genuinely safe to be honest. Maybe you shared a mistake, named a fear, or said something unpopular.

Jot a few notes:

- O Where were you, and who was there?

- O What were you willing to say that you normally wouldn't?

- O What did you notice in your body, breath, or energy when you realized, "I'm okay here?"

Safety the Foundation for Courage & Growth

2. Name your safety signals

Look closely at what told you it was safe. Complete these in your own words:

In a conversation where I feel safe, the other person...

- I notice myself...
- The pace of the conversation feels...
- It feels okay for me to...
- What is not happening in those conversations is...

Be specific. You might name tone of voice, pausing, not being interrupted, being asked what you want from the time together, or having your feelings acknowledged instead of fixed.

3. Flip the lens: how do you signal safety?

Shift from "me in the safe space" to "me creating the safe space."

Write:

- When I am the coach or leader, people probably feel safer with me when I...
- One thing I already do that supports safety is...
- One habit I have that might quietly erode safety is...

If you get stuck, look back at your answers from step two and ask, "Do I offer this to others?"

4. Choose one micro-shift

Circle one behavior you want to turn up, for example:

- Asking, "What would help this feel safe enough to be honest today?"
- Checking in before exploring something tender: "Is it okay if we stay with this a bit longer?"
- Letting silence do its job instead of filling every gap.

5. Write an intention:

- Over the next three conversations, I will practice…
- So that others can feel safe enough to…

Reflecting in this way trains your nervous system, and theirs, to recognize that this is a place for courage and growth, not performance.

CHAPTER FOURTEEN

PRESENCE IS A PRACTICE

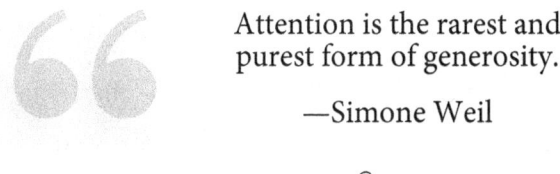

Attention is the rarest and purest form of generosity.

—Simone Weil

Let's start with this simple truth: you can't fake presence. People feel when you're with them, and they feel when you're somewhere else, in your head, in your notes, in your grocery list. So the quality of our attention is important to the coaching relationship we are creating.

In coaching, presence is what makes everything else possible. Without it, you can ask a technically solid question and still miss the moment. You can track it to an outcome—the thinker has done XYZ—but not actually be attuned to the person in front of you. Presence is what allows a thinker to feel seen and heard, think clearly, and trust that the space is truly theirs.

And here's the rub: we aren't just doing coaching. We're being with someone. That means not multitasking. Not crafting your next brilliant question while the person in front of you is still speaking. Presence means truly listening, not just to their words but to what's underneath those words: the meaning, the weight, the patterns, the thing they might not have said yet.

It reminds me of that quote by Maya Angelou: "Courage is the most important of all the virtues because without it, you can't practice any other virtue consistently." Presence is like courage. Without presence, you can't consistently practice any other coaching behavior. Presence is how you manage yourself, how you regulate yourself. To quote Wayne Dyer, "Be here now," not worried about the next question or proving your value, but here with the person in front of you.

As you read in Chapter 9 of my sad 2015 coaching demo, I did that. I missed that the thinker wanted to work on their *stumbling blocks*. Instead, I stepped completely over the deeper, meaningful issue and asked about their business, because I was so focused on doing coaching, on doing it right, that I missed what really needed attention. I was listening for content—what I felt I needed to understand—but that was surface stuff. I was not listening for what mattered: *the stumbling blocks* that were getting in the way.

When you're present, you can hear things like the stumbling blocks when they show up. You can notice when someone says they want to build a business, but what they're actually talking about are all the ways they're getting in their own way. If you miss that and just ask them to tell you more about their business, you're not coaching them anymore; you're just talking about a topic.

I think presence starts before the session ever begins. Some people say coaching starts the minute we begin talking, even in the small check-in, "Do you need anything in order to be fully present today?" And it does. But here's an important question for you: *Do you ask that of yourself, too? I think it starts before we even step on the call. Have I taken a bio break, do I have my water, have I turned off my phone, or shut off my notifications?* All these pieces play into how available we are and how focused on the person in front of us we can be.

Which begs the question, what do you need to be fully present? A break? A snack? Water? To lie down for five minutes between sessions? To dance it out? To wash your hands and shake off the energy from the last conversation? Or something else, like supervision or mentor coaching?

For me, it's also about reducing my distractibility. I close my browser, close all the tabs, turn off notifications, and pin my thinker so I am looking directly at them. I also make sure I'm not multitasking because, let's be honest, humans don't multitask well. The human brain is not designed for multitasking; what we think of as multitasking is really task-switching, and every switch costs us focus, accuracy, and time (Levitin 2014; American Psychological Association 2006). We might think we are great at switching between tasks quickly, but our brains are built for one thing at a time. If I want

Presence is a Practice

to show up fully for someone, I have to stop expecting myself to do two things at once, regardless of any time pressures nudging me in the back. I have to say, "Stop that. Go away for the next hour. I want/need to focus, and I'll be back soon!"

Presence a Working Definition

Doug Silsbee's work offers a nice perspective on presence. He invites us to see presence as both an experience and a skill, something we can cultivate by learning to witness ourselves while staying in relationship with others. His writing reminds us that presence isn't just something we have; it's a continual work in progress, something we return to again and again (Silsbee 2008).

Presence in coaching is your way of being. It's how you're showing up, not just physically, but emotionally, mentally, and relationally. It's also everything you bring into the room with you, whether you mean to or not.

Presence can show up as staying neutral or calm. I think it has more to do with being real and responsive to the person in front of you. That means you can track your own inner experience—what's happening in you—and stay attuned to what's happening with the thinker without getting swept up in either. You can notice your own thoughts, judgments, or emotional responses and still stay with the person in front of you. I think we can mine what's coming up for us by asking questions. This is where, in mentor coaching, the thinker will have said something, and I ask the coach, "What did you notice here?" They often notice something like an energy shift or that they heard a powerful belief emerge. Yet they asked something unrelated. I am always curious, "What stopped you from sharing what you noticed?"

We can use ourselves as a conduit of curiosity. "As you shared that, my stomach tightened. What did you notice in yourself?" Or maybe, as the thinker is sharing, a word pops into our brain, and we can test the hypothesis: "The word *integrity* came to mind; is there something there?" These sorts of questions come directly from our full presence in the conversation.

At other times, presence is letting silence stretch a little longer than is comfortable. Sometimes it means naming what's happening in the room, even when it's awkward. Sometimes it means not knowing and being okay with not knowing. "What is the next question that needs to be asked here?"

Presence is what grounds us; it could be in our breath so that we can sit in the unknown long enough for the thinker to hear themselves. We talked about safety and courage in the last chapter; I think presence is courage and safety in ourselves. It asks something real from us. It asks us to stop managing how to ask the perfect question or how to look like we know a lot or anything at all. Instead, it demonstrates deep respect and full attention to how the thinker is experiencing their life, which actually makes the coaching easier, more fluid, and, yes, more partnered.

Common Disruptors to Presence

There's a whole host of things that can yank us out of presence. Some are obvious, such as hunger, fatigue, responding to crises, and the ungodly number of daily distractions. Others are like that little voice whispering that you need to perform or that you need to offer something brilliant to prove your value.

We all have experienced these moments. You're halfway through a coaching conversation, and your brain starts chasing a question you want to ask, or you're wondering if the session is even helping, or if you're doing a *good enough job*. Or maybe you stayed up too late writing a book, or answering emails, or just binging on a TV series because you needed some downtime, and now your body is in the room, but your mind is longing for your pillow. And that internal chaos? You may think you are good at hiding it, but people pick up on your distraction (Rogers 1951; Bachkirova and Borrington 2018).

And, we all know, you can't support someone else if you're completely drained. The old oxygen mask analogy still kind of works here. But really, it's about capacity. If you're not resourced, you can't offer the kind of grounded attention that presence requires.

The hard truth? We live in a world that pulls us in a thousand directions. Productivity culture tells us to hustle harder and grind more. Wellness culture tells us to slow down, take time, and breathe. Then there are the fears that AI is coming for your job, so you must do more. And don't forget you should be exercising more or less.

Presence is a Practice

Eating differently/healthy. Making sure you are spending more time with the people you love, your friends, doing fun things like walking the dogs, dancing, or doing art. And somehow still being present for everyone. It's a lot. So ask yourself, "What helps me settle into the *now*? What lets me feel resourced so that I can be present with myself and others?"

Most of us are not living four-hour workweeks. We're juggling real things, with real pressure, in real time. And even knowing how important presence is, it's not always easy to access. That's why presence requires the giving of grace. Grace for yourself when your focus slips or your energy is low. Grace for your thinker when they're tangled in their own patterns. And grace for the whole messy, beautiful process of coaching—but probably even more importantly, being alive.

> **You can't control everything. But you can choose where you spend your energy.**

You can't control everything. But you can choose where you spend your energy. In palliative care, they talk about energy in the form of spoons. One of my thinkers is an MD and brought this into the coaching we were doing. If you get one hundred spoons a day, everything you do takes at least one spoon. If you use up all your spoons, then the energy is gone, and you have to wait until the next day, when you get the next one hundred spoons.

I think there is a correlation between presence and energy. And to be present means you need to spend your spoons wisely. Presence in coaching isn't about being *zen'ed* out or calm and relaxed at all times. It's about being human and recognizing the need to find our spoons and our equilibrium, which requires us to return to balance again and again. And when you do, you may find the energy to be fully present and find a way of saying: "I'm here now, let's begin."

Why Presence Matters

Say this three times fast: ***performance kills presence.***

When we stay with the thinker, not just their words but their whole self, we help them stay with themselves. That's where their insights live. That's where the shift happens. And that's what coaching makes possible. You've heard me say, if a tree falls in the forest and no one is there to hear it, did it make a sound? In coaching, our capacity to be present is what lets us hear the falling trees.

Often, if no one truly hears the thinker's message from the lens of deep listening and reflects it back to them, they may not fully hear it either. And when that happens, they miss the chance to get curious about how those beliefs, values, or longings are shaping (or obstructing) the outcomes they want.

This is why presence and deep listening matter. Not to catch or correct, but to reflect. So the thinker can hear themselves more clearly and begin to make choices that align with what really matters.

Example from Practice

I worked with a divisional president who had just been informed on Wednesday that they needed to fire a vice president by Friday. They came into the session highly upset and anxious. There had been no succession planning, no turnover plan, and now they were in a very real state of overwhelm. After downloading the details, they looked at me and said, "I don't know how to move forward."

My first question was simple and clean: "Given the circumstances, what is the first thing you need to focus on?" Then I sat quietly. The silence gave them room to take several deep breaths and collect themselves. After a pause, they were able to articulate where it was most important to focus.

This moment reflected both the beginning of agreement-setting and a powerful demonstration of presence. By staying calm, resisting the pull into the scramble, and not diving into the details, I was able to create a container where the leader could slow down, re-center, and begin to move forward with clarity.

Presence is a Practice

Presence supports leaders in:

- **Co-Regulation:** They calm their own system through the grounded presence of the coach.

- **Slowing Down:** They break free from urgency to reflect more deeply. Stephen Covey talked about urgent and important and, not urgent but important. We want to try our best to be in a state of "not urgent but important."

- **Authentic Connection:** They genuinely meet others as human beings, not just their roles.

- **Modeling Presence:** Experiencing presence can give the leader insights into how they want to show up.

With executives, presence often means resisting the pull into urgency. Coaches can model calm responsiveness by slowing down, listening fully, pausing, and allowing silence. This demonstrates that grounded presence is possible—and presence is powerful in leadership.

Activity: Resourcing Ourselves

If presence is the foundation of transformational coaching, then tending to our own presence is not optional; it's the work. Here's a practice to close this chapter and center yourself before any session:

Three-Minute Presence Reset

1. Pause. Close your laptop. Turn away from your notes. Let your eyes land on one still thing in the room. Breathe.

2. Feel your body. Notice any tightness. Release your jaw. Drop your shoulders. Plant your feet on the floor. Wiggle your fingers.

3. Ask yourself: "What do I need right now to feel a little more present?"

- Maybe it's a sip of water.
- Maybe it's a walk
- Maybe it's naming the thing that's tugging at your

attention.

○ Maybe it's reminding yourself, *I don't need to perform. I just need to be present.*

This isn't about emptying your mind or forcing calm. It's about noticing and awareness. Choosing to come back to this moment. So that when the thinker arrives, you're already present with yourself and available for someone else. Presence is not something we achieve; it is something we practice. And it is always and ever about who we are working on being in the present now.

CHAPTER FIFTEEN

LISTENING ISN'T WAITING TO SPEAK

> Blindness separates people from things; deafness separates people from people.
>
> —Helen Keller

Listening isn't the same thing as hearing. We all know how to hear. The action of sound waves hitting an eardrum, even making our bodies or an entire car vibrate, at its most fundamental, is hearing. Those waves have frequency, measured in hertz, and amplitude, which we experience as volume. High frequencies come through the ears alone, while very low frequencies can be felt in the body, like the deep bass that thumps in your chest from the car radio four cars back. Every time we hear or feel vibration, we're perceiving sound.

So, when we say, "I hear you," it's passive; it's only describing the action of how we process sound waves. And think about it, we hear all sorts of things: our spouse speaking, kids laughing, horns beeping, dogs barking—or even very subtle things, like the sound of wind through the trees.

Sound waves are all around us. But listening is different; it's the process by which we intentionally attune to meaning. It requires presence, focus, choice, and attunement. When we listen, we're not just taking in sound. We are paying attention to meaning. And since humans are meaning-making, this is important to our work as coaches. Listening will ask you to suspend your own agenda long enough to let the other person's words, emotions, and perspective matter. It's not automatic. It's active, intentional, and generous.

In coaching, this difference matters. When we are only hearing, we might catch the words but miss the meaning. We might nod at the surface of a story and never touch what's bubbling below the surface. Listening, the kind that shows up in Competency 6, is about focusing on what the thinker is and isn't saying. It's being curious about their words, their pauses, their tone, and even the shifts in their energy. It's letting them discover what they really mean as they speak it out loud.

Listening at this level isn't about us gathering data as coaches so we can solve something. It's not listening to prepare our next brilliant question or to find the "answer." It's listening so fully that the thinker hears themselves more clearly. That shift, when someone suddenly catches their own insight in the reflection of their words, is a moment that has the potential to shift how people see and experience themselves. Think about how many people you have in your life who listen to you with no agenda, no attachment to the outcome; if you're like most of us, there are very few who have zero attachment to your choices and actions.

If hearing is passive, then listening is participatory. It's another facet of how we create a full partnership. It's how we show the thinker that their words matter, their meaning matters, and that we are listening to their ideas, perceptions, and beliefs. Listening is also how we escape the trap of directing or fixing. Because when we're truly listening, we don't need to take over. Because as we listen, we can get curious about what they say, what they notice, and what they want to explore to move the conversation forward.

Predictive Brains

Most people don't realize the brain isn't just taking in reality like your mobile phone camera set to video. Your brain is not recording, it's predicting. Karl Friston, a leading neuroscientist, suggests our brains are always modeling what we expect to happen, not what is actually happening.

This idea comes from what he calls the *Free Energy Principle*. In a nutshell, the brain tries to reduce surprise. And this isn't the surprise of a birthday cake, it's the surprise of the brain failing to accurately predict what's happening in the environment, especially anything it might interpret as a potential threat. It does this by filtering out anything that doesn't line up with its internal predictions. So, we end up seeing what we expect to see. That's why familiar problems jump

Listening Isn't Waiting to Speak

out at us, or we notice what isn't working, or if we buy a car, we see it everywhere. It's also why real change can feel almost invisible; if we aren't primed to notice it, we tend to tune it out. Unless we interrupt the pattern, we miss what's new. Friston's work hints that even small disruptions, such as a well-placed question, a metaphor, or a shift in perspective, can shake things loose enough for the brain to update its story.

And most of us have grown up in cultures that celebrate fixing things. Spot the issue, jump in, and fix it. We get that little dopamine hit, and our brain lights up. But if we're only listening for what's not working, the challenge, then sadly, that's all we'll hear. Before we know it, we're knee-deep in the negative emotional attractors (Boyatzis et al. 2018). Coaching offers an opportunity to shift the focus, in a safe way, which lets our patterns get interrupted so we can consciously choose something new.

The Speed at Which We Speak

Conversations move at the speed of light. Research shows that across languages, the average gap between one person finishing and the next jumping in is about 200 milliseconds, barely enough time to say a single syllable. In Danish, people take their time with a pause of around 470 milliseconds, but in Japanese, it can be as fast as seven milliseconds (Levinson et al. 2015). It's a little crazy when you realize it takes about 600 milliseconds for someone to produce a word from scratch. Which means we can't possibly be waiting until the person finishes speaking before we start preparing our response—our brains are already predicting, filling in, and lining up our reactions, responses, and interjections.

Daniel Yon points to this in his book *A Trick of the Mind: How the Brain Invents Your Reality*. He explains that the speed of natural conversation shows just how much prediction is baked into the way we listen (Yon 2025). It isn't that we're being rude—it's that the brain doesn't sit idle. It gets ahead of itself. And yet, that same quick-draw system is exactly why coaching requires so much discipline. This is why we must intentionally slow ourselves down. By being fully present in our listening, we can throttle back on our predictions and sit in curiosity instead. This requires us to recognize the speed at which our predictions are working and consciously choose to zipper-emoji our mouth and listen to all the words.

Linguistic research adds another layer here. Edward Gibson and colleagues have shown that even in comprehension itself, our predictive brains can pull us off course. When we hear a word or phrase, the mind doesn't just sit back and neutrally receive it without judgment; it reaches for the most frequent or expected meaning for the listener. In Gibson's 2006 study, readers sometimes misparsed sentences, hanging on to an interpretation that the grammar didn't actually support, simply because their predictive bias was so strong (Gibson 2006). In other words, our brains will cling to the expected pattern even when the sentence structure contradicts it.

For coaches, this matters greatly. Because this means we may not only jump ahead in conversation, but we may also subtly mishear what's being said because our brain is already "auto-correcting" the thinker's words into something familiar. That's why slowing down, testing hypotheses out loud, and letting the thinker guide meaning is so important. Otherwise, we risk coaching our own prediction instead of their reality.

If I am primed to hear problems and challenges, I will notice everything that is shared through the lens of what challenges need to be addressed. If my ears are tuned to solutions, I might push hard toward solving before enough exploration has been done. There is a balance to be struck: we need the purpose or outcome, and we also need to explore the challenges that get in the way of that happening. While this filtering is efficient for our brains, it is also problematic if we aren't mindful. This means that unless we are intentional, we might miss the quieter signals, the desires, the values, the dreams beneath the surface (Felleman et al. 1991; Grady et al. 1998).

Think of it this way: when a thinker says, "I feel stuck," our brain will start predicting solutions, and we could spend thirty minutes untangling the details of the stuckness. Or we could break the pattern and listen below the surface and explore the stuckness, becoming curious about what forward might look like. "If you weren't stuck, what would be happening instead?" The conversation shifts from stuck to a new direction.

Listening for direction doesn't mean ignoring struggle. It means honoring the struggle while staying tuned to the deeper current of where the thinker wants to head. When we listen that way, we're not

Listening Isn't Waiting to Speak

just hearing their problems—we're hearing their potential. And that's where coaching lives, at the intersection of what is and what *could* be.

The competencies spell it out. A coach who is listening actively doesn't just capture the words. They consider the thinker's context, their values, their identity, the bigger story of their life—so the coach's understanding doesn't flatten down to problem and solution. They reflect or lightly summarize the underlying meaning that the thinker is communicating to make sure they've really caught it, but not to show off their memory. What no one needs is a long list, *I heard you say a, b, c, d, l, m, n, o, and x, y, z—did I get that right?*

When we are listening, we recognize the "more" under the surface and stay curious about what's important rather than skating past it to the tactical or superficial. We notice shifts in energy, emotion, or even silence—and then trust those signals enough to name them and invite the meaning to emerge.

And trust me, you can hear the difference in a recording. When a coach is only hearing, the conversation moves along like a checklist. The thinker says something important, but the coach presses ahead with the next prepared question. When a coach is listening actively, the pace slows. There are pauses. The coach's responses feel tethered to what just happened—sometimes even to what wasn't said. The thinker begins to slow down too, hearing themselves in new ways.

So active listening, in the competency model and in the PCC markers, is less about the coach performing attentiveness and more about creating space where the thinker's meaning comes forward. It's not enough to say back what was said. The markers remind us that listening means weaving together tone, words, body language, and patterns across time, so the thinker can see themselves more fully in the mirror of the conversation.

Radical Listening

The ideas in *Radical Listening* by Christian van Nieuwerburgh and Robert Biswas-Diener remind us that listening is never neutral. It can either open doors or quietly shut them. Their work shows how quickly listening gets hijacked by habits that feel normal but become barriers.

Sticky Outcomes!

Think of the classic responses. "That happened to me, too." On the surface, it sounds empathetic, but really, it shifts the attention back to us. Or "That's nothing, I've seen worse." That one dismisses the thinker's experience altogether. Then there is mind-reading, the assumption that we already know what they mean. We are all probably guilty of this when we talk to people we know well. Or the quick draw of unsolicited advice, which says, "I know best." The one many of us feel most keenly: time poverty. That little tick, tick, tick that subtly triggers a sense of *I don't have time for this* that makes us rush, interrupt, and listen only for the exit ramp. Each of these responses quietly steals the thinker's voice.

van Nieuwerburgh and Biswas-Diener talk about the anatomy of a conversation, and once you start noticing it, you can't unsee it. There is the interjecting, or back-channeling, all those "mhms," "uh-huhs," and "yeahs." They are intended to show we are paying attention, but they can just as easily nudge conversations in directions we, or the thinker, do not intend.

I have a good friend who does a lot of coaching assessments. He counts how many "mhms," "yeahs," and other verbal tics show up, and on one demonstration of 30 minutes counted 222 back-channel noises. I can only assume there wasn't any empty air on that call.

Then there are the interruptions. Sometimes they are meant to help, sometimes they come out of our own impatience, but either way, they break the thinker's flow. And then there's the big one, the full takeover. The moment the coach grabs the microphone and starts telling a story about themselves. That is the point where listening has stopped and performing has begun (van Nieuwerburgh et al. 2025).

The challenge: our brains are wired with selective listening filters (Schacter 2001). If you walk into a conversation expecting problems, your perception will spotlight problem-related cues and downplay others:

- Problems or obstacles
- Challenges or struggles
- Solutions or fixes
- Intended actions or outcomes

Listening Isn't Waiting to Speak

In other words, if I'm unconsciously listening for problems, that's what I'll hear. If I'm listening for solutions, I'll steer the conversation that way. Carol Kauffman put it beautifully: "In coaching, we are following a trail of dreams" (Kauffman 2025). My question is, if we are not listening for the dreams, how on earth will we, or the thinker, find them?

Neuroscience points the same way. Our brains don't have unlimited capacity... They filter. Attention and bias step in like little gatekeepers, letting some things through and blocking others (Felleman & Van Essen, 1991; Grady et al., 1998). That keeps us from being overwhelmed, but it also means we miss things. Those unconscious filters trap us, circling around resistance or obstacles, instead of leaning toward the thinker's dream direction of growth and possibility.

Listening Actively

Listening actively is not just about "being a good listener." It is about creating a relational mirror so the thinker hears themselves more clearly.

When we listen with depth, something shifts. The thinker begins to catch the sound of their own beliefs, the weight of their emotions, or the possibility tucked inside a half-formed thought. That is why we listen: not simply to understand, but to reflect meaning, to offer observations, and to help the thinker see the choices in front of them.

And when do we miss it? When we paraphrase too quickly, move on too soon, or change the subject to follow our agenda, we walk right past their awareness. Listening keeps us at the threshold of transformation. That is why Competency 6, actively listening, matters: it's fundamental to partnership and to the importance of being heard. I think being heard is the point of coaching, so our listening is crucial.

On *The Tonight Show Starring Jimmy Fallon* in 2025, Stephen Bartlett said, "To be a good interviewer, your job isn't to lead, it's to follow. And if you listen, people will take you where they want to go." I loved that so much because I was writing this chapter, and it felt like the universe saying yes to listening. So, what are we actually listening for?

What Are You Listening For?

Focus Area	What to Notice in the Session
Words	The thinker's language, especially words that repeat or carry emotional weight
Voice	Tone, volume, and pace, how something is said, as much as what is said
Body	Shifts in posture, breath, gestures, or facial expression
Energy	Changes in emotional resonance, intensity, or presence
Beliefs	What the thinker reveals about how they see themselves and the world
Values and Strengths	Clues about what matters most and what their natural resources and character strengths are
Coach Awareness	Your own internal responses: what you notice, what stirs in you, and how you stay curious

The Universal Themes Beneath the Surface

In my years as both a therapist and a coach, I've noticed that people, whether they're executives running multibillion-dollar divisions, founders juggling two start-ups, or managers leading small teams, tend to bring the same underlying themes into coaching. The content changes, but the currents beneath the water are remarkably universal.

Here are some of the themes that often show up:

Listening Isn't Waiting to Speak

- **Insecurities and Self-Doubt:** Am I enough? Am I capable? Will I be found out? I feel like an impostor.

- **Overwhelm and Chaos:** I can't keep up. There's too much on my plate. I'm drowning.

- **Meaning and Purpose:** Why am I doing this? Does it matter?

- **Hopes and Dreams:** What's possible for me? What do I long for?

- **Expectations and Pressure:** I should be further ahead. Others expect more of me. I expect more from others.

- **Acknowledgment and Appreciation:** Does anyone see what I've done? Do I matter here? Are you trying to change me?

- **Ethics, Integrity, and Values:** Am I living in alignment with who I say I am? What do I do when people's words and actions are out of alignment? What if my words and actions are out of alignment?

- **Boundaries and Autonomy:** How do I hold my space? Where do I say no? How do I choose to say yes or no? How do I stop crossing my own line in the sand?

- **Safety and Threat:** Is this a risk I can afford to take? Am I safe to say this out loud?

- **Grace and Forgiveness:** Can I let myself off the hook? Can I let others? I need to give myself the same wiggle room I give to others.

- **Connection and Disconnection:** Am I in or out? Belonging or alone?

- **Growth and Change:** Who do I want to be? What sort of leader do I want to be? How do I step into a new way of being?

- **Energy:** I feel depleted and close to burnout. How do I capture energy? How am I spending energy?

Sticky Outcomes!

O **Beginnings and Endings:** How do I start? How do I let go? How do I close this chapter?

Thinkers may not use these exact words, but the themes are there. Beneath the topic about a frazzled week or a conflict at work, you'll hear the deeper story. This isn't a model. These are just things to be listening for, because they point the way toward what's important.

Coaching Demo: Everything Everywhere

In this session, the thinker began with what sounded like a straightforward business request: "prioritizing next steps" and making decisions about potential partners. If the coach had stayed with that surface agenda, the conversation might have focused on timelines, pros and cons, or action steps. Instead, by listening below the waterline for what else was present, her anxiety, desire for ease, and the tension in her body, the conversation deepened into clarity about identity, boundaries, and values.

> Coach: "What is showing up for you as something that would be useful to coach around today?"
>
> Thinker: "I think I would like to use this time to talk about how to... *What my next steps* are on the business development side. We had a conversation about that a couple sessions back, and I want to talk through *prioritizing next steps*. It's the same issue. How do I *prioritize* not doing everything at once? There was a crazy movie, *Everything Everywhere All at Once*. And sometimes *that's what my life feels like*, and I need not to make that reality. So it's about scaling."

It's not the coach's job to repeat everything back to the thinker. Remember, we are listening, and several themes are emerging in this first sharing. "… my next steps are on the business development, prioritizing next steps, and there was a crazy movie, *Everything Everywhere All at Once. And sometimes that's what my life feels like.*"

As the listener, I am hearing all of this, my brain is predicting options, and I am also really focusing in on words that sound

Listening Isn't Waiting to Speak

important. The "everything, everywhere, all at once sounds like the deeper overwhelm, and the steps sound like a way to organize the chaos. But it is not my job to determine, so I ask another question to get more guidance from the thinker:

> Coach: "As you're saying this, is there anything that's really bubbling up as the most important element to focus on?"

> Thinker: "It's going to be really good to focus on one thing in the time that we have. And I think that one thing is thinking about a partnership with two people, inviting two people as partners to my business. So that's a focus. I can think of a hundred things, but that's the problem. Right. I believe this is a crucial decision to operationalize within the next six months, ensuring we're ready to make the shift at the start of the new year. And I just would like a safe space to talk through that."

As I am listening, I am noting one thing, which is thinking about a partnership with two people, and also noting that I just would like a safe space to talk. There are a lot of ideas being shared that could take a coach who is listening to the surface straight down the proverbial rabbit hole. "Business development," "prioritizing steps," "deciding between partners," and "operationalizing the next six months." I need more information.

> Coach: "And then as we have the safe space that we create and we talk through this, how will you know this has been a meaningful or useful conversation for this exploration?"

> Thinker: "I think if I feel less anxious about having the next conversation, I need to have with the two of them, there is an anxiety for me about that conversation and that meeting. And I would like to feel less anxious and more at ease about the conversation."

On the surface, the concern is about planning and partnerships

Sticky Outcomes!

for her business. But notice the deeper currents: the thinker is preparing to bring potential partners together and is worried about how she will show up in the room. Beneath the swirl of logistics lives the potential question the thinker is asking themselves:

- "Can I hold my own?"
- "Will this conversation go off the rails?"
- "How can I feel more ease?"

And these questions have now come from her, not from me.

> Coach: "At ease. What is the experience of at ease for you? Where does it reside within or around you?"

This question shifts the conversation away from external planning toward internal experience. The thinker describes the tightness in her solar plexus, the way anxiety shrinks her breath, and what it would mean to feel "easeful."

> Thinker: "To feel at ease would be to breathe fully into my lungs and relax my abdomen. Easeful… that's my word of the day. I'd like to feel spaciousness in my core."

By naming ease and spaciousness, the thinker begins connecting the business challenge (partner negotiations) with the deeper personal challenge (holding ground, owning authority, not collapsing under pressure).

As the conversation unfolds, she steps into greater clarity and self-awareness:

> Thinker: "*I need to show up as the savvy business woman that I am*, I also need to take care of myself because I have a lot of sh*t going on in my life right now, and my other insights are that I need to get a meeting on the calendar with my potential partners and the awareness that under stress I really revert to my old habits and I need to be mindful that my anxiety is a signal. It's not anything else."

Listening Isn't Waiting to Speak

If early in the conversation I had latched onto "prioritizing steps," we would have missed the more important issue that shows up later about how she shows up as a savvy businesswoman. So rub your tummy and repeat, "It's okay, it's okay, it's okay to wait, predict, and set it to the side, and keep listening deeply."

Directionality: Listening Toward Dreams

This is where *directionality* shows up as so important. When we listen, we're not just attending to the words; we are orienting ourselves and our thinker toward a destination. So we need, and I mean need, to make sure we understand what the thinker wants to explore and where they want to be when we are done. Coaching conversations that get stuck often do so because the coach unconsciously follows the wrong thread, digging into resistance or problem-solving before clarifying where the thinker actually wants to move.

True listening requires us to:

1. Notice what we tend to listen for.

2. Expand our listening to include what the thinker longs for, the direction they want to go, not just what they're struggling with.

3. Partner with the thinker to establish where "forward" actually is and how they want to explore getting there.

As one of my thinkers once said, "I want to move the needle a tick forward." That became our compass, not the resistance itself, but the desire to move the needle, motivation, and energy as we ticked along.

Listening as Partnering

From a coaching perspective, listening is not a test of memory or attentiveness. It is an invitation to shape the kind of partnering where the thinker hears themselves more fully. Listening actively means tuning into words, tone, body, energy, and silence, not to collect evidence, but to reflect meaning. When we do this, the thinker begins to recognize their own beliefs, their own themes, their own way forward.

From a practical lens, this requires restraint. We don't rush to paraphrase every detail or interrupt with a clever next question. We lean into curiosity and stay with what has just emerged, however small or subtle it may seem. That pause, that reflection, is often where the door to awareness opens.

Listening at this level is not about performance. Remember, it's about holding the mirror in which the thinker recognizes themselves, and it is through our capacity to listen deeply and actively that we can hold up that mirror for them. So few people have anyone who listens to them for longer than a few minutes, and to feel heard and understood is an important gift that we give when we practice this ability.

Listen Forward

We started this chapter with Helen Keller's reminder that deafness separates people from people. By now, you've seen why—hearing may happen automatically, but listening is a deliberate choice.

As coaches, when we choose to listen beyond the surface, we're creating a space where the thinker can actually hear themselves. That's the shift, from everyday conversation to coaching partnership. We listen so the thinker has a chance to really hear themselves. Sometimes that means catching the word they repeat three times. Sometimes it means noticing the pause, the waving arms, or the shift in energy. Sometimes it is just being quiet long enough for them to keep going. And it means catching our brain predicting outcomes and solutions, so we can set aside our ideas to invite the thinker's ideas to emerge, so they can move forward.

CHAPTER SIXTEEN

Coaching Is Both Brain-Based & Meaning-Making

> We cannot solve our problems with the same thinking we used when we created them.
>
> —Albert Einstein (maybe)

In recent years, neuroscience has become a buzzword in the coaching world. Terms like "amygdala hijack," "neuroplasticity," and "limbic system" appear frequently in workshops, articles, and coach training. But what does it really mean to say coaching is "brain-based"? And how do we use neuroscience responsibly without reducing coaching to a series of biological reactions? The first thing I would say is that coaching is not something we do to the brain; it is something we do with a person. In this chapter, we explore the integration of neuroscience and coaching in a grounded, accessible, and ethical way.

Coaching Is Neurobiological by Nature

All human experience is processed through the brain. As coaches, we engage with thinkers' thoughts, feelings, memories, and bodily sensations, all of which are aggregated, interpreted, and responded to by the brain. Our capacity to self-reflect, plan, take perspective, and even hold awareness of the coaching process itself are functions of the brain's prefrontal cortex.

However, the brain does not operate in isolation. It is constantly influenced by hormones (such as cortisol, oxytocin, and adrenaline), the autonomic nervous system, and the social and emotional cues of the environment. When the brain perceives threat or uncertainty, even subtle cues such as judgment, disconnection, or confusion, it activates protective responses that reduce a thinker's access to insight and creativity (Brown et al. 2012).

This is why safety is not just a "nice to have" in coaching; it is a neurological necessity. Since our brain doesn't know the difference between a real physical threat, like a tiger, and an imagined threat, like an existential tiger, threats are threats. Eisenberger, Lieberman, and Williams (2003) studied how social exclusion activates the same brain regions associated with physical pain. Social exclusion will not eat you like a real tiger, but the brain still activates the same regions involved with pain sensing. When people feel seen, heard, and accepted, their nervous systems calm, and their brains become more receptive to new possibilities. Emotional regulation opens the door to perspective-shifting, deeper insight, and behavioral change (Boyatzis et al. 2018).

Discovering the "I" Within

Who are we really? Our sense of self is shaped by the events happening around us and how we process them. Our past experiences, beliefs, values, habits, and even physical sensations all play a role in how we perceive the world and react to it.

Our sense of self, or "I," develops as external events move through our filtration system of experiences, expectations, attitudes, desires, preferences, beliefs, biases, values, habits, the systems that we operate within, and even our internal physical responses (embodied experience) to situations, such as feeling hot or cold, noticing how we are breathing, or being aware of our heart rate.

The result of the external event is that we perceive it as either positive or negative. We experience it on a spectrum from threat to safety. Because of this threat-safety spectrum, we develop an emotional response, positive or negative. Emotions accompany behavior directed toward a goal.

Threat------------------------Safety
            continuum

Coaching is Both Brain-Based & Meaning Making

Emotions are related to the perceived significance created uniquely by each person. We cannot make assumptions; we must ask questions to evoke individual awareness. What triggers my fear and what triggers yours will always be different.

Behaviors are adopted because they are consistent in some way with a person's sense of self. From a coaching perspective, it is important to be curious, not necessarily about the origin of the behavior, which is the realm of therapy, but about whether the behavior serves the thinker's current goals.

If an experience challenges someone's identity or threatens their self-concept, it may be perceived as dangerous. In such cases, emotional and cognitive resources shift toward protection rather than curiosity or creativity. And remember, threats can be existential or real. The brain doesn't recognize the difference; it reacts based on the need to survive. So while we understand that a difference of opinion isn't typically as deadly as a tiger, the brain may respond to the difference of opinion as if it were a tiger. This is one reason why safety and presence are so essential in how we create the container of the conversation: we are creating a safe space for the thinker's meaning-making process to reemerge.

Behaviors do not happen in a vacuum; they emerge because they were once helpful or protective. We adopt ways of responding because they worked, maybe when we were five, but they worked. From a coaching perspective, it is important to be curious, not necessarily about the origin of the behavior, which is the realm of therapy, but about whether the behavior serves the thinker's current goals.

When people disown their behavior (e.g., a micromanager who says, "I just want things done correctly"), they often adjust their sense of self to rationalize the behavior. These adjustments keep them consistent with their internal narrative and can distance them from recognizing the impact of their actions. This rationalization reflects the brain's drive for coherence and safety.

The image below illustrates how external events are filtered through internal lenses, such as past experiences, beliefs, and body states. So, going back to someone who micromanages their team, past experiences may evoke "you better do this right," as a result of having gotten positive or negative consequences based on "doing it right" when we were five. This can lead to the belief that things always have to be done right in order to avoid being shamed or scolded.

Sticky Outcomes!

This belief becomes codified in the brain and, over time, becomes the unconscious response that shapes how this person leads. These filters influence how individuals perceive safety or threats, which in turn shape their sense of self, emotional states, physical states, and ultimately, behavior. Coaching supports thinkers in discovering and working with these filters consciously. Now that I am twenty-five, thirty-five, or 105, does what worked when I was five still make sense?

As mentioned earlier, if an experience challenges someone's identity or threatens their sense of self, shames them, or sparks self-judgment or the perception of external negative judgment, it is often perceived as dangerous—an existential threat. And in such cases, emotional and cognitive resources shift toward protection rather than curiosity or creativity.

Not Just Brain-Based

While coaching is absolutely influenced by neurobiological processes, it is also a psychological and relational process. As Brown and Brown (2012) caution, treating the brain as the direct object of coaching is not useful. What they call "brain talk" and coaching, needs to be done with a consideration of the whole person, in context, with meaning, not just with their neurology. The human experience of meaning—how thinkers interpret their stories, values, identities, and goals—cannot be reduced to neural pathways alone.

This distinction matters. When coaches over-rely on "brain talk" without grounding it in accurate science, it can lead to confusion, misinformation, and ethical concerns. Responsible integration of neuroscience means drawing on validated insights (such as neuroplasticity and the stress response) while staying attuned to the thinker's lived experience and language.

Bridging the Two Worlds: Neuroscience and Meaning-Making

Effective coaching lives at the intersection of the brain and the human. It honors how the brain functions and how humans make meaning. Coaches can integrate this understanding in several ways:

> **Safety First:** Recognize that emotional safety is the foundation of access to the prefrontal cortex, where reflection, planning, and insight occur.
>
> **Directionality:** Ask questions that invite ownership, anchor what is important, and prime for indicators of success. This moves people from dysregulation, that is, from the struggle, toward an outcome they want.
>
> **Metaphor and Memory:** Use the thinker's metaphors to support integrated processing between emotion and cognition, as metaphors activate multiple brain regions and help reduce cognitive load. They also increase safety, because full plates are

not as scary as "I have no boundaries."

Trauma-Informed Practice: Be aware that your thinkers carry unresolved experiences. The goal is not to coach the trauma specifically, but to understand that trauma may be in the mix. So we need to create a container where the thinker can safely explore what is in the way of reaching their goals. A client-led approach helps this, in that people typically do not bring up things they are not ready to name. We are not here to drag people below the waterline.

As coaches, we support the conditions for insight and change through safety, presence, curiosity, and partnership.

Why this Matters

Coaching is more than a conversation; it is a relational process grounded in presence, trust, and exploration. At its most powerful, coaching activates the brain in ways that foster insight, creativity, and long-term behavioral change. Neuroscience helps us understand why this works. When we align our coaching approach with the way the brain naturally learns and grows, we help the thinker move from insight to action and from awareness to integration.

The Brain's Dual States: PEA vs. NEA

Dr. Richard Boyatzis's research on **Positive Emotional Attractors (PEA)** and **Negative Emotional Attractors (NEA)** offers a compelling framework for understanding the emotional landscape of coaching.

- PEA states, such as hope, compassion, curiosity, and vision, activate the *parasympathetic nervous system*, which fosters calm, openness, and receptivity. These states are neurologically aligned with learning, creativity, and intrinsic motivation.

- NEA states, such as fear, shame, anxiety, and frustration, activate the *sympathetic nervous system*, preparing the body for survival by narrowing attention and reducing access to higher-order thinking.

Coaching is Both Brain-Based & Meaning Making

Boyatzis's longitudinal studies in leadership and coaching consistently show that individuals and teams make more sustainable changes when supported by experiences that activate PEA. These states create a kind of neurological "fertile soil," ideal conditions for insight, reflection, and growth. Coaching conversations grounded in PEA increase psychological resilience, foster innovation, and strengthen relational bonds.

Importantly, Boyatzis emphasizes that PEA isn't about avoiding the hard stuff. Effective coaching integrates NEA when necessary, for example, to highlight urgency or surface accountability, but then intentionally returns to a PEA foundation. He calls this emotional resonance, the ability to move fluidly between emotion and cognition in ways that support sustainable change.

When a thinker feels emotionally anchored to their own goals, the brain shifts from resistance to receptivity. The relationship becomes more than safe; it becomes generative. And the coaching process, rather than simply solving a problem, becomes a pathway toward possibility.

Boyatzis's research reinforces what masterful coaches intuitively understand: when you coach toward a vision, you unlock energy, creativity, and the capacity for lasting transformation. In this way, PEA is a biological invitation to thrive.

The Polyvagal Lens

Stephen Porges's polyvagal theory gives us a simple but powerful lens for coaching. At its core, it says the autonomic nervous system isn't just reactive; it's adaptive. Beneath our awareness, it's always scanning for cues of safety or danger, a process Porges calls neuroception.

Think of it like a ladder with three rungs. At the top is the ventral vagal state, where we feel safe and social; it's often referred to as the parasympathetic state. In this place, the prefrontal cortex is fully online. We can reflect, connect, and stay open. Drop down a rung, and you find the sympathetic state. That's where the body gears up to fight, flight, fawn, or freak out. Energy is high, but it's fueled by urgency. At the bottom is dorsal vagal collapse. Here, everything shuts down: we freeze, left with numbness, withdrawal, and a sense that "it's too much, I just can't…"

Sticky Outcomes!

These aren't just moods. They're neural platforms that shape what kind of thinking is even possible. A thinker in collapse can't brainstorm their future. A thinker in sympathetic drive may look productive, but often they're running on stress rather than alignment. Only in the parasympathetic state can we really access choice, creativity, and integration.

State	Physiology & Experience	Internal Story	Coaching Implications
Ventral Vagal (Safe & Social, Parasympathetic)	Regulated, connected, curious; prefrontal cortex online	I feel seen. I can think clearly. I'm open.	The best state for coaching. The thinker has access to reflection, learning, and choice. Coach presence & co-regulation keep them here.
Sympathetic (Mobilized)	Fight, flight, or fawn; energy high, driven by urgency	I need to fix, flee, prove, or protect.	The thinker may sound motivated, but actions often come from stress, not alignment. The coach can slow the pace and invite grounding.
Dorsal Vagal (Collapsed/Shutdown)	Freeze, numb, withdrawn; system overwhelm	It's too much. I just can't.	Insight & planning are not available. The coach focuses on safety, gentle presence, & small openings for connection.

Polyvagal theory illuminates when coaching is most effective. How the thinker feels in their body shapes what they can do with their thinking. Coaches who bring presence, respect, and safety, even without naming polyvagal theory, are already working in alignment with it. The simple things we do as coaches make a difference: a grounded tone of voice, a steady gaze (or a soft one on Zoom), noticing energy shifts without pushing, reflecting emotion without trying to fix. These gestures of presence create co-regulation, helping the thinker climb back up the ladder into a state where they can actually think, feel, create, and choose.

If you have ever heard "The thinking that got you here won't get you out of here," then you can see how the stuck brain needs safety so that it can start to do the work of getting unstuck. From this perspective, professional coaching emphasizes that trust and presence are biological prerequisites for transformation. That's why questions like *What are you noticing in your body right now?*, *What would help you feel a little more settled as we talk?*, or *What do you need right now?* are doorways. When the nervous system feels safe, the brain can finally get to work.

Polyvagal theory reminds us that the state precedes the story.

Coaching is Both Brain-Based & Meaning Making

In other words, a thinker's interpretation of events is shaped by their physiological state. In a calm, regulated body, they may tell a story of possibility. In a defensive or collapsed state, that same story may feel hopeless or overwhelming.

By helping the thinker shift state from survival to safety, the door opens to new creativity, new narratives, new perspectives, and ultimately, new choices.

The Brain Can Make a New Groove

Neuroplasticity is the brain's ability to form new neural connections across a lifetime. Every time a thinker has a new insight, notices a pattern, or takes a different action, they are quite literally rewiring their brain. Neural networks, pathways made of electrical and chemical signals, are not fixed. They change in response to focused attention, emotional salience, and repeated practice.

As Norman Doidge explores in *The Brain That Changes Itself,* even deeply ingrained behaviors can be reshaped through awareness, intention, and repetition. This has profound implications for coaching. We are not simply helping someone think differently; we are helping them build different neural grooves that make new ways of being more accessible and sustainable.

Coaching leverages neuroplasticity by supporting the thinker in interrupting automatic or conditioned responses. These moments of reflective awareness serve to unstick habitual patterns. And, fingers crossed, this supports repeated experimentation with new behaviors, thoughts, or perspectives that come from insights the thinker develops through inquiry.

These moments may seem small—a pause, a reframe, maybe a new metaphor, or an insight/awareness—but in the brain, they are significant. Every time the thinker says something new aloud, especially something that resonates with meaning and autonomy, it strengthens the neural groove. We have all heard neurons that fire together wire together (Hebb 1949). These grooves are how change becomes sticky. Like water and wind carving a deeper channel with each pass, client-owned insights and choices etch their way into the thinker's system.

And the more those insights are embodied, spoken in the

thinker's language, aligned with their values, and explored in their body, the more durable those grooves become. This is where real transformation lives: not just in what is said, but in what becomes lived experience.

The Brain as a Body Budgeting System

Dr. Lisa Feldman Barrett offers a compelling frame: the brain's primary job is not thinking, it is regulating the body's energy. She calls this body budgeting.

According to Barrett, the brain constantly predicts how much energy we will need in the moments ahead. It does this by drawing on past experiences, reading current sensory input, and assessing internal physiological states. These predictions determine everything from our ability to focus to our mood, motivation, and behavior.

When the brain anticipates that our body budget is in deficit, whether due to poor sleep, unresolved stress, emotional strain, or even too many decisions, it begins conserving resources.

This often looks like:

- Diminished access to higher-order thinking (the prefrontal cortex)
- Heightened reactivity or irritability
- Reduced emotional flexibility and creativity

This explains why, under stress, people often say things like *I just can't think straight* or *I'm too overwhelmed to decide*. Their body budget is overdrawn. No amount of encouragement to *just be positive* will work if the nervous system is signaling danger, depletion, protection, or lack of safety.

Coaching, when practiced with somatic awareness and attunement, supports body-budget repair and resilience.

We can do this by:

- Slowing the pace: Coaching often moves at the speed of insight, not urgency. Spaciousness gives the nervous system time to settle.

Coaching is Both Brain-Based & Meaning Making

- Tracking and reflecting somatic cues: Tuning into breath, posture, energy shifts, or tension helps the thinker attune to their own body budget.

- Exploring meaning, values, and strengths: When a thinker connects with purpose or personal agency, it stabilizes the nervous system and refuels energy.

Barrett's research underscores why coaching must work with the nervous system, not against it. It is not just about *changing thoughts* but about helping the whole system regain balance so that creative, empowered thinking can reemerge. Coaches who understand body budgeting are better able to hold space for both insight and integration, especially when working with thinkers under stress or navigating transitions.

In many ways, coaching becomes a co-regulatory process: the coach's presence, calm, and curiosity offer a template for the thinker's own regulation. From there, new choices become possible, not because the brain was told to think differently, but because the body was supported in feeling safe enough to do so.

One of the ways the brain manages this body budget is through the senses. Every sensory channel—sight, sound, touch, taste, balance, even the subtle signals of heartbeat and breath—acts like a data stream feeding into the nervous system. These signals tell the brain whether to conserve or spend energy, whether to lean into curiosity or brace for defense. For coaches, this means that paying attention to what the body is sensing is not a side note; it is how we invite the exploration of safety, meaning, and possibility to emerge in the conversation.

The Senses and Coaching Presence

We often talk about five senses, but neuroscience recognizes at least eight sensory systems, each contributing to how a thinker navigates and interprets their inner and outer world. These senses act as data channels, constantly informing the brain's assessment of safety, context, and meaning.

The brain is an aggregator of information, a dynamic processor that pulls from both internal and external stimuli, weaving them into our perceptions, reactions, and decisions. Understanding these senses gives us deeper access to how change is experienced in the whole body, not just cognitively (Porges 2011).

Let's take a closer look at the three most relevant senses in coaching:

1. Exteroception – External Awareness

This is our ability to perceive and make meaning from stimuli outside the body: sights, sounds, smells, touch, and taste. It's how we stay oriented to our environment. In coaching, exteroceptive awareness may be heightened when a thinker becomes attuned to external cues that trigger stress or softened when invited to focus inward.

Coaches might use this by asking:

- "What are you noticing around you right now?"
- "Is there a sound or sight that's contributing to how you're feeling?"

2. Proprioception – Awareness of the Body in Space

This sense allows us to detect our body's position, motion, and balance, even with our eyes closed. It's what helps us know where our limbs are and how we are grounded. In coaching, proprioceptive awareness can be a doorway to grounding presence. For example, noticing how someone sits or holds themselves can indicate whether they feel safe, stuck, or open.

Coaches might invite:

- "What happens if you sit back or plant your feet?"
- "As you say that, how is your body positioning itself?"

3. Interoception – Internal Sensation Awareness

This is the awareness of internal bodily states—heartbeat, hunger, breath, tension, digestion. It is central to emotional self-awareness. Interoceptive signals are often the first indicators of stress, truth, or resonance. Coaching into interoception can increase self-trust and presence.

Questions may include:

- "What are you noticing in your body as you say that?"

Coaching is Both Brain-Based & Meaning Making

- "Where do you feel this in your system?"

- "If that feeling had a texture or temperature, what would it be?"

Other senses relevant to coaching include:

- Vestibular sense – Balance and spatial orientation.

- Nociception – Perception of pain, discomfort, or threat.

When coaches work with the whole sensory system, they support the thinker in engaging not just the thinking brain, but the sensing, feeling, and intuitive self. This sensory integration allows insight to become more than a good idea. It becomes a felt experience, anchored in the body, available for memory, and ready for action.

This depth of inquiry honors the **whole person** and supports full-body integration of insight.

Just as we invite the thinker to notice their internal and external experience, we as coaches must also cultivate awareness of our own sensory and emotional states. A coach's breath, posture, tension, or intuitive nudge can serve as subtle signals, information that something important is unfolding. When a coach notices, for example, a tightness in their chest or a sudden drop in energy, it may be a cue to pause, reflect, or gently bring curiosity to the space. This self-awareness is not for interpretation or projection but rather to support attunement, the coach's ability to stay present and responsive to what is happening in the relational field. In this way, our own bodies become part of the listening system, expanding our capacity to hold safe, responsive, and generative space.

Head, Heart, and Gut Intelligence in Coaching

When we talk about intelligence, we often picture the head with little legs walking around doing all the thinking, little neurons analyzing, planning, and telling stories. But we live within bodies that are whole, interconnected systems. Our intelligence is more like a distributed network than a single command center. Alongside the head, or cephalic brain, are two other centers of intelligence that matter just as much in coaching: the heart and the gut.

Sticky Outcomes!

The head helps us with aggregating information, logic, body budgeting, survival, and conscious thought (Barrett 2017; Damasio 1994). The heart interprets emotional resonance, signaling whether our choices align with what we care about, as supported by research on the intrinsic cardiac nervous system and its network of neurons (Armour 1991). And the gut offers a quieter kind of knowing, a sensing of safety, risk, or intuition that often precedes conscious reasoning, grounded in the enteric nervous system's hundreds of millions of neurons and its close connection with the vagus nerve (Gershon 1998; Porges 2011). Together, these three centers form a whole-human intelligence that a coach can tap into to support the thinker in getting curious and making integrated meaning. This is not only a metaphor. The heart contains its own network of neurons capable of local processing and communication with the brain (Armour 1991), and the enteric nervous system in the gut houses hundreds of millions of neurons tied directly into the vagus nerve (Gershon 1998; Porges 2011). These systems shape mood, perception, and even how safe or threatened we feel. From my experience, human behavior, and arguably behavior across species, tends to respond according to where we find ourselves on the threat-to-safety spectrum.

This can be observed in high-stakes environments, such as the financial markets, including the London Stock Exchange. In a 2016 study, John Coates and colleagues tested traders' ability to sense their own heartbeats, a measure of interoceptive awareness. Those who were more accurate not only made more money but also lasted longer in the profession. The takeaway? The body's signals, the so-called *gut feelings* of trading lore, can give a real edge in uncertain conditions.

When we ask not only *What do you think?* But also *What are you noticing in your body?* And *What does your gut say?* We support the thinker in accessing their full intelligence. Decisions become more grounded, aligned, and resilient when the head, heart, and gut are in conversation with each other.

From Reactive to Proactive

The foundational distinction between reactive and proactive behavior is not new. Long before Stephen Covey made the terms popular in *The 7 Habits of Highly Effective People*, psychologist Viktor Frankl laid the groundwork with his powerful insight: "Between stimulus and response, there is a space. In that space is our power to choose

Coaching is Both Brain-Based & Meaning Making

our response. In our response lies our growth and our freedom." Frankl's work, grounded in existential psychology, emphasized the capacity for self-awareness and intentional action even under extreme stress.

Later research in behavioral psychology and emotional regulation echoed these findings, highlighting that proactive behavior stems from internalized values and self-direction, while reactive behavior is typically driven by external triggers and conditioned responses. In coaching, helping a thinker move from reactive to proactive is about restoring access to that space—the reflective pause, if you will—where choice becomes available.

Reactive ------------------->Proactive
the space to choose

In a reactive state, the thinker is tethered to habitual, protective behaviors. The nervous system, detecting a threat (real or perceived), prioritizes safety over self-reflection. In this mode, the thinker may react with old habitual patterns.

In a proactive state, by contrast, the thinker gains access to curiosity, possibility, and choice. Their prefrontal cortex comes back online, and they are more able to explore nuance, sit with discomfort, and imagine new futures.

The shift is often subtle, but the impact is profound. Reflective presence co-regulates the nervous system and makes space for integration. But the shift is not just psychological; it's fundamental to thinking. Coaching supports the conditions that allow for both neuroplasticity and body-budget rebalancing. It helps thinkers move from instinctive reaction to intentional response. It is, at its best, a laboratory for self-directed neural rewiring.

The emphasis is on partnership, presence, and evoking awareness, not just as ethical imperatives but as neurologically sound practices that support the thinker's transformation. The core competencies are not just professional standards; they are invitations to co-create the internal conditions needed for growth, integration, and sustained sticky change.

Sticky Changes

Lasting, or sticky, changes do not come from being told what to do—you know that, I know that. So consider: how do you like it when people tell you what to do? Or how you *should* feel? If I think of the things that lie below most disagreements, I would say that even more than differences, there are assumptions.

If we assume we know something without getting clarity, it is problematic 99.99999 percent of the time. Most of us like ideas being shared with us. But lasting changes are earned through the lived experience of discovering something for yourself, the *aha moment*. When a coaching conversation evokes a felt, embodied shift—where insight meets ownership—it lays down new grooves in the brain or deepens grooves that already exist.

I like to say, if I am building a chicken coop, then yes, I want the directions—how much wood to buy, screws, and so on. But in my thinking, I am not building a chicken coop; I am formulating ideas, mindsets, and ways of handling a wild, messy world of experiences.

When insight is paired with agency, it sticks. And when that insight is expressed in the thinker's own words, metaphors, and body, the neural groove deepens. This is the signature of competency-based coaching: not just temporary change, but transformation that lasts because it lives in the nervous system, not just the notebook.

Expressed in the thinker's own words, metaphors, and body, the neural groove deepens. This is the signature of competency-based coaching: not just temporary change, but transformation that lasts because it lives in the nervous system, not just the notebook.

Activity: Integrating the Neuroscience of Coaching

Take a moment to notice how these ideas show up in your life.

- When do you feel yourself shift from reactivity to reflection in safe relationships?
- What signals does your body give you that let you know you're grounded or unsettled?

Coaching is Both Brain-Based & Meaning Making

- Recall a time you or a thinker truly owned an insight. What made that moment stick?

These prompts aren't homework; they're opportunities to explore through your lived experience. I hope they support you in connecting the science with your lived experience so that neuroscience isn't just something you *know*, it's something you *embody* in your coaching presence.

One Last Thing

The neuroscience of coaching is still evolving, but what we already know is clear: Coaching works because it aligns with how humans grow. It honors the body as wise, the brain as plastic, and the person as the expert in their own life.

When coaches create safe, attuned, and client-led spaces, we activate the natural conditions for change—biological, emotional, and behavioral.

And in that space, the thinker can not only find their way forward… **they can become the person who walks it with clarity, creativity, and choice.**

Chapter Seventeen

Awareness Follows Where Questions Lead

> A question is not a bolt of lightning, it's a seed.
> You never know what may grow.
>
> —Amos Oz

The first thing I want to acknowledge here is that every question is leading. *What color is the sky?* Leading. *What is important to you?* Less leading, but still the question points toward what is important to you. So when we think about questions, it is important to be aware that you, as the questioner, are always leading.

Which leads to the reality that there is power in a question. In fact, the person asking the question always has more power than the one answering. From childhood, we are trained to respond when asked, and while some of us eventually learn to resist, the social wiring runs deep. This means every question we ask in coaching is directional. Even when we do not intend it, our questions point the thinker somewhere.

The question we must ask ourselves, then, is, where are we leading the thinker? Into questions that are for our sake, our curiosity, or for their sake, their insight?

For many coaches, especially in the beginning, questions tend to come out wrapped in preambles, stacked with multiple options, or layered with the coach's own assumptions. They often come from our own need to process and understand. And yet, these tendencies can work against us. Instead of opening space, they overload or confuse people. What if we do not actually need all the details, and we do not need to understand all the external stuff?

Sticky Outcomes!

So let's explore how to ask a better question.

Why Fewer Words Matter

Cognitive science has been clear on this point: working memory is limited. John Sweller's Cognitive Load Theory demonstrated that human beings can only hold so much at once. Nelson Cowan's research later pinned that number down to about four chunks of information at a time, give or take one. That is it.

When a coach asks a question with three parts, a long lead-in, and a trailing commentary, the thinker has to juggle: *Which part should I answer? What did they mean by that phrase? Where do I even start?* In the shuffle, the core of the question, and the insight it could have sparked, can get lost.

This is what Sweller described as **extraneous load.** The thinker already brings the intrinsic load (the complexity of the situation itself). Our job as coaches is to minimize anything extra that clutters the process. A concise, clean, open-ended question reduces the noise so that their cognitive effort can go where it matters most: germane load, the meaning-making. That is where awareness emerges.

Once, my husband teased me after a long-winded explanation: You flood me with your words. That statement lodged in my brain. Because in coaching, **flooding a thinker** with words is one of the **fastest ways to block insight.** So if fewer words protect working memory, what replaces them? *The secret lies in asking one clear question.*

The Power of One Clear Question

Educational psychologist Dylan Wiliam has said that the depth of learning depends more on the quality of the question than on the quality of the explanation. Coaching is no different. One well-placed, open, clear question is exponentially more powerful than three cluttered ones.

Every question carries weight, which is why asking one question at a time matters. It allows the thinker to hold it fully, digest it, and respond without the mental labor of sorting through options. It may feel unnatural at first—most conversations in life are fast, overlapping, and layered. But coaching is not an everyday conversation. It is a practice of creating the space for insights and awareness.

The Social Brain at Work

Remember that every question is leading; what matters is where your questions are leading the thinker to explore. This is important because human brains are wired to treat questions as social cues. Developmental psychologist Michael Tomasello and others in social cognition have shown that we feel compelled to respond when asked. That compulsion means our questions do not just open space; they actively direct attention.

Which is why leading questions can become problematic. Because if every question directs attention, then a poorly placed one can unintentionally drag someone into pain or trauma. Most of us carry some of that history. So the real issue is not whether to explore, but how to explore, and whether the direction serves the thinker's desired outcome and growth.

A question like *I heard you say, the elephant in the room was scary, tell me more about that?* Does more than invite exploration. It points the thinker's brain toward scary, whether or not that was truly the center of their experience. **This question points in an outward direction**, and the thinker follows, even if it leads them away from what matters to them.

Contrast that with: *In reflecting on what you just shared—the elephant in the room—what feels most important to explore?*

Now the coach's **question points inward**. The thinker not only chooses what is important; they also choose the direction.

When we point the thinker toward something, we need to ensure that it serves their outcome and not just our curiosity. If we are pointing to the scary elephant in the room, for what purpose are we doing that? If it is to explore emotions, then we need to be certain that the thinker wants to explore that scary emotion on their way to what they have stated they want. Which, of course, means we need to get at what they want before we dive too deeply into evoking awareness.

Sticky Outcomes!

Coaching Demo: Elephant in the Room

Let's look at how this plays out in practice. The thinker brings in a metaphor, the elephant in the room, and you'll see how easily a coach could slip into poking at the fear or amplifying the drama. Instead, notice how the coach keeps testing alignment, circling back to what the thinker wants, and letting the thinker decide where to go. This is directionality in action: holding curiosity with care, without dragging the thinker into the scary parts unless they choose to go there.

> Thinker: "It's like there is this elephant in the room that is this looming conversation. And I start to freak out, like we are dancing around the really important issue, but I don't want to bring it up, because what if the conversation goes off the rails and I am left with a new problem I have to deal with."
>
> Coach: "I hear what sounds like a lot of energy here, what would you like to be different?"
>
> Thinker: "I guess I would like the tools and confidence to have a grown-up conversation that doesn't lead to more problems."
>
> Coach: "When you have difficult conversations like a grown-up and you feel confident, what are the indicators that tell you this is working?"
>
> Thinker: "Well, I am able to stay calm, I am able to communicate that I am not against them, but on their side, and we still need to deal with this elephant. I can breathe, and my throat doesn't close down."
>
> Coach: "Then, if I am hearing you correctly, you would want to show up calm, able to breathe, and to deal with the elephant?"
>
> Thinker: "Yep, that sums it up."
>
> Coach: "Where would you like to start so you can

Awareness Follows Where Questions Lead

show up calm and confident and able to deal with the elephant?"

Thinker: "I think I need to really look at the elephant so that I can start to think about how to approach it calmly."

Coach: "Perfect. What part of the elephant do you want to look at first?"

What are you noticing as you read the transcript? I notice the coach is not dragging the thinker into the heavy negative feelings or pointing at a path the coach believes the thinker needs to explore. They have not said *Tell me more about the elephant or the looming conversation.* Think back to the idea that we all have trauma, and we do not need to activate it with the NEA.

Testing Hypotheses

As the thought partner, the coach is testing a hypothesis by staying curious, checking for alignment, and letting the thinker choose what is important, what change would look like, and how they want to explore dealing with the elephant from the position of being the expert on themselves. Clear agreements make evoking awareness easier for the coach, safer for the thinker, and genuinely thinker-led. Without a full agreement, it is much easier for the coach to lead, maybe into dangerous waters. Evoking awareness comes from exploring what is important to the thinker, and the coach sits firmly in the seat of asking questions that support the growing insights, learning, and awareness that emerge through the process.

> We must always test our hypothesis versus assuming anything. Ask and test. Non-attached curiosity is needed.

And since we can never know another person fully, we must test our observations and offerings to see if we are being useful or heading in the wrong direction. We test our hypotheses along the way, checking in, being curious, and staying non-attached. The biggest

Sticky Outcomes!

problems in coaching and therapy occur because of the assumptions, assertions, and, ultimately, the telling we do.

Share your observations, intuitions, or guesses with very open hands. We want the thinker to be able to say yes, no, or offer a different perspective, their perspective. They can and need to create the dots. We want to ask, not tell, another person what they are thinking, feeling, experiencing, or knowing. When we ask, we invite the thinker's knowledge, insights, wisdom, thoughts, and feelings to be named by them, not us. These then become the dots they need for awareness.

● ● ●

So, as the conversation continues:

> Thinker: "I think I need to look at why I am feeling so intimidated by this conversation with this person. We have a long history, and while I know they are great at what they do, they are not always a team player. This isn't the first time I have tried to address this issue; it's just the first time I am addressing it as their boss. So, I think there are a bunch of things coming together. I am the boss, they are part of my team, and this is impacting our team outcomes. They can't go all 'lone wolf' and just say or do things without considering the team goals. And I guess I am also pissed, they went off and did and said things, that now I have to go and clean up… I am not sure I have said that before, I am really angry."
>
> Coach: "That sounds like some clarity, how might this inform you on this elephant conversation?"
>
> Thinker: "Well, going in hot isn't going to help. I could, literally, make matters a lot worse. I don't want to get into a power struggle, but I do need to be clear about how this is impacting me and the team. Also, I can't have this happening again. It's taken hours of my time, time that I needed for other projects I am responsible for, all my other responsibilities got sidelined, so I could deal with the fallout from this situation."
>
> Coach: "What do you need right now, as you name this?"

Awareness Follows Where Questions Lead

Thinker: "I think I first need to shake some of my anger off, then I need to consolidate the impact that I am experiencing, so that I don't babble angrily, but get concise and clear about how this has impacted the team, to include me. I am also wondering if I need to have this conversation as a team or individually?"

Coach: "That's an interesting question, what is emerging as you hear yourself say that out loud?"

Thinker: "I think there are pros and cons to doing this individually and as a team. One part of me likes the team being in on the conversation, One, I wouldn't be alone, and two, the team can name their own impact from this experience, instead of me relaying it. I always hate it when people say stuff like, 'You stepped in it and everyone on the team agrees with me…' it's BS. So, I like the idea of people naming for themselves their experience.

"On the other hand, I don't want the conversation to escalate because this person feels ganged up on by the team, and there is something to having the conversation in private, rather than calling them out in a group…"

Coach: "Are those the only two ways to have this conversation?"

Thinker: "I don't know… hmm… maybe there could be another option. I mean does it have to be one or the other, I don't think so. Let me just play with this for a second… What if I have the one-on-one and really get clarity about their thinking and expectation of what they thought was going to happen by their actions, then share my personal experience, then lay it out that we are going to discuss this as a team, so we can learn and grow from what happened?"

Coach: "What just happened with the elephant here?"

Thinker: "(Laughs) I feel like the elephant is shrinking…"

Sticky Outcomes!

The important thing here is not the elephant, per se. It is how the coach used questions as a compass, testing their hypothesis rather than spotlighting any particular thing or directing the thinking in a specific direction. Each question was for clarity, reaffirmed the thinker's direction, and invited awareness to emerge on their terms. That is why the elephant started to "shrink"—not because the coach solved it, but because the thinker explored it from a calmer, chosen stance.

This is the essence of evoking awareness: questions that reduce noise, honor safety, and create space for the thinker's insights to unfold. And the coach who invites rather than points.

A Story of Too Many Words

Here's a quick example of what flooding with words can look like in practice.

> Thinker: "The awareness is I'm putting a lot of pressure on myself to be an expert in a job I literally just started. Mhm. When I'm not feeling confident, I'm not feeling confident, and that makes me want to just fix the problem. Fix the problem. They're coming to me, they need it, it's my job to fix it."
>
> Coach: "I heard you're putting a lot of pressure on yourself. That's a really good insight. You're right, and what are you feeling as you say that? What just showed up? I wonder if it's important to look at how you're not feeling confident? Or, what are you noticing?"

This is a flood. Too, too many words, too many questions, too much for the thinker to carry. Working memory gets overloaded. The brilliance of what the thinker actually said gets buried under the verbal clutter, or what I call the "word salad."

Here's what one simple, concise CP might have sounded like:

CP: As you share these insights, what is emerging for you?

CP: That sounds like a lot of pressure. Fix it. What's driving that, do you think?"

Awareness Follows Where Questions Lead

CP: What do you want to do with this awareness?

Each of these questions is clean and open, and they honor the thinker's words, but notice: none of them is a word salad. Each is a simple invitation.

Why We Babble and Ramble

So why do we ask the long-winded, stacked questions in the first place? Sometimes it is because we are external processors, thinking as we talk. Sometimes it is because we do not want to sound too direct, or we are afraid of being misunderstood. Sometimes we simply get caught in the flow of our own curiosity. Or we are constructing the question as we ask it. There are probably as many reasons as there are coaches.

But here is the reflective question for you: When you find yourself asking stacked or rambling questions, what is going on for you?

Awareness here matters. The more you can notice your own tendency to flood the thinker with words, the more you can step back, pare down, and trust them. Their mind, not yours, is where the answers live. And this is where Nancy Kline's work reminds us that thinking needs space. If we fill that space with our own words, we choke out the very conditions that allow new insight to emerge. Silence, paired with a clean question, often does more to ignite the thinker's mind than any string of sentences and explanations ever could.

Why it Matters

Asking questions and evoking awareness isn't about perfect questions or perfect language. It's about practicing restraint, asking a simple question, inviting the thinker inward rather than toward the external, trusting the thinker's capacity, and remembering that awareness follows where the questions lead. Each time you pare back a leading question into an open one, you create space, what Nancy Kline calls "the conditions for real thinking to happen." I invite you to start playing with creating these sorts of creative spaces.

Sticky Outcomes!

Activity: Turning Leading Questions into Open Ones

Purpose: To strengthen your ability to spot and reframe leading or directive questions into open, nondirective questions that foster autonomy and agency for the thinker.

Part 1: Spot the Leading Question

Read each question below. Ask yourself

- **?** Does this question direct the thinker toward a specific topic, feeling, or solution?
- **?** Does it subtly suggest what I think is important?

Part 2: Rewrite for Openness

Rephrase each question so that it

- **O** Opens space for the thinker to choose the focus
- **O** Avoids embedding assumptions or judgments
- **O** Invites reflection and self-direction

Example:

Leading: "I heard you say the elephant was scary. Can you tell me more about that?"

Open: "I hear what sounds like a lot of energy here. What would you like to be different?

Practice Questions – Rewrite Each of These Questions so They are Open and Thinker-led.

1. "You seemed upset when your colleague interrupted you. How did that make you feel?"
2. "It sounds like you've already decided to leave your job, what's your plan?"
3. "Why didn't you talk to your manager about it?"
4. "You said the meeting was frustrating. Was it because

Awareness Follows Where Questions Lead

people weren't listening to you?"

5. "Do you think you should focus more on time management?"

6. "Since you're unhappy in your relationship, have you thought about breaking up?"

7. "It seems like you're avoiding the real issue. What's holding you back?"

8. "Are you worried you'll fail if you try that?"

9. "Do you think you're being too hard on yourself?"

10. "Given how stressful this is, wouldn't it be better to take a break?"

After Rewriting These Ten Questions, Consider:

- ? How does the new question allow the thinker to lead us instead?
- ? How does the language change the power dynamic?
- ? How does the new open question give more options to the thinker to take the question anywhere they choose?
- ? How might the rewritten question create more space for the thinker's own insights?
- ? How does it feel in your body to hold the question lightly, without attachment to where it goes?

CHAPTER EIGHTEEN

Emotional Intelligence is a Mindset

Safety is not the absence of threat;
it is the presence of connection.

—Stephen Porges

The phrase emotional intelligence gets bandied about a lot these days. People sometimes confuse this with being a nice person. Being nice might be nice, but this sort of intelligence is actually a whole lot more nuanced. Though being a nice human being is still a decent thing to navigate toward.

Psychologists Peter Salovey and John Mayer first defined emotional intelligence in 1990 as the ability to perceive, use, understand, and regulate one's emotions. Their research positioned emotions not as messy distractions but as sources of data, signals the brain and body use to guide thought and action. Daniel Goleman later popularized the idea in his 1995 book, showing how emotional intelligence shapes leadership, relationships, and performance.

Over the years, the models have multiplied, but most agree on this core: emotional intelligence is about noticing feelings, your own and others', and working with them wisely rather than being overwhelmed by them. On an episode of the *Mindhack* podcast (McClain 2025), neuroscientist Daniel Yon reminded us that perception itself is an active construction, not a passive recording. In his book *A Trick of the Mind* and in a *Scientific American* interview, he describes the brain as a "brilliant illusionist," constantly predicting and shaping what we experience as reality (Yon 2025; Feltman et al. 2025). Our brains are constantly making predictions about whether we're safe or threatened, budgeting energy accordingly (Barrett 2017). Emotions are not noise in the system; they are the system's way of keeping us aware, connected, learning, and most importantly... alive

So, what does this mean for coaches?

My take is that it aligns with a coaching mindset based on the idea that we are committed to being open, curious, flexible, and client-centered. This means we need to do our own work so we can use our emotional intelligence to be with, and sense into, not just others but ourselves. Without at least some emotional intelligence, we are tone-deaf. We don't hear the undercurrent of themes or concerns running below the surface. We hear "I need a strategy" or "I need a list," and we stop there. Fundamentally, our curiosity stays in the shallows, and our capacity to be fully present is compromised. Empathy can easily slip into either pulling out the pom-poms or trying to save someone. Here is a common chant for me in coaching: *performance kills presence*.

> **Performance kills Presence!**

When our focus is on doing it right or giving value, we are more focused on ourselves than we are present with what is emerging in the human relationship in which we are participating. When a coach has a healthy level of emotional intelligence, the coaching relationship becomes a steady, safe, grounded space where the thinker is center stage.

I think most of us learn these skills through experiences with family, friends, and then with work. The following anecdote illustrates a context in which I used my tools.

The Airman and the Late Nights

When I worked as a clinical social worker for the Air Force, I worked with Family Advocacy. In our office I was one of two clinicians who assessed for domestic violence and child abuse and neglect. I also ran several groups: Anger Management, Parenting, Healthy Relationships, and Empowerment. The office was set up to have an officer/commander who was the main leader in that unit. Then we had the clinicians, then the support staff. There was a young airman in my office whose job was to answer phones and sign people in for their sessions. Because she was a military member and I was a

Emotional Intelligence is a Mindset

civilian, this also included staying with me if something came up and we couldn't leave at 4 p.m., which was the end of our day. This meant that if one of my sessions ran past 4 p.m., she had to stay late.

There was a personal value I abided by: during an assessment of something as serious as an allegation of domestic violence or child abuse, if someone was still talking, I didn't just end the session when the clock struck four. If we needed to run ten minutes long, so be it. This happened very infrequently, because we would plan for one and a half hours for an intake. But on a few occasions, I might run over ten to twenty minutes.

One day, as the office manager, the airman, and I sat eating some lunch, she decided to let me know exactly how she felt about my behavior. She started by telling me that it was rude and disrespectful of me to keep her late, and that *everybody said so*. Then she kept going and going. She unpacked two years' worth of grievances about every little thing I had ever done that annoyed her. She was clearly mad, she felt entitled to tell me off, and as I sat there, I could feel my face getting hot and my heart pounding in my chest. I was definitely feeling a strong emotional reaction myself. I knew that if I responded in any way other than with a firm hand on my mouth, I would probably escalate the situation. So I sat there quietly while she waxed on.

By the time she was finished, I knew several things. First, I was stunned, and also really mad. I wasn't her boss, but she worked for me, and this power difference activated some feelings, right or wrong. Swirling in my mind was my judgment that I would never talk to anyone like this, but especially not someone I worked for. I didn't like the delivery, and I certainly didn't like sitting through a laundry list of complaints. I didn't appreciate that this was done with an audience, and that I was the sole target of the finger-pointing. But I also knew enough to realize I couldn't just snap back. I mean, I taught anger management; I had to put my tool belt on and use every one of my tools.

I knew I needed to disengage, cool down, and get my head straight before we had any more conversation.

I said, "Okay, if that's all, I am going to my office."

I was very aware of my state. I could feel and recognize my anger, and I remember closing the door to my office, lying down, and breathing through the intense emotions. I am a redheaded Irish Leo, and my first response is not to calmly find my equilibrium.

Sticky Outcomes!

I had to choose consciously not to fire back at her, *I know you are, but what am I?* Or *I'm rubber, you're glue...* I knew I didn't want to turn into an angry monster. Honestly, in retrospect, she was a teenager and I was an adult, so I needed to respond like one. So I went to my office, shut my door and started to self-regulate.

The office manager knocked on my door a while later and asked, "Are you okay?"

I said, "Oh, I am pissed, but I am okay, and I don't think it will do anyone any good if I say more right now."

I left at 4 p.m., reminding myself to breathe the whole drive home. I was obsessively playing the conversation over in my head, then breathing some more. I am not ashamed to say I also thought through quite a few clapbacks that would have felt good in the moment, and I was glad that I hadn't said any of them. Though I did enjoy how laser-like my zingers were.

When I got home, I vented to my husband, who was a master sergeant at the time. He got fired up that she would speak to a superior that way, and then we both had to throttle back, breathing again. I have a pattern of writing "the angry letters," letters I will never send, but pretty much express everything I am feeling on the page with little to no censoring.

After I worked through the initial anger, wrote my angry letter, and had gotten back to some sort of balance, I started thinking about the whole situation from her perspective. She literally was a teenager. I probably wouldn't like it if I felt like someone in the office was *making me* stay late either. It might feel like they were stealing my personal time. She was also the person with the least amount of positional power in the office. She was eighteen years old. What was I like at that age? Again, redheaded, Irish, Leo… I am sure I had some entitled opinions. Her frustration wasn't invalid; of course she had things she wanted to do after work. But the issue wasn't whether I would stop doing my job to the best of my ability, it was how we were going to move forward together without turning every conversation into a shit show.

I spoke to my commanding officer, let him know what had happened, and said that I didn't need him to do anything. We discussed that I did want to have a conversation with the airman, and I asked that he join for that follow-up, to avoid any misunderstanding or drama. It took about two weeks before we could all sit down.

Emotional Intelligence is a Mindset

When we did have our sit down, I started by acknowledging her perspective: yes, I could see how it would be frustrating when her day got extended. I heard her feelings and repeated quite a lot back to her so she knew I was listening. I also acknowledged her underlying feelings and apologized that I hadn't considered her in my mental calculus for when to let a conversation go longer. Listening and understanding does not equal agreement, though, and I was very clear that we were never going to have a similar conversation again. I was very okay with her coming to me, shutting the door, and speaking to me the way she would want to be spoken to if I were angry at her. Exactly like we were doing right then, in my office.

Then I set two clear boundaries: the mission came first, assessments were people's lives in the balance and sometimes sessions would run late, and that was part of the job. Second, the way she had approached me, unloading a couple of years' worth of complaints in one sitting, with an audience, wasn't acceptable. I wasn't going to retaliate with my own laundry list, but I was also not willing to be treated that way again. If she had a problem with me, my door was open, and we could close it so that neither of us would be publicly attacked, which had been my experience with her delivery.

We ultimately agreed to address concerns as they came up. If something bothered her, she could raise it respectfully, and we'd talk it through without stockpiling resentment. I stayed calm during this conversation because I had taken the time I needed to come back with a balanced mindset. I acknowledged her position, and I was crystal clear about my own position.

It was an uncomfortable process, but it cleared the air. It gave both of us a way forward. Funny enough, after our conversation, I felt good. The air didn't feel tense, and I had no anger left about the situation. This experience confirmed several essential things: we only have control over what we say, think, and do; emotional intelligence doesn't mean it feels great when someone lays out a laundry list of what they don't like about you; and if we prioritize the relationship, we have a better-than-average shot at a long-term solution. All of that means noticing our reactions, taking the time we need to self-regulate, coming back with clarity and empathy, and setting boundaries that honor both the relationship and the work that needs to be done.

I have had similar experiences of these sorts of conversations through the years, and they are rarely comfortable, but they're important. They are skill-building for our relational toolkit, as we learn and develop how we want to be with people when it's hard. It's the difference between creating work drama and escalating negativity around you or creating safe working environments and safe relationships.

If I hadn't done my own work, how easy might it have been to do harm, get hooked, simmer in my anger, or create an environment that would have been toxic?

Coaching Demo: Spinning To Calm

Let's look at how this might show up in a coaching conversation. In this session, the thinker arrived having just gotten off an unsettling call with her boss. There was a bunch of leadership drama at work, her boss was probably getting fired, and the conversation had left her doubting her organization, doubting her role, fearing for her team, and spiraling into anxiety. She named it for herself: *I am spinning*.

> Coach: "What is showing up as important to have a conversation around?"
>
> Thinker: "There have been a lot of changes on my team. Our boss was fired right after our second meeting, and since then everything's been in flux. Lori, our acting director and the founder of our team, has been pulling us into the drama. It looks like she may be exited from the organization too, because she's been fighting leadership.
>
> "All of this leaves me discouraged and uncertain. I'm doubting the work we do, and I feel some imposter syndrome. There's always been tension between our community team, which does culture work and facilitation. Now that we're reporting into HR, that tension feels sharper.
>
> "I'm losing faith in leadership because I'm not seeing good leadership anywhere. I feel discouraged, unsure of what to do, and I'm worried about the future of our team. Will I even have a job? Do they value our work? I don't know where to go with all of this." **The thinker's**

Emotional Intelligence is a Mindset

hands were waving around her head through much of this part of the conversation.

If you're human, you've had these moments, the intense emotions, the feeling that the world around you is out of control, and the worry about how to respond. When we get hooked or dysregulated, we become unbalanced. We may be uncomfortable with the emotions, or we may get hooked because we *totally understand* and it's part of our story too, or we start feeling an internal pressure to help get the other person out of the spin so that we, or they, can feel okay.

I checked in internally, I was fine, and I chose not to meet that spin with anything other than calm curiosity and tested my hypothesis. Emotional intelligence begins with self-awareness, checking in with your own nervous system.

> Coach: "I'm hearing that. And if you were no longer in this space of discouragement, where would you want to be jostling over towards?" *My hands were waving similarly to how her hands had been.*

> Thinker: "I think, um, I was struck by what you're doing with your hand, waving and mimicking me. I'm like, gosh, is that the energy I have? I think I want to move to a place of serenity or acceptance that the work I do, that my team does, is valuable. And whatever is going to happen. (Sigh.)"

Mirror Neurons and Co-regulation

Mirror neurons were first identified in monkeys: these are cells that fire both when an animal performs an action and when it observes another performing the same action (Rizzolatti et al. 1996; Gallese et al. 1996). In humans, brain imaging shows that similar networks—especially in premotor and parietal areas—are active when we see, imagine, or experience others' actions and emotions (Iacoboni et al. 1999; Rizzolatti et al. 2004). This response system is thought to instigate empathy, imitation, and learning. In other words, our brains "mirror" others' states, allowing us to resonate emotionally and behaviorally.

Sticky Outcomes!

Co-regulation is about how the nervous systems of people sync up in relationships. According to Polyvagal Theory (Stephen Porges 2011), genuine social interaction is beyond words; it's a subconscious exchange of physiological signals. Our voice tone, vocal speed, facial expressions, overall energy, and body language influence others' autonomic state. When we're around someone calm and safe, our nervous system begins to downshift too; when we're around stress, our system may activate in response. Research shows us that emotions are contagious; our predictive brains scan others for safety cues before we even know we are doing that (Saxbe et al. 2010; Hudson et al. 2014).

Back to the Coaching Demo

So a coach's presence becomes an important data point for the other person. If we are acting like everything is okay and we are simply curious, the other person will begin to feel like everything is okay. If it feels okay, our curiosity can lead to insight. As people co-regulate with us, this invites them into a space where they can be curious with themselves. My waving my hands the way she had became an important data point for her, an insight into the energy she was bringing. Remember, we don't want to activate fight, flight, freeze, fawning, freakout, or NEA.

> Coach: "What just happened there with that big sigh?"
>
> Thinker: "I know that I have no control over all this nonsense going on. Right. So intellectually, I know it here. And so the sigh was, Susan, when are you going to just accept and know that you'll be okay and sort of let go of all the spin that is happening?"

This small exchange captured exactly what I am talking about. The sigh is information. I heard it and got curious. Because I didn't ignore it, the thinker didn't ignore it, and that resulted in a profound insight. I wasn't trying to fix the drama at work. I was curious about her response. That curiosity invited her to explore a deeper truth she already knew: she's not in control, and there is a place of acceptance she needs to reach. She also named the spin.

From my perspective, if I had been anxious or felt like I needed to rush toward a solution, I would have stepped out of presence

Emotional Intelligence is a Mindset

and into performance, which would have led to dysregulation, the opposite of a coaching mindset or emotional intelligence.

> Coach: "Is that what's important is to kind of go from the spin and jangle toward. I think I heard you use the word serenity or calm. And that deep sigh?"
>
> Thinker: "I think that would be a good goal for us to get to today."
>
> Coach: "How will you know that we've made it to that calm serenity?"
>
> Thinker: "I'll be able to feel it. The spin in my head, instead of being this, (hands waving) it'll be a nice, calm lake or pool, you know, serenity."
>
> Coach: Then where do we need to begin in this movement toward serenity?

As she explored this image, she began to look more closely at what was instigating the spin and turbulence, and she started to regulate herself. As we continued, she was able to release the spin by recalling her own tools and practices: listening to music that helped her let emotions move through, taking walks, and giving herself permission to pause. By the close of the session, she remembered a ritual from earlier in her life, placing a hand on her heart center to ground herself.

> Thinker: "I forgot about that. This is what grounds me. I have what I need to get through all the craziness."
>
> Coach: "What have you just relearned about yourself?"
>
> Thinker: "That I have what I need to get through all the craziness and the drama and the spin, and I just have to come here (hand on heart) and slow down and breathe and connect with me."

It isn't about coaches displaying empathy or managing the

thinker's feelings. It's about being fully human, present enough to notice, steady enough to be useful, curious, and not getting hooked into the drama and spin that arrived at the beginning of the conversation.

Why this Matters Beyond Coaching

What shows up in coaching conversations doesn't stay there. Thinkers carry their new awareness back into their teams, families, and organizations. And here's where the research is striking: emotional intelligence and empathy don't just make individuals feel better; they reshape how groups function.

A 2025 study on organizational life found that emotional intelligence works like a buffer when workplaces get political or conflict-heavy. Employees with stronger emotional intelligence were less likely to disengage or spiral into stress. Instead, they reframed challenges, stayed grounded, and kept collaborating, even when the environment was messy (Bhatia et al. 2025).

Empathy played a special role. It transformed conflict from destructive to constructive. When empathy was present, teams communicated more openly, trusted one another more deeply, and worked toward shared goals rather than retreating into silos. In other words, empathy wasn't just a "nice" leadership quality; it became the bridge that turned a group of individuals into a cohesive team.

When we embody emotional intelligence and nurture it in our Thinkers, we're equipping them with capacities that ripple outward. Self-awareness helps them see their triggers before those triggers spill into team dynamics. Self-regulation allows them to hold steady during tension rather than escalate. Empathy opens the door to psychological safety, where innovation and collaboration can actually thrive.

Spinning to Calm shows how the coach's self-regulation and empathy supported one person's journey back to steadiness. The broader evidence reminds us: these same skills fuel all systems. Coaching with an emotionally intelligent mindset doesn't just change the conversation in front of us, it prepares leaders, parents, and partners to bring steadiness and humanity into every space they inhabit.

Emotional Intelligence is a Mindset

The Five Clusters of Emotional Intelligence

Researchers often frame emotional intelligence as five interconnected clusters that capture both the personal and the relational (Goleman 1995, 1998; Boyatzis et al. 2000). It's tempting to read them like a checklist, but that misses the point. These aren't discrete skills you master one by one; they're a living system. You move back and forth through the different elements, and they shape how we move through the world and how we meet others. In coaching, they're part of the foundation that makes a coaching mindset more than words on a page.

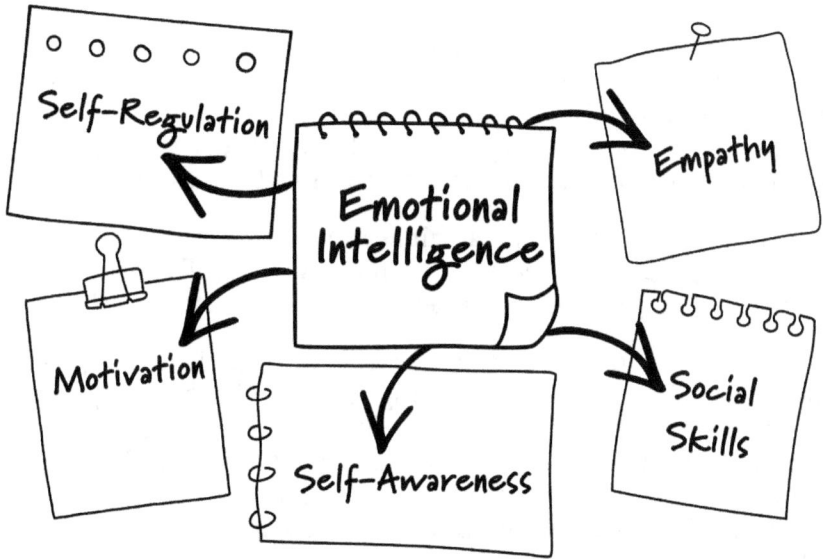

Self-Awareness

Self-awareness is where everything begins. Without it, we're at the mercy of impulses we don't even notice. In coaching, I see this when a thinker suddenly recognizes the story underneath their frustration. Maybe their "irritation" with a team member is really about something else in their personal life, or something they've ignored for too long. That noticing doesn't fix the problem, but it changes the focus. Once something is seen, it can be worked with.

Lisa Feldman Barrett's theory of constructed emotion shows that what we call "anger", "joy", or "anxiety" isn't a raw signal; it's the brain constructing meaning from bodily sensations and context

(Barrett 2017). Awareness, then, is the practice of catching those constructions in the act.

For leaders and employees, the payoff is enormous. A 2025 study showed that employees with greater emotional awareness and regulation perceived organizational politics as less threatening and were more resilient in the face of conflict (Bhatia et al. 2025). They didn't get pulled into defensive spirals as quickly, which meant they stayed engaged and collaborative when others checked out.

Motivation

Emotions aren't just something to manage; they're also fuel. Motivation, from the perspective of emotional intelligence, is about harnessing that fuel in the service of a purpose. A leader driven by fear may try to control every detail, but a leader driven by purpose and values can inspire and sustain commitment across a team.

Coaches see this when a thinker reconnects with why a goal matters. That spark of meaning shifts focus; it pulls them out of compliance and back into alignment.

Research shows that this capacity is what helps employees stay engaged instead of withdrawing. People with high degrees of emotional intelligence reframe challenges, stay psychologically present, and keep working toward solutions (Bhatia et al. 2025). That reframing is itself a resilience practice, because it redirects energy away from defensiveness or spin and into a focus that is actually useful.

Self-Regulation

Of course, awareness without regulation is knowing what something is without knowing how to use it. Regulation is the hinge that lets us move from noticing to choosing. As coaches, we live this every time we sit in silence that feels uncomfortable, resisting the urge to rescue the thinker. Leaders live it when they hold their ground in a tough negotiation instead of snapping back in anger or rolling over.

Self-regulation isn't suppression. It's not about forcing yourself to be calm or plastering on a fake smile. It's about being flexible, breathing, taking a pause, and responding in a way that serves your

Emotional Intelligence is a Mindset

values rather than your impulses. Again, it's the space between "reactive" and "proactive."

Empathy

Empathy isn't about feeling sorry for someone or wanting to take care of them. Empathy is the ability to put ourselves in someone's shoes. This is different from sympathy or over-identification. Sometimes empathy is silence. Sometimes it's a word or a nod. Sometimes it's curiosity that widens the lens: "I hear you. What do you need right now?"

Organizational research confirms what we sense in the coaching room: empathy is a game-changer. In 2025, studies showed that empathy transformed destructive conflict into constructive dialogue. Employees who used empathy reduced misunderstandings, bridged across differences, and created the trust that made collaboration possible (Jordan and Troth 2002; Bhatia et al. 2025).

To circle back to "The Airman and the Late Nights," we need to ask ourselves questions like: *What happens if we don't find our balance? Do we care about feeling connected? Do we care how our choice to hold onto anger or resolve it impacts the people on our team? How does a fractured team meet goals or the mission? Who wants to be the identified problem?*

I ask these because sometimes one person, or both, will be so entrenched in their own perspective that they lose sight of the system. None of us work or live in silos. We are interconnected. If I were coaching the airman and myself, and we had found ourselves in an impasse, these are the sorts of questions I would be asking.

Many years ago, someone shared with me that they never trusted someone they hadn't had an argument with. How people show up with disagreement, discomfort, and anger tells us a great deal about their level of emotional intelligence, self-awareness, and self-regulation.

Feldman Barrett offers a fascinating layer here, too. Empathy is built on the brain's predictive machinery. When we empathize, we're simulating another person's state, constructing what we think they might be feeling based on cues and context. That means empathy literally changes both nervous systems in the room. In coaching, when I sit steady with a thinker's anxiety, grief, or fear, my calm isn't just for show; it's the biological data their brain uses to calibrate.

Social Skills (Relationship Management)

Finally, there's relationship management, the expression of all the other clusters in action. It's about trust, collaboration, influence, and the capacity to repair when things fracture. For coaches, it often looks like helping a thinker learn to have a difficult conversation with a colleague, friend, spouse, or child without rupturing the relationship. Or it can look like supporting a leader as they rebuild trust with a team after a misstep.

It also requires developing both self- and other-perspective. To coach effectively, we have to learn to listen to disagreement, track the relational field, and keep the relationship as the goal rather than our personal need to win. These are the same social skills we lean on in our own lives, in our families, and in everyday conflict.

In organizations, this is the systemic glue. Leaders high in emotional intelligence foster loyalty, adaptability, and stronger team climates, even when resources are scarce or tensions run high, which is pretty much a daily thing (Goleman et al. 2013). Relationship management isn't about charm; it's about sustaining the conditions in which people can work together effectively, even in the face of stress and negative experiences.

Activity: Building Your Emotional Intelligence Muscles

Think back to a recent conversation—coaching or other. Try this reflection:

1. Self-Awareness

What was happening inside you during that situation or conversation? Did you notice your own inner critic, judgment, strong emotional responses, or even checking out? Take a minute to write it down without editing. Then ask yourself: *What triggered that?* Journaling this over time helps you see your patterns.

Emotional Intelligence is a Mindset

2. Self-Regulation

What did you do with that awareness? Did you push it aside, get swept up in it, or take a breath and choose how to respond? If you could replay that moment, what would one notch more regulation look like? Consider experimenting with a quick reset tool, like 4x4 breathing, journaling, or letter writing, or putting yourself in the other person's shoes as much as possible before you respond.

3. Motivation

What was your goal? What allowed you to stay present? Was it your curiosity, your commitment to growth, or your overarching goal? Notice where you felt energy running low. What helps you renew it: a quick body check-in, or simply reminding yourself, *I have something to learn here.*

4. Empathy

Where did you understand the thinker the most? Where did you fit in their shoes, not just their words, but the emotions underneath? How did you show that awareness without explaining, rationalizing, or rushing? Practicing empathy might mean asking one open-ended question or reflecting a single feeling word and then giving space.

5. Relationship Management (Social Skills)

Looking back, how did you help strengthen the relationship? Did you co-create safety, name something important, or support a boundary? Think about how your tone, presence, or even your willingness to listen shaped the trust between you.

Take one insight from your reflection and set a small practice goal for yourself. Keep it tiny and specific, like:

- ? "Notice when my shoulders tighten and take a breath before I speak."
- ? "When people seem stuck, notice my response or reaction."
- ? "Invite feedback at the end of the conversation about what felt most useful."

Sticky Outcomes!

The Invitation Is Simple, Not Easy

Emotional intelligence isn't a tool in a coach's kit; it's the foundation of how we work to show up. Self-awareness, regulation, motivation, empathy, and social skills or relationship management are part of the living system that shapes how we show up with every person around us, including ourselves, in our coaching relationships.

In *Spinning to Calm*, we saw how a steady presence gave a thinker space to find her own grounding. When the coach can self-regulate and stay present, we create the conditions for thinkers to see themselves clearly and either recognize where they are hooked or take responsibility for what's theirs to own.

The invitation is simple, but not easy: keep practicing your own emotional intelligence. Notice your patterns. Slow your reactions. Practice empathy. Shift your perspective to look at the situation from many angles. And show up to build relationships that can hold truth, flexibility, and respect. That's the coaching mindset.

Chapter Nineteen

Tuning into Metaphors

> Ordinary words convey only what we know already; it is from metaphor that we can best get hold of something fresh.
>
> —Aristotle

Metaphors are insights into how human beings experience and perceive their world. They are idea containers for a way of thinking and conceptualizing our situations. George Lakoff and Mark Johnson's work began exploring how people use metaphors in everyday life. What they discovered was that metaphors revealed how we understand and navigate our lives. More than a poetic trick, these metaphors were meaning-making. When someone says, "I'm stuck," they're not only describing their felt experience; they're revealing a mental schema that communicates how they are making sense of themselves in their world or situation. I write about this at length in my 2024 book, *Light Up: The Science of Coaching with Metaphors.*

Michael Reddy, one of the early linguists in this space, described what he called the "conduit metaphor." He suggested that ideas are objects, language is a container for those idea-objects, and communication is sending those idea-objects in containers. It's simple and clean. What matters here is that metaphors aren't random; they are the way human beings package their experiences and send them out into the world. To repeat a point Lakoff made years later: the locus of metaphor is thought, not language. And that's why they matter so much in coaching.

In coaching, hearing these unconscious but very intentional words is golden on multiple levels. When we hear phrases like "I have a full plate" or "I am spinning," these statements serve as the conduit or package of an experience, communicating the experience the thinker is having. It's an expression of life that is being experienced in the moment. *I'm drowning in work.* Or, *I feel like I'm running on a hamster wheel.* These aren't throwaway phrases. They're windows into the thinker's internal landscape. Each phrase reveals the thinker's reality, showing how they perceive their world and how their somatic systems are being impacted.

Let's take the word *doormat.* If I say to you, "I am going to the store to buy a doormat," we both know exactly what that means. I am getting a mat to put in front of my door. That's an object. But if I say to you, *"I feel like a doormat,"* something significant shifted. We are no longer talking about a thing; we are talking about my experience, and I have packaged the idea container as feeling like a doormat.

> **Metaphors are Idea Containers**
> **They point to the thinkers inner landscape & meaning making.**

As a coach, if I hear this nuance, I can ask, "And if you weren't a doormat, what would you rather be?" Which might lead to any number of interesting things:

"I would rather be a door," the thinker might say.

"What does it mean to be a door?" the coach might ask.

The thinker might share an insight, "Well, doors open and close, I can lock a door, I can stand in the door, but not let someone in, there are peepholes, and I don't even have to answer the door if I don't want to."

Now we have a direction, and the movement becomes the shift from doormat to door. We will ask other questions to reach a full agreement, such as, *What is different for you when you become the door?* And *What are the indicators you notice when you are the door?* The metaphor becomes a powerful and safe way to explore the movement or directionality that takes the thinker from one state to another.

As coaches, we don't need to insert our own clever imagery. If you say to me, "I feel like a doormat," and I respond with "Yeah, it's like bugs on a windshield," it's going to create a disconnect. By inserting my metaphor, I pulled you out of your own conduit of meaning. This is how we create cognitive load in a conversation; you now have to translate your lived experience into my words, see if it's correct, decide whether I understood you, or you might start down a path of explaining the metaphor of being a doormat, or even worse, you just don't feel heard. If I stick with your metaphor, you remain within your own thinking and flow. We can continue to explore more deeply.

Listening at this level asks us to tune our ears not only to the surface of the story but also to the specific language being used to communicate the story. Noticing the metaphors in the thinker's words and treating those words as opportunities to safely explore is where the magic happens.

Which would you prefer: to explore your problematic boundaries, or to explore what you would like to do with this full plate? In this way, metaphors create clarity of distance and reduce the likelihood of negative self-judgment. We're just looking at full plates. Nothing to fear here.

It's a Dance

Fiona Mathieson's work adds another layer to how we understand the role of metaphors in conversations involving change. In her study, *The Metaphoric Dance: Co-construction of Metaphor in Cognitive Behaviour Therapy* (2015), she and her colleagues analyzed transcripts from early CBT sessions to see what really happens when metaphors show up in the room. What they found is that metaphors aren't just sprinkled in and forgotten. They come in bursts, with both therapist and client actively responding—repeating, rephrasing, clarifying, extending, or simply agreeing within just a few turns of dialogue.

Mathieson describes this back-and-forth as a "metaphoric dance." Neither party owns the floor; both step into and shape the imagery together. And that's important. When metaphors are taken up and developed, they become a kind of shared language, a shorthand that organizes large amounts of meaning and experience. Instead of slipping past unnoticed, these metaphors anchor the conversation in a way that helps the thinker see their own concerns more clearly.

For coaches, the parallels are striking. We talk about client-led, client-owned metaphors, but Mathieson shows that how we respond matters just as much as whether we notice them. If we "swap out" a thinker's metaphor for one of our own, rapport suffers; it can sound like "my metaphor is better than yours." However, if we stay within their imagery, repeating or elaborating on it, we align ourselves with the emotional weight and lived experience embedded in their words.

This research supports what Lakoff and Johnson argued years ago, that metaphors structure thought, not just speech. Mathieson demonstrates that, in practice, when we notice and use those structures, we join the dance. As we play with the thinker and their words, we strengthen safety and create the environment for more meaningful and deeper exploration. This, too, has been my experience.

Owning It

Owned metaphors are especially important. These are often expressed as "I am" or "I feel" metaphors, such as *I am on the fence, I'm wrestling with this, I'm at a crossroads, or I feel like a doormat*. They surface from the unconscious, yet they are intentional containers of meaning. They show how a person conceives of themselves, their identity, and their place in the world. When I hear a thinker say I feel driven or I am in a rut, that isn't small talk. That is their sense of self and life experience speaking. And if we miss it, it's like a tree falling in a forest with no one there to hear.

I recently had a coaching session in which the thinker was discussing the desire to write a book. They mentioned that they had already tried many things, including blocking time on the calendar to visit the library every week. However, despite the calendar block, they hadn't gone. They talked about how they had to find the time or make the time, and that something was keeping them from just doing it. As I asked about what was important for us to explore in this, what emerged was: "I need to create space. It reminds me of how sometimes people use a bell or a chime to start an activity and then again to end it. I think I need a gong, and I need to create space between the gongs, so that I can have that set time to write."

I asked, "Is that what's important, to find the space between the gongs?"

"Yes, that is what I want to do," she responded.

Tuning into Metaphors

"I need space" was conceptualized as "the space between the gongs." As we continued the conversation, the thinker was able to explore what needed attention, not only regarding the creation of this space but also how to use it effectively.

Some of the space was needed to determine what was important enough to write about and spend this time on. This became an important insight: the space between the gongs wasn't just about writing. It was about discovering what mattered to the thinker, what would become part of their legacy, the mark they would leave in the world.

Suppose I had missed the metaphor. I might have helped them craft another gorgeous calendar, blocking time in yellow, green, or blue, without addressing the underlying question of what was important enough to spend the time on, so they were actually motivated to write. Basically, I would have missed the mark.

Partnering with metaphors in this way is exactly what Carl Rogers emphasized in his client-centered theory. He believed people already hold the resources for growth, and our role is to attune to those resources. When we follow the thinker's metaphors, we are saying, "I am listening, and I hear you. I trust you. I trust your brain. I trust your way of making meaning." That stance is partnership, and it's what allows people to create the dot, connect the dots, and ultimately own the dots.

Biased Brains

In coaching, we're never dealing in certainties. We're always testing hypotheses. A thinker may tell us XYZ, and even if we think we know what XYZ means, that's our predictive brain jumping in. Daniel Yon, in his book A Trick of the Mind (2025), discusses how the brain pieces together the world based on our perspective, preferences, patterns, experiences, and what our brain focuses on or doesn't focus on. This means we are all primed to hear what our brain expects to hear based on our experiences. That's bias at work, not good, bad, or indifferent, just the brain's way of managing the world, filtering out the stuff it decides doesn't matter. Even if we're careful, those biases shape the questions we ask and the direction we take a conversation.

Sticky Outcomes!

Imagine a leader coming in upset about an upcoming hard conversation with a direct report. They're worried they'll lose their cool. If our bias is leaning toward being helpful, we might rush to offer tools and strategies. But that may not be what matters most to them. What matters might sit beneath the surface of their worry. If we stay in "I don't know" mode, we slow down. We listen for what's actually being said, not just what our brain predicts is coming next.

This slowing down matters because the brain loves shortcuts. Yon gives an example: if I say, *I am going to the forest to forage some 'mushr...,'* your brain is already filling in *'...ooms.'* So, when I finish with *mushrocks*, your brain may flash an alarm. That prediction error is disorienting. Coaching works a lot like that. The thinker may bring us the proverbial "mushr...," in their words, their story, their concern. We may already be supplying the ending. But if we leave room for surprise, we hear the "mushrocks" moments, the unexpected meanings that belong to them, not us.

Awareness of our bias is so important. Biases filter what we notice and ignore. They can make us assume sameness where none exists, cultural background, political leaning, or even something as ordinary as how families eat dinner. Remember that first time you went to a friend's house and realized not everyone has the same rules, food, or rhythms as your family? Coaching asks us to remember that moment again and again. No one else's house is exactly like ours. No one else's mind is either. So, always test your hypothesis.

This is why I love metaphors so much. They give context, safety, and a peek into the internal landscape of the thinker; when we are talking about *full plates, juggling, spinning, or doormats*, it also helps us avoid our immediate assumptions and predictions. We linger longer in the realm of curiosity and non-predictive judgment. What do we know about what another person wants on or off their plate anyway? Nothing. And that's exactly right.

The Brain's Fast-Forward Button

Listening isn't neutral. Our brains are constantly stitching together what comes in through the ears (bottom-up signals) with what we expect to hear (top-down predictions). Yon, in *A Trick of the Mind*, points to Matt Davis's research at Cambridge, which shows how quickly listeners combine raw speech sounds with predictions. The brain is essentially running a real-time hypothesis test: Is the sound I'm hearing matching the word I already expect? And, as noted earlier in Chapter 15 on listening, we are already formulating responses before the speaker has even finished their words.

Bottom-up refers to the raw data: the tone, timing, and acoustic features of what we hear. Top-down is all the context we bring with us: the topic of the conversation (and here's where expertise can trip you up), the grammar of the language, and even the cultural patterns we know (Gibson 2006; Matar et al. 2021). Put those together with raw sounds, and suddenly we "hear" things that may not have been said at all. It's like being on a Zoom call with someone whose bandwidth is faltering. Words might drop, but we still follow the thread because our brain fills in the missing pieces.

This was demonstrated in a 2024 study using magnetoencephalography (MEG), a technology that detects the faint magnetic fields produced when neurons fire. In this study, researchers observed the brain navigating grammar and context, parsing meaning from scrambled sentences in about 200 milliseconds. The brain was busy predicting and filling in the missing syllables and words, treating them as if they were present and fully understandable (Flower and Pylkkänen 2024). The brain doesn't concern itself with what's missing. It rushes ahead, rewriting what we hear so that it fits the story we expect. This shows up in conversations when we nod rapidly in agreement or are already preparing our counterpoint. We "yeah, yeah, yeah" or "no, no, no" the other person because we've predicted where they're going. Sometimes we're right, and sometimes we are wildly off.

Gibson (2006) showed that our brains can even misunderstand meaning itself; we cling to the interpretation that fits our expectations, even when structure or usage points elsewhere. This is why metaphors matter so much. They interrupt the brain's autocorrect function and give us a chance to linger in curiosity instead of racing toward assumption.

Once, in a mentor coaching group, the coach asked what the thinker would have if they discussed the topic fully. The thinker answered, "Enlightenment."

In this situation, enlightenment wasn't about sitting on a lotus blossom as an enlightened being. It was about shining a light on their struggle.

When the coach responded, "Enlightenment, that's a big word," it did two things. First, it shut down the thinker's flow, prompting them to backtrack and explain. Second, it revealed the coach's bias and assumptions about the meaning of *enlightenment*—not wrong in general but incorrect for this moment with this thinker. The perfect move would have been to test a hypothesis: "What do you mean by enlightenment here?" That question would have moved the conversation forward in partnership, leveraging the metaphor instead of flattening it.

In friendly conversations, especially when we agree, we can get away with predictions. In arguments or in non-argumentative coaching conversations, we have to train our brains to slow down. Predictions will still happen, but we need to keep our mouths closed and our minds open until the other person finishes their thought.

The added layer is that we're not only predicting words; we're also predicting ideas, beliefs, and meaning. If a thinker says something and our bias primes us to hear something altogether different, we tend to default to our interpretation. The brain autocorrects the sentence. Now we "fix" what we thought they meant into something that fits our worldview. If we don't slow down, we risk coaching our prediction instead of their reality.

In some coaching arenas, this top-down/bottom-up theory has been co-opted into classifications of "levels of listening." Coaches use the terms metaphorically to distinguish between focusing on the bigger picture (top-down) and the details—beliefs, words, body language, tone, pace, energy (bottom-up). As metaphors, these definitions are fine. But the scientific theory is about how our brains predict words and meaning, not about attentional focus. We're not only listening to content; we're predicting and often hearing things that were never said. Understanding this process matters because our predictions can steer the conversation into coach-led territory, pulling the thinker away from their intended path.

This is where metaphors are powerful. They interrupt the urge to predict and auto-complete meaning. Instead, they let us suspend what we think we know. We don't have to fully understand the metaphor the thinker brings. Our ability to recall it helps us hold the conversation with more latitude and fewer assumptions. When a thinker offers an owned metaphor, we can set aside the "certitude" of prediction. If someone says, "I feel like a doormat," that idea container has no predictable direction. There's no obvious next step. If we let it, our brain gets curious: "If you were no longer a doormat, what would you prefer to be?"

Coaching Demo: Prickles

We've just looked at how our brains run ahead of us, predicting, filling in blanks, assuming, and sometimes pulling us in directions before we've even realized it. This coaching conversation shows what happens when a thinker names their experience in a metaphor. Notice how the metaphor interrupts the rush to interpret. The word *prickles* lands in the space. That one word carries somatic and psychological weight and becomes a container for exploring the relationship with her older sister from a different angle.

> Coach: "What's showing up for you today for a coaching conversation?"
>
> Thinker: "Well, I just came back from a cruise with my sister. Seven days in Italy and Spain, it was lovely. The thing I'd like some coaching on is my relationship with my sister, where I'm struggling.
>
> "I'm the youngest of four. Susan is three years older, we grew up close, doing a lot together.
>
> "One day, I said to her, "It always feels like a competition."
>
> "She said, 'Well, I don't see it that way.'
>
> "And I thought, 'What are you talking about? It's always a competition with you.'
>
> "Then I thought, maybe I'm the one making it feel like a competition. That stopped me in my tracks. What am I bringing to this relationship that creates this tension? That's what I want to explore."

Notice that the word *struggle* has emerged, and I am hearing it. However, before I pounce on this, I need to ask more questions. I also need a full agreement before we dive into the deep end of this pool.

Sticky Outcomes!

I don't have enough information about what is important. Several themes are emerging: "What I am bringing to the relationship," "competition," and "maybe I am the one creating the tension."

>Coach: "So, what would you like to be bringing to this relationship?"
>
>Thinker: "Friendship, love, kindness, support. Feeling like I have a confidant or that I can be a confidant."
>
>Coach: "What is the experience of that, friendship, kindness, being a confidant, for you?"
>
>Thinker: "In the ideal version, it's a feeling of trust. Friendship. Knowing the other person cares. It flows, it feels comfortable. It's not that struggle feeling."
>
>Coach: "And what is the importance of that in this moment?"

I am still not making any guesses as to what we need to do or where we need to explore; I am suspending my assumptions and judgment. I am still hearing that this is a real struggle. I'm sitting with the ambiguity, continuing to ask questions that invite the thinker to name what's important.

>Thinker: "I'm sick of the struggle. It makes me stressed and uncomfortable. My older sister said, "What else is new? You two have always been that way." I love her and care about her friendship, but it feels like a struggle for control. I don't want to be doing that, but I am."
>
>Coach: "Is that what's important for today's conversation? Exploring that struggle and maybe letting go of the control?"

Testing my hypothesis out loud, no hidden agenda. The thinker is at choice to direct me.

>Thinker: "Partly, yes. To look in the mirror and realize

Tuning into Metaphors

I'm at least 50% responsible. What am I bringing that's not helpful? And also, how do I shift it? Her comment really surprised me. I've always thought she was the competitive one, and I just learned it from her. Now I wonder, maybe it's me."

Coach: "If we explore this deeply today, what would be different for you at the end?"

Thinker: "Two things. One, a better understanding of where I'm coming from—am I really the competitive one? And two, having a sense of what I'd like to choose in my relationship with my sister."

Coach: "So, acceptance and the capacity to choose. Would those be the indicators of a shift?"

Thinker: "Yes."

Coach: "Where do we begin this exploration?"

Thinker: "With acceptance of self. Am I the competitive one? I like to achieve and be successful, but I always felt like I had to catch up with her. She was good at sports, good at math, successful. Her style is not like mine. She can feel like a bulldozer, not very empathetic, and she just drives forward with her perspective. That rubs me the wrong way. Maybe I interpret that as competitiveness."

Coach: "What's bubbling to the surface as you share this awareness?"

Thinker: "This might sound funny, but maybe that's my need for control. I want her to be softer. I don't like it when she's brusque and demanding. I want more softness in interactions. That's different from competitiveness."

Coach: "What is the difference?"

Thinker: "Competitiveness is more about winning or

Sticky Outcomes!

losing, being better than someone. Style is about how you show up in the world, how you treat people. At times, I feel like she pricks me. Like I'm handling a rose with thorns. It's prickly. I got pricked again."

The metaphors abound as she talks about wanting her sister to be softer and wanting more softness in the relationship, but they are externally focused. In naming *She pricks me, it's prickly, and I got pricked again,* we are hearing an owned metaphor of her experience. This reaches deeper than the surface-level *struggle* and into the hurt itself, pointing to what might be her 50 percent of the relationship, her response to the hurt.

> Coach: "May I share an observation? How do you become when you're handling something prickly?"
>
> Thinker: "Defensive, because it hurts."
>
> Coach: "How does that impact what you want for your relationship?"
>
> Thinker: "It's a block."
>
> Coach: "If the block were shifted, how would you like to handle prickles?"
>
> Thinker: "There's our metaphor. I'd put on some gloves. In fact, I was handling roses this morning. If I could protect myself from the prickles, I might not feel so attacked or defensive."

Now she is starting to think more creatively. If she is handling a rose, something cherished but covered in thorns, then she can begin to protect herself so she doesn't need to react to her prediction of attack or competition. She is constructing a new way to think about her 50 percent, which gives her a more empowered position. It's no longer just an external locus of control, *She's the problem.* It becomes an internal locus of control; *I can protect myself so I can be in the relationship safely.*

Novel versus Conventional Metaphors

Not all metaphors are created equal. Some phrases slip by almost unnoticed because they're part of everyday talk, such as "lean in," "full plate," "at a crossroads," or simply "I'm struggling." Others feel fresh or unusual, a little odd even, and they ask more of us. Vicky Lai and her colleagues found that these novel metaphors actually demand more from the brain. They take more effort to process, which is exactly why they can jolt us into new ways of seeing.

The findings show how the brain processes novel versus conventional metaphors (Lai 2009), which is why staying with the thinker's metaphor is crucial. Familiar metaphors run on automatic and require very little energy from the brain. The new ones make us pause; they take more processing and create cognitive load.

In coaching, the concept of "novelty" isn't universal. A metaphor may be novel to the coach, but if the thinker generated it, it may be unique, yet it is not novel to them; their brain processes it in a conventional way. It flows from their internal landscape, and they unconsciously understand its meaning. So, the thinker is not experiencing cognitive load. The coach might be, but that is simply an invitation to check in and get curious.

And metaphors don't stay new forever. Eileen Cardillo's team showed that repeated use tunes the brain. Initially, a metaphor sparks widespread connections across both hemispheres, but over time, as it becomes familiar, processing settles into the more efficient language systems. In coaching terms, a thinker's owned metaphor might begin as a brand-new spark and then, as they return to it session after session, become a shorthand for their lived experience.

There's also what happens between people. Fiona Mathieson's work highlights metaphor co-construction, the process by which meaning evolves as coach and thinker jointly explore the image, as seen in the coaching demo discussing "prickles." Instead of ignoring the prickles or steering the conversation toward solving the struggle, we explored the metaphor together. That is when metaphors do their best work. These are not clever turns of phrase but living containers of meaning that both people can touch and turn over until something important spills out, something that might lead to deeper insights.

Activity: Tune Your Ear for Metaphors

For your next few coaching conversations, just listen and notice the metaphors that naturally emerge from the thinker. Your only job is to notice what shows up. Listen for phrases like "my plate is full," "I feel like a…," "I'm the one who…," or even single words used symbolically, like "doormat," "anchor," "struggle," or "storm."

You don't need to analyze anything or turn it into a coaching moment. Just catch the metaphors. Notice how much emotional weight, identity, energy, and possibility can sit inside even a tiny phrase.

If you feel a natural opening, ask one curious question using the thinker's metaphor and language. Keep it simple. For example, "If your plate is full, what's taking up the most space?" Or "When you say it feels like a storm, what sort of weather are you seeking?"

This is practice. You're training your ear to tune itself when meaning arrives wrapped in everyday language. The more you tune in, the easier it becomes to hear what's really being offered beneath the words.

CHAPTER TWENTY

THE WILD WILD WEST

> The true test of a man's character is what he does when no one is watching.
>
> —H. Jackson Brown, Jr.

The reason coaches need a code of ethics is simple: coaching is an unregulated industry. There isn't a license, and there isn't a single governing board that decides who can call themselves a coach and who can't. Given that coaching is an international profession and it didn't evolve from a medical model more than one hundred years ago, having states, provinces, and countries all determining licensure would be a literal dumpster fire. Unfortunately, this means that no matter where you look, you can throw a rock and you'll probably hit someone calling themselves a coach, and possibly a certified coach, an executive coach, or a master coach. *Yeehaw!*

Some of those people are excellent, while others have never been trained in professional coaching at all. From the outside, it's hard for consumers to tell the difference. What they often end up getting is a consultant, an adviser, or a "if you want what I have, do what I do" person, and then they walk away thinking that's coaching. It isn't, but how would they know?

Let's just say the quiet part out loud—coaching is easy to claim and hard to verify. So if coaching is largely unregulated, what keeps it professional?

Ethics.

What's important for coaches to understand is that, to be part of a professional body such as the International Coaching Federation

Sticky Outcomes!

(ICF), the European Mentoring and Coaching Council (EMCC), or the Board Certified Coach (BCC), you are agreeing to follow a set of ethics, values, and standards for the professional representation of coaching. These professional bodies, and others, have codes of ethics that outline those standards. This creates a significant difference between you and everybody else who calls themselves a coach, who may or may not have any training, and who is not aligned with a professional organization.

Coaching as a Profession

Part of the reason this is so important is that coaching is an unregulated industry. If you get your haircut, the stylist has a license that shows they've been trained and are legally allowed to cut your hair. The same is true for the massage therapist who works the kink out of your neck, or your real estate agent, accountant, lawyer, therapist, doctor, or any number of professions that require a license to practice.

Coaching isn't like that. Unlike these other fields—where you're working with people, engaging in deep work, and navigating the intricacies of the human experience—in coaching, you're doing all of that without a degree that guarantees you have a master's in psychology, social work, or another therapeutic discipline. And you're doing it without a license issued by the state, province, or country where you live. That's a big hole. Which means you, and the people who choose to hire you, need to know you have serious training behind you, and you adhere to an ethical framework.

The reason coaching is unregulated is that coaching spans the globe, and regulating "the world" would be nearly impossible. Let's say Washington State passed a law requiring coaches to have a license, what would that mean for coaches in Colorado or New York? Or in Canada? Or throughout Central and South America? Or in Asia, India, the Middle East, Africa, or Europe? Nothing. Washington law applies only to Washington. There is no shared governing body across all the places where coaches train and practice. Only coaches in Washington State would be impacted. This is in part why regulation hasn't happened, and as much as I wish it could be licensed, I don't have a clear idea how to do it in a way that is fair across the planet.

What we have instead are professional organizations like the ICF, the EMCC, and the BCC that work to regulate, as best they can, the standards of coach education and credentialing. This matters because it differentiates those with credentials from those without, similar to how an associate's degree differs from a bachelor's, a master's, or a doctorate. These levels reflect increasing degrees of learning and experience.

The ICF and BCC accredit Continuing Coach Education (CCE) units and regulate coach training organizations. Ideally, this creates a level playing field so that if you attend an ICF- or BCC-accredited school, your education aligns with the professional standards of coaching. Coaches also have to renew their credentials and complete a specific number of CCEs every three years, including ethics. This is very similar to my clinical license in social work.

Why This Helps You Practically

This is useful to you as a coach on a number of levels. Many organizations now require that you have a minimum of a ACC in order to work within their organization. If you want to work for a coaching organization like BetterUp or ERZA, you need to have a certain level of credentialing certified through the ICF. This ensures that you are qualified to even apply for a job with one of these organizations.

I haven't seen it as much with small businesses, but with large businesses—organizations such as Microsoft, Procter and Gamble, NASA, Coca-Cola, or Google, you name it—they often require that you have at least an ACC credential. Some require PCC before they're willing to have you be on their roster of coaches. And, of late, I am hearing some require an MCC.

Guardrails, Not Handcuffs

The code of ethics is a guide to the fundamentals of how we do our work. When you read through the code of ethics, you will see sections on core values and ethical principles, commitments, ethical standards, and a pledge of commitment to those ethics. For the full and official ICF Code of Ethics, visit www.coachingfederation.org and search "Code of Ethics" to download the current version.

Ethics protects us in a lot of other ways, too. Without ethics, we don't have a framework for how we set up agreements, how we handle confidentiality, how we establish the parameters of working together, and what is required of me as the coach and you as the client or thinker. While it's not exactly a juicy topic, it is hugely important for being a professional coach.

I think a lot of people hear "ethics" and think of all the things they can't do. I don't see ethics that way. I see them more as guardrails.

Ethics says it's important that you continue to learn and grow, that you're making a commitment to your thinkers, yourself, and your business, and that you're continuing to develop yourself as a coach. It also says you need to take care of yourself as a human being so you can show up fully and be fully present with the people you're working with.

Note: For these scenarios, I'll be referring to the thinker as "the client" since that is the language ICF uses on their exams.

> **1. External engagement, supervisor requests a debrief**
>
> **Scenario:** You're coaching within an organization through an external coaching company, and you're four sessions in. The client has several organizational goals and one personal goal. The supervisor calls you to debrief on how the client is doing and what the goals are. What should you do?
>
> Choose the **BEST** of These Options
>
> 1. Acknowledge the supervisor's request and set up a meeting between the coach, client, and supervisor, ensuring transparency.
>
> 2. Acknowledge the supervisor's request and explain that, due to confidentiality agreements, you cannot share anything without the client's explicit consent.
>
> 3. Acknowledge the supervisor's request and explain that the supervisor will need to ask the client for consent before discussing any details.
>
> 4. Acknowledge the supervisor's request and agree to provide a debrief on the organizational goals without mentioning the personal goals.

The Wild Wild West

? Why did you pick the answer you chose?

? How did you determine that was the best choice?

Answers at the end of the chapter.

The Four Values (Quick Pass)

There are four main values that matter for professional coaches: Professionalism, Collaboration, Humanity, and Equity. I'm going to go through them briefly.

Professionalism

This is about committing to being professional. It's not about "I wear a blazer"; it's about the values we bring into our interactions with other coaches, people in other professions, and the people and organizations we work with. We demonstrate our professionalism by being responsible, respectful, and working with people and organizations with integrity and competence. We show up as our best selves. Professionalism includes recognizing potential ethical dilemmas or conflicts of interest, being accurate about our training and credential level, and making sure our conduct aligns with both a coaching mindset and, frankly, basic humanity. We deliver on our commitments. We are resilient and take care of ourselves so that when challenges arise, we can handle them. We commit to the highest standards of the profession and to lifelong learning and personal development.

Collaboration

This value is about social connection and community building. Within the ICF, there are chapters. You likely have one where you live, or at least one that spans your province, state, or country. Local chapters often offer learning and networking opportunities, which help create community so you can meet other coaches. You can support them; they can support you. Collaboration also means partnering across multiple groups. You might be involved with the ICF, BCC, or EMCC, or be a member of other professional organizations. Collaboration keeps you from being in a silo. You're not alone; we're all out here.

Humanity

This usually reflects who people drawn to coaching already are at their core. It's about being kind, compassionate, and respectful. It's owning and acknowledging our mistakes and taking responsibility for our actions. It recognizes that we're all on a lifelong journey of self-awareness. It includes being transparent and honest about who we are and owning it when we fall short (spoiler: we all do). It's a commitment to inclusivity, dignity, self-worth, and human rights, while avoiding anything that suggests we're superior to anyone else.

Equity

This value emphasizes recognizing and respecting different identities and groups and their contributions, both in the world and in coaching. As best we can, we work to recognize our biases and treat people with dignity and fairness. We explore and bring awareness to social diversity, systemic inequality, and oppression, and how these forces may show up in coaching.

If you have a brain, you have bias. Since we all have brains, we're all biased. The work is recognizing those biases and choosing to ask questions instead of assuming. Equity means working toward equality and partnership in all our relationships: thinker and coach, training participant and educator, mentor coach and coach client, supervisor and coach client. Adult-to-adult. Equal-to-equal. Or sometimes trying on the stance of "novice-to-their-expert." At its core, this value reminds us that we each have a responsibility to the greater good.

Transparency

Because we're an unregulated industry, having a code of ethics is crucial for our work with individuals and organizations. We need clear agreements to support our work with a client or sponsor and to clarify the limits of confidentiality and our legal capacity to hold secrets. These are also critical for our own safety.

A lot of what the Code of Ethics requires of us can be summed up with one idea: transparency. Be transparent. Honestly, I could beat the transparency drum all day, because transparency often determines whether something is an ethics violation.

- Your role
- Confidentiality
- Boundaries
- Affiliates

The Wild Wild West

- Scope
- Discrimination
- Power Dynamics

We need to be transparent about what role we are in, whether we are coaching or acting as something else. We need to be transparent about who we refer to and whether we receive affiliate payments. It's fine to have affiliates, but we must make that transparent.

We also need to be clear about confidentiality. We can keep some things private, and we need to clearly state up front the few situations where we may not be able to protect confidentiality. For example, I am a mandated reporter of child abuse and neglect, and I cannot maintain confidentiality if you threaten harm to yourself or others. Coaching has no legal client privilege, so if required by law, or by a valid court order or subpoena, I will break confidentiality. And, the limits of confidentiality in a world where information is rarely fully safeguarded.

You must be clear about our legal requirements and boundaries at the outset. Put them in your agreements and say them out loud. Every coach needs to ask: How will I protect, or at least be transparent about, what I can and cannot do, my role, the thinkers' role, and our relationship boundaries in the work as we are embarking upon? And, how we will discuss things, if needed. I have agreements with the people I work with, so that should something come up, we have a plan on how we will resolve anything messy.

Discrimination, meaning unfair discrimination, is when our prejudices and biases impact the work we are doing. It is totally appropriate to say, *I don't work with kids,* or *Substance use and addiction are outside my scope,* or *I prefer to work with people who share my spiritual belief system.* A coach may determine that they prefer not to work with certain people due to value differences that would make the coaching difficult. But this needs to be determined up front, before the engagement begins. What's not okay is knowing, *I don't want to work with X, but I need some paying coaching clients,* then delivering biased and judgmental coaching.

If an issue emerges in a coaching relationship—for example, a significant values difference between the coach and the thinker—then this becomes something the coach needs to discuss with the thinker and, if needed, make the appropriate referral to another coach, or end the coaching engagement.

Sticky Outcomes!

I have worked with people from every major religion and from both sides of the aisle politically, and I have typically learned something from each of these engagements. Yet this requires that we aren't overly attached to our perspective. I can imagine that all of us have a few perspectives that are deal breakers. We need to know what those are, because we owe it to ourselves and to those we work with to use our energy wisely and to be of service.

Finally, power dynamics are inherently in coaching relationships, no matter how hard we work to mitigate them by meeting as adults to adults. Seeing the thinker as whole, capable, resourceful, and creative. Things can still get muddy very fast when we coach friends, partners, or people we are close to. And, if romantic or sexual relationship attraction enters the picture, watch out. If you genuinely fall in love, then for the love of Pete, refer the thinker to another coach and do not attempt to navigate a dual relationship. Those almost always go poorly for everyone involved.

> **2. Hidden relationship conflict**
>
> **Scenario:** You and the client have been working together a little over a year. You used to work in the same organization where the client now works. The client shares less-than-favorable details about their manager, someone you know and like. The client doesn't know that you and the manager are friends. What should you do?
>
> Choose the **WORST**
>
> 1. Acknowledge the client's feelings about their manager without revealing your relationship.
>
> 2. Ask the client what they'd like to achieve with their manager and explore actions.
>
> 3. Share that you know the client's manager but remain neutral, focusing on how the client can navigate their situation.
>
> 4. Share your friendship with the manager and discuss how the client would like to move forward.

- **?** Why did you pick the answer you chose?
- **?** How did you determine that was the best choice?

Answers at the end of the chapter.

Most ethical problems don't start as "big ethical concerns." They start small: a casual comment, a fuzzy boundary, a tiny conflict of interest, a sponsor request you handle a bit loosely, a client moving into therapy territory, and you trying to be nice instead of being clear.

I was talking with a coaching friend; he has been working with a big coaching platform and had a coaching engagement through that platform. The thinker shared that they were leaving the position and would no longer be able to continue the coaching through the organizational coaching contract. They then asked about hiring the coach on their own, to continue the coaching. This immediately sent some electricity through my friend's brain. How to handle this with integrity and compassion. This sort of request requires us to know what our contracts say about client engagement after termination. We probably need to talk to the platform about options for the thinker. And there may even be a piece about letting go of the ego that says, *I'm the only one who can support positive change with this person.*

How we decide to move forward with this sort of situation will determine if we are in alignment with our ethical responsibilities.

Referring to Other Professionals

What I love about a code of ethics is that it keeps our lane really clear when we work with people. For example, I am not an attorney, nor do I play one on TV, so I do not give legal advice. It is simply not something I am going to do.

We must accurately identify our coaching qualifications and work within the boundaries of our level of competency, expertise, experience, training, certifications, and our ICF credential (ICF 2025).

I also understand that ICF professionals often serve in multiple professional roles based on prior training or experience, such as mentor, therapist, HR specialist, or assessor, and it is my responsibility to disclose to the client when I am acting in any capacity other than the role of an ICF professional coach (ICF 2025).

Maybe you have a background as a CEO, or you spent twenty

years in human resources, or you are an MD or JD, or you are a recovering therapist like me. These are all very different fields, and when someone comes to us for coaching, we still need to remain in the role of coach. Otherwise, we must be transparent that we are acting as an adviser, an HR professional, a lawyer, a doctor, or a therapist. And if we want to preserve the coaching relationship, we may need to explore whether a referral would better serve the thinker.

Often, in my chemistry sessions, I suss out the folks who need therapy more than coaching. I can coach people who are also in therapy, and I have, but we must understand the scope of our work.

A big part of learning to coach in a thinker-led way is recognizing how easy it is to slip into therapy, advising, mentoring, or teaching. We are not doing those things when we are asking open-ended questions anchored in an agreement and an outcome. And ethics reminds us that we are accountable to professional behavior that reflects that boundary.

> **3. Trauma content, scope concerns**
>
> **Scenario:** A client begins to share deeply traumatic family experiences, suggesting unresolved trauma. They insist on continuing coaching rather than therapy. You're concerned the issues may be beyond scope, yet fear disrupting the trust. What should you do?
>
> Choose the **BEST**
>
> 1. Listen empathetically but avoid discussing the trauma further to prevent overwhelm.
>
> 2. Invite the client to discuss how these issues in coaching might hinder progress.
>
> 3. Acknowledge the client for sharing; explore how these experiences relate to their current goals.
>
> 4. Listen as the client continues sharing while you document details for later reflection in supervision.

? Why did you pick the answer you chose?

? How did you determine that was the best choice?
Answers at the end of the chapter.

Decision Tree for "I'm Not Sure What to Do"

Ethics problems usually don't show up as "ethics problems." They show up as feeling uncomfortable: a niggling worry in the back of your brain, the hairs standing up on the back of your neck, a stab of concern, maybe you notice yourself minimizing, or you notice yourself wanting to avoid something. That's your signal to slow down and take a deeper look.

I was the Director of Learning for an ICF chapter in 2017. I was working to pull together a large training opportunity for about twenty chapters, where we could all come together. Each chapter could make money or offer value to its members, and the "big-name" presenter would have enough people on the webinar to make it worth their time. I worked hours and hours on this, working with little chapters that had never hosted a big webinar, and with large chapters that had. We ended up with close to 1,000 people on the call from around twenty chapters. It was a big deal, as this was before COVID, and people weren't as used to Zoom yet. So I worked and worked, and it went off without a hitch. It was my first big event success. It felt great.

The presenter was giving away a free seat in their big training, valued at around $3,000. After the presentation, they reached out to me and offered me a seat in the training as well, for all my hard work. My first desire was to say, "YES!!" It was a wonderful opportunity. But it felt weird. I had a little feeling: Do I need to keep this a secret? Do I say "yes" and then never talk about it again? Those concerns were my first indicator that I had stepped into a hazy ethical space, maybe a conflict of interest?

So I took it to my ICF chapter board, laid it all out, and said, "Whatever decision the board feels is appropriate, I will honor." They discussed it, came back and said they didn't feel it was a problem. I hadn't brought the speaker in with the intention of getting the training, and I had worked hard. This was a nice outcome, yet even if they had said, "No, that's not okay," I would have been fine. I didn't want to live with the secret. Plus, very few secrets stay secret forever . . . and it wasn't worth my integrity.

Steps for ethical decisions

1. Pause. Take a breath.

Name what's happening in you: I feel uneasy. I feel pressure. I want to avoid this. I'm not sure what the right move is.

Don't argue with the feeling. Use it as a signal to stop, drop and roll. Look or feel into what this discomfort is trying to tell you.

2. Name the concern.

What kind of issue is this? Usually it's one (or more) of these:

- confidentiality or privacy
- power dynamics or dependency
- competence/scope (am I out of depth here?)
- conflicts of interest
- dual roles
- risk of harm to self or others
- bias, or a personal line you're not willing to cross

At this stage, you're not fixing anything, you are sorting it out. Naming it so that you can decide the best next step.

3. Go back to the agreement.

What did you and the thinker agree to? What is in writing in the overarching coaching contract?

What did you say about confidentiality, sponsor involvement, boundaries, records, referrals, and limits around confidentiality and legalities?

If your agreements are vague, or missing vital information, or don't state what you're responsible for in the code of ethics, then you may need to add information and tighten up your contracts to create more clarity for both you and the stakeholders.

4. Talk it out. Don't keep it in your own head.

A stressed brain is not good brain for ethical decisions. Also, secrecy often makes things worse, because if you choose poorly, you're on your own. In these complex situations, we need other brains to help us.

Talk to someone:

- a mentor coach or supervisor
- a trusted peer, maybe more than one
- an attorney (if it's a legal question)
- your professional associations
- the ICF Ethics Department, if you're a member of ICF and need clarity

This isn't about making your decision for you; it's about getting different perspectives and options.

5. Straight talk.

Once you're clear about what's going on for you, say it in plain language:

- Here are my concerns
- These are my boundaries
- And here are some possible next steps

This is where simple concise language is useful. No long speeches or confusing and unclear messaging. Apply the KISS (keep it simple stupid) acronym, when laying out what, where, when, who, and how of next steps.

6. Document.

Write down what happened, who all you spoke to, dates and times are helpful, what you decided, and why. Keep it factual. From years of working with the state and Military organizations, when it comes to things that may become legal issues, don't work alone, and write it down.

Sticky Outcomes!

I often will share a brief written summary of what we discussed with the thinker, or relevant stakeholders, so we're all clear on what we've agreed to.

At the End of the Day

As professional coaches, we're agreeing to be professional in our conduct, committed to delivering consistent value, and grounded in integrity and accountability. Having a code of ethics is fundamental to our professional standing. If someone is upset with us, they have the avenue of filing a complaint with the ICF about an ethical problem. The ICF will do an investigation, and we'll get to have a conversation.

There have been times when something came up and I didn't know whether it was an ethical dilemma or not. I called the ICF ethics line and talked through my concerns with a person. One time, I literally made up an ethical dilemma where there actually was none. Another time it was, yeah, that might be a dilemma if I don't do X, Y, Z. These conversations helped, because I could bounce the idea around and develop a plan. These situations are not typically enjoyable, yet they are so important and, in my case, kept my actions aligned with my professional guidelines.

When you decide to become a professional coach, you're signing a pledge to a code of ethics. I did, and every professional coach I know who belongs to the ICF, the EMCC, or the BCC has done this as well. We are upholding the standards ourselves.

So, while coaching may still be like the Wild Wild West in some ways, you don't have to practice like it's a lawless profession. Instead, our code of ethics means this is a profession with standards, responsibilities, transparency, and integrity. You can choose to be the kind of coach people can trust. And this, my friends, is a very different thing from not having a Professional Code of Ethics. It's the striking difference between those who call themselves a professional coach and those who are professional coaches.

Answers to the Scenarios:

1. External engagement, supervisor requests a debrief

The Wild Wild West

Scenario: You're coaching within an organization through an external coaching company and you're four sessions in. The client has several organizational goals and one personal goal. The supervisor calls you to debrief on how the client is doing and what the goals are. What do you do?

Best: Explain you cannot share anything without the client's explicit consent.

Why: Honors confidentiality and protects trust. Client remains in control of information. Clear, professional boundaries.

2. Hidden relationship conflict

Scenario: You and the client have been working together a little over a year. You used to work in the same organization where the client now works. Client shares less-than-favorable details about their manager—someone you know and like. The client doesn't know you and the manager are friends. What do you do?

Worst: Acknowledge feelings without revealing the relationship.

Why: Hides a relevant conflict. If they find out later, you'll have a trust problem you can't walk back

3. Trauma content, scope concerns

Scenario: A client begins to share deeply traumatic family experiences, suggesting unresolved trauma. They insist on continuing coaching rather than therapy. You're concerned the issues may be beyond scope yet fear disrupting the trust.

Best: Acknowledge and explore how it relates to current goals.

Why: You honor what they shared and keep coaching aligned with agreed outcomes. You can then discuss scope and support, including referral options, without abruptly shutting them down.

CHAPTER TWENTY-ONE

Purposeful Play

Laughter is the shortest distance between two people.

— Victor Borge

I know we have discussed so many things that coaching might not sound as fun and playful as you might have wished. The competencies and the ethics can feel like rules. I don't see them that way, but I can see how some people might. I will go back to the idea that Mozart had to learn his scales, maybe when he was one year old, but still he had to learn his scales before he could create The Magic Flute. Every craft has a learning curve, be it writing, art, leadership, sports, or coaching. We have to learn to crawl, then walk, before we can skip, run, and hula-hoop.

That said, I think there are so many amazing ways we can have fun with the people we work with, and I want to share a few that I love.

Fast Method to an Open Creative Brain

Laughter is an imperative to living a happy life. In a 1999 study, psychologist Robert Provine found that adults actually laugh a lot more often than the old "four laughs a day" myth suggests, on average around eighteen times a day, though the range was huge. Some people had zero laughs, and some had almost ninety (Provine 1999). More recently, a 2014 study using daily diaries found that adults average 2–3 belly laughs a day, with bigger laughing fits showing up only every few days (Martin et al. 2014). And science tells us that laughter reduces cortisol and stimulates serotonin, dopamine, oxytocin, and endorphins, all chemicals that help us remember better, focus more clearly, and open up to creative problem solving (Dunbar et al. 2012; Berk et al. 1989).

Psychology researcher Barbara Fredrickson showed that positive emotions broaden attention and open up creative, flexible thinking, which she called the broaden-and-build theory. What she found was that joy sparks the urge to play; interest sparks the urge to explore; contentment sparks the urge to savor and integrate; and love sparks a recurring cycle of each of these urges within safe, close relationships. Experiencing positive emotions fosters more positivity and resilience over time, creating self-reinforcing cycles (Fredrickson 2001, 2004). And, while we don't fall in love in an intimate way with the people we work with, we do still find ourselves loving and caring for them. And we are working to create safe, close relationships. Coaching is a relational space. The love is platonic, but still, it represents the care and concern that we hold for another human being. It can expand us, and them.

So, when we say laughter, joy, and a positive mindset are linked to an "open brain," it's not just a metaphor; it's science. The risk is that as adults, we get out of the habit of laughing. Somewhere between four years old and forty, that wide-open playfulness and creativity narrow. And yet, those are precisely the capacities leaders, executives, and coaches need in order to navigate the wild changes of life and work.

Laughter Yoga

I discovered laughter yoga in the late 1990s. I was working with a lot of depressed and angry people, and I saw a show with Dr. Madan Kataria talking about laughter yoga. It looked sort of insane, so I had to know more. At that time, there was a 1-800 number you could call, and people were just laughing. It was infectious; I would call every day and laugh. I didn't have time to stay on for an hour, but I would get a ten-minute laughter fix. I also brought it into my anger management group with the Air Force. We would spend five minutes just laughing. And when you start, it might feel forced, but pretty quickly people can't stop laughing. It just feels good.

When I went into private practice, I was still working with angry, traumatized, and depressed people, so of course one of the things we would do in therapy was laugh. I even prescribed that 1-800 number to people, even if all they did was call and listen to people laugh. We would do it in my office together. They might think I was crazy to begin with, but then watching me laugh had them laughing too.

Dr. Sophie Scott, in an interview on the *This Is Your Brain Podcast*, shared that "emotions are meant to be emotionally contagious. That's the job of an emotion quite often, to make somebody else react emotionally to what you're doing. Laughter is behaviorally contagious. So, people will laugh even if they don't know why they're laughing." This is exactly what happened in my groups and with my thinkers.

One of the things I noticed through this practice was that laughter was actually exercise. You get the same movement in your diaphragm and your core with laughter as you do with sobbing. Only laughter feels better emotionally.

I don't do laughter yoga with clients or groups as often, but I still do it myself. Before I have a big presentation, or have to have a difficult conversation, or if I am feeling nervous about a live coaching demo, I will do a few minutes of laughter to move the chemicals in my body all around and bring my energy back into alignment with how I want to show up in the world. *I am deep belly laughs.* That is my personal motto.

Improv for Coaches

I have a couple of coach friends, Betsy Salkind and Amy Warshawsky, who were on my podcast. They recently published a book called *Coaching with a Twist,* about using improv in coaching. Coaching, how we set agreements, our presence, and partnership are all improvisational acts.

There are several "rules" that we have to follow in improv, starting with actively listening so that we can build on what's been offered. "Yes, and…" is fundamental; we have to take what is offered and play with it and build on it. Being spontaneous can be risky, so we have to let go of judgment and just play. And we have to be fully present in the moment; otherwise, we risk missing the moment (Salkind et al. 2025).

Think about it, we don't use scripts in life. We don't have a book of questions sitting next to us. I mean, do you have a script when

Sticky Outcomes!

you're talking to a friend? Do you carry with you a list of questions to ask your friends? Maybe for game night, but normally, we are quite capable of being interested in people and spontaneously creating conversations. So, you already have the skills to ask questions. In coaching, this improvisational collaboration between you and the thinker plays it forward, in the moment.

When Amy and Betsy visited as teaching guests in one of my courses, they shared the three-word coaching Improv game. Each coach and thinker go back and forth and have a coaching conversation using only three words or fewer.

Coach: What's important today?

Thinker: Want explore dreams.

Coach: Dreams about?

Thinker: Want write book.

Coach: What important book?

Thinker: My life legacy.

Coach: How know successful?

Thinker: Finish book.

Coach: What changes then?

Thinker: Feel accomplished, complete.

Coach: How know accomplished?

Thinker: Calm, confident, empowered.

Coach: That our direction?

Thinker: Yes, empowered.

Coach: Empowered, what notice?

The entire coaching conversation goes on like this, three words, back and forth. This isn't for everyday coaching, but as a learning exercise, it is a brilliant thing to practice. This exercise requires us to slow down, both the coach and the thinker, as sharing meaning in three words is hard. What my students said about the experience was that they had to be really present to both what was said and how to ask the essence of what was most important. That's a pretty important lesson to learn from this cool exercise.

LEGO® Serious Play®

I was introduced to LEGO® Serious Play® (LSP) through a good friend of mine, also a coach, Gideon Culman, MCC. We had been talking about fun ways to support insight and growth. I was waxing on about metaphors, and he started telling me about how amazing LSP was. The ICF DC Metro Chapter was holding a webinar, and Gideon said I had to attend. It happened to work out timing-wise, so I joined. It reminded me of doing Sand Play Therapy, without the sand and all the toys. I loved it. Then Gideon made me join the longer training, and it was awesome.

Basically, my experience is that LSP is a three-dimensional metaphor. LSP's methodology was developed in 1996 by Institute for Management Development professors Johan Roos and Bart Victor with LEGO Group owner Kjeld Kirk Kristiansen. They wanted an alternative to traditional strategic planning and found that using LEGO bricks to model ideas created more adaptive, participatory strategies.

In 2010, LEGO released LSP under an open-source model. The methodology is available freely for use and adaptation, as long as facilitators respect its guiding principles.

Core Principles

- Constructionism: People learn and think better when building physical models to represent their ideas. Seymour Papert framed learning as "hands-on, minds-on," and LSP is 100 percent that.

- Metaphor: LEGO models act as metaphors, allowing abstract concepts to become concrete and easier to discuss.

- Storytelling: Builders explain their artifacts to others, which deepens reflection and collective understanding.

- Everyone participates: The method ensures that all voices are heard, reducing dominance by louder participants.

My husband is not a guy who likes to talk about his feelings.

Sticky Outcomes!

When I went through the training, I had to do a coaching demonstration with someone, so I asked him if he would let me practice LSP coaching with him. His first words were, "You're not going to make me talk about myself, are you?"

"No, of course not, don't be silly," I said, "you're just going to play with LEGOs."

With serious reservations, he said, "Okay."

He had just started a new position in an industry he didn't know anything about and was a bit stressed. He was in his first ninety days in his role, and he decided that's what he wanted to do coaching around. I gave him his LEGO kit, and he had about ten minutes to build his challenge. Each kit comes with a little mini-me LEGO body, a bunch of blocks, and a flat building panel. So, he went to work building his challenge.

When he was ready, he had a pointer, and I asked him to tell me what he had created. He talked about some of the blockers. He had built a wall—he was on one side—and it was rich with meaning. New people, not understanding all the politics at play, unspoken expectations, unspoken rules, and the spoken rules: he had thirty days to get his high school diploma, thirty days to get his college degree, and thirty days to get his Ph.D. In the new industry he had joined. Behind the wall was everything that he couldn't yet see that he had to master. He talked for about thirty minutes straight, which blew my mind. After I asked a few questions and he finished really looking at his build, being curious about what he was looking at, and starting to play with some ideas, I asked him what might need to shift. Then he went off to work on it for another ten minutes.

When he came back, the artifact was completely different. He was transformed—he had wings on his feet, he was in a chariot, and he was aiming toward the future. Using his pointer, he spent another thirty minutes telling me about what had changed on the build and what was meaningful to him. And, somewhere in the conversation, his deep belief in Stoicism kicked in and the idea that the obstacle is the path lit up in his mind: if the way is blocked, take a different path. Instead of focusing on the wall, he realized all he needed to do was focus on the learning, and that wasn't a big deal.

Since this experience, I have used LSP for members of groups to get to know each other and in coaching with leaders who typically might not talk about the struggles. Something happens with the safety of the blocks. No one is scared of a LEGO—except if they are left out on the floor in the middle of the night and you step on one… then they suck.

Humor Gives Humans an Edge

Humor is one area where humans still have an edge over AI. Not because AI cannot produce something "funny," but because real humor isn't just the ability to say a sequence of words that make up a joke. It's about timing, relationship, and playing with what just showed up in the conversation; it's contextual.

In an interview with Prof. Jonathan Passmore on *the Coaching Studio* podcast, he shared that while AI might be able to coach at an ACC level, it's missing something very human: humor. He shared that AI can tell a joke on command, but it's usually a canned, dad-joke punchline.

For example: An AI walks into a bar.

The bartender asks, "What'll you have?"

The AI looks around the bar and says, "What everyone else is having." Ba-dump-bump.

Or, "I tried to start a professional development group for procrastinators. We're meeting next week, as soon as everyone's ready."

If you're lucky, that might get a polite laugh (more likely an eye roll); it's just not very funny, and either would be out of context in a shared conversation.

But human-to-human humor is different. In a coaching conversation, it is a nuanced exchange between two people, bringing themselves and their funny bones into the conversation. It is about context, timing, empathy, and the experience between two people. It comes from the conversation, and both people are in on what was funny, creating a "you had to be there" moment that becomes an inside joke. If someone else walked into the room, they might not even understand what we're laughing about. We laugh about it because (a) it was funny and (b) it's now something that we share.

One of my executive thinkers wanted more connection with his teenage son, and somehow in the conversation, he brought up the old movie Airplane! and the blow-up doll that was the co-pilot. For whatever reason, when he said this, we both started laughing, and it became a pivot point for him to really look for those funny "blow-up" moments with his son, where they could laugh and connect.

And it's not just what we say, it's when we say it. Timing is crucial for humor. Human beings are constantly making micro-judgments around humor. Is this the moment to bring levity or laugh at what was just said? Do we have enough trust that a playful comment is safe and connecting? Jonathan named that, too: humor can deepen the relationship, but it only works when it serves the thinker, not the coach's need to be clever (deHart 2026).

When we talk about what humans can do that AI can't, humor matters because it's one of the ways we co-regulate and build a "we-ness." Humor builds and deepens our relationships. AI can generate jokes. What it can't truly replicate is the lived, mutual, in-the-moment relational energy that makes humor funny and connecting, the way a person can.

Oh, the Places You'll Go!

Play has this sneaky way of teaching us the very skills we need for mastery without us noticing. When we laugh, when we build, when we improvise, our brains and bodies get the workout they need to become more flexible, more resilient, and more creative. This is the work of coaching, to open our minds so we can learn to explore with people. Play builds the muscle of curiosity, the capacity to sit with uncertainty, and the courage to explore what we don't yet know. Plus, it builds connections and deepens relationships.

So, if the competencies are the scales, playfulness is the music. It keeps us fresh, available, and willing to experiment. It reminds us that coaching is a human-to-human encounter, and we have the opportunity to do really useful and important work with people through many different lenses. I hope you choose the paths that light you up and light up those you work with.

CHAPTER TWENTY-TWO

Continuing Your Coach Development

> To be truly visionary we have to root our imagination in our concrete reality while simultaneously imagining possibilities beyond that reality.
>
> —bell hooks

As we come to the conclusion of this book, I want to start by saying thank you for reading all the way through, and I genuinely hope that this book has been of use to you on your journey toward becoming a professional coach, a coach leader, or reaching the next level of your coach development. I wanted to use this final chapter to really widen the lens on how we continue to grow and develop as professional coaches with an open, growth mindset.

Coaching doesn't end when you're done with your training. After you earn your credential, you enter the space of continual development for the rest of your life, which is a wonderful thing. I live by the motto "Every day is a school day!" This approach will keep your mind flexible and open.

There are three things that I did not specifically address in the prior chapters but that are fundamental to any working coach, and I will cover them here.

Cultural Fluency

Why do we need this? The ICF Code of Ethics has the four values we talked about in the last chapter, and one of these is equity. From a framework of being a professional coach with a code of ethics, we are already paying attention to the reality that the world is bigger than the one we personally live in. We are codifying the idea that we have respect for differences.

Cultural fluency is not just a platitude for being nice to everyone; it is essential for trust, safety, and effective coaching. It's the fluency in which we communicate through differences. We cannot separate people from their context, their identity, or the way they think and believe. All of these elements are tied together and interact with how people see themselves and how they move through the world. If we miss culture, if we miss identity, we are missing the human being in front of us.

For me, the question becomes: what is your capacity to be open to the multitude of different people and perspectives in the world? One of the things I feel blessed by is the work I did with the U.S. Air Force. There were people from every possible part of the country and many different parts of the world, with all sorts of belief systems and cultural identities. This gave me experience far greater than my own personal world. I won't say you need my exact perspective, but I do think these differences, and our capacity to be with people who are very different from us, is an enriching opportunity. It forces us, or invites us, into that place of not knowing, curiosity, and wonder. That's what I hope you take with you as you think about becoming fluent in navigating the many elements of cultural identity.

Cultural fluency means recognizing that every thinker arrives carrying far more than their surface challenge. As Peter Hawkins notes, no one comes into a conversation alone. Their unique individual identity, histories, families, communities, workplaces, belief systems, and the teams they work with all show up inside them (deHart 2026). In other words, identity is nested within many different systems. When we miss the systems moving through a person, we miss pieces of their humanity. Seeing people in this fuller, interconnected way strengthens trust and safety and helps us coach with a wider lens.

So, what does cultural fluency mean in our daily conversations? For me, it's the idea that every unique individual you meet is connected to more than one identity. Their sense of self may be tied to the area of the world they're from, or even more tied to the specific community inside that place. They may be tied to a religious or spiritual belief system. They may be tied to other things, such as diet: gluten-free, keto, vegetarian. Maybe they love to run or swim. Maybe they're dog people, cat people, horse people. The list of identities is far too long to list, so write down a list of every group you feel connected to, and start by looking at your own complex identity.

Continuing Your Coach Development

Supervision

One way we keep checking ourselves as coaches is through a practice called coaching supervision. Supervision isn't the same thing as mentor coaching. Mentor coaching is about your observable skills and getting feedback on your coaching against the ICF Core Competencies. Supervision is about something different: our relationship to the work that we're doing with the people we are working with.

Sometimes a thinker comes back session after session, circling the same issue, and you feel stuck. Maybe they say "no" to every idea you toss out to them. Sometimes you care so much about a thinker that you hold back from asking hard questions because you don't want to risk the relationship. Sometimes it's the opposite: you don't like them much at all, and you notice judgment creeping in—often negative judgment—about pretty much everything they say, think, and do. Supervision is where we get curious about those reactions. It's a mirror we hold up to ourselves so that we are actively blind spotting our over-attachments, judgments, frustrations, and our over-desire to provide value in the coaching space.

Peter Hawkins talks about supervision as systemic and multilayered. His Seven-Eyed Model invites us to look through "lenses," not just at the client, but at what is happening in the relationship between coach and client, what is going on inside the coach and the thinker, and the larger organizational or cultural system around the work and the people. Hawkins says his Seven-Eyed Model is often misinterpreted as "look through seven individual lenses," but that misses the real point: noticing the relational dance between coach–thinker, thinker–system, and coach–system (deHart 2026). All of us live within a multitude of circles and systems. As coaches we need to keep that front of mine.

This is a perfect moment to clarify why supervision matters beyond skill refinement. These lenses give supervision great value as we stretch to see the bigger picture that we are working in, not just the story we're telling ourselves.

I especially love group supervision. You bring in a case that's keeping you up at night, and suddenly you're in a circle of colleagues who get it. Someone else has been through something similar. Someone else has a fresh angle. Maybe the entire group is like, "Yep, I am in that too, and I am looking forward to seeing what comes

245

up." You realize you're not alone. Coaching can be isolating work, especially if you're in private practice.

Group supervision becomes a unique biofeedback system where we can bounce our perspectives off others, and new possibilities open up. It can be an amazingly creative way to work through coaching relationships and discover new ways to handle situations that might otherwise have us pulling our hair out.

At its heart, supervision is about three things: reflection, learning, and support. It gives us a place to lay down the pressure to be "perfect" and instead pick up curiosity. It helps prevent burnout. And it keeps us resourced so we can keep showing up with clarity, courage, and compassion for the people we coach.

Mentor Coaching

Mentor coaching is the way we formally look at our coaching practice and begin to develop a sharper understanding of how we're listening, what threads we're following, and what kinds of questions we're asking in response to what the thinker has offered us. It's a developmental, skill-building relationship. In mentor coaching, we'll often have a focus, maybe agreement setting, crafting concise questions, or listening beneath the surface to the deeper currents below the waterline.

One of the most powerful ways to do this is through transcript analysis. In fact, that's the only way I mentor coach. A transcript lets us slow down a conversation and see what's happening line by line. The coach can begin to notice which elements of the ICF Core Competencies are showing up in their questions and which are not. Plus, we have the opportunity to play with choice points. Yay.

Here's an example:

> Thinker: "There are a lot of reasons this matters to me. One is my history of overreacting in ways that can be hurtful and leave me feeling regretful afterward. Another is that I may be feeling something positive, something complimentary or kind, but for whatever reason, I don't always create the space to let what I'm feeling inside come out in the way I'd want it to.

Continuing Your Coach Development

"What I really want is to interact with people from a place where I have more control over what comes out, how it comes out, when it comes out, and to whom it comes out. As I've thought about this and worked on it, I can see progress. I'm not where I ultimately want to be yet, but I'm moving in that direction."

Now, let's look at how a coach might respond:

Coach 1: "I'm hearing that there's either overreaction at times, and then other times you don't share what's important, positive, or kind. And that you want to make progress. Am I understanding you?"

Coach 2: "Suppose you were to get to where you ultimately wanted to be, how would you be showing up?"

Both responses are fine, but in mentor coaching, we slow down and ask, What choice did the coach make here? Coach 1 reflects back and then asks a closed question. That may meet some competency indicators, but not many. The curiosity is focused mostly on getting the details right; there is no forwarding of the conversation. Coach 2, on the other hand, is asking about the dream, the future state, inviting the thinker to imagine what's possible. That kind of question demonstrates multiple competencies, especially Agreement Setting, Trust and Safety, Presence, Listening, and Evoking Awareness.

This is what we do in mentor coaching: we look at these "choice points." We ask, How is the coach partnering? Are the questions open? Are they evoking awareness or simply gathering information?

The ICF defines mentor coaching as "a collaborative learning process through which coaches receive feedback based on observed or recorded sessions to support them in further developing their unique coaching style and coaching skills in alignment with the ICF Core Competencies." Coach 2 is following this approach to a T.

Every Day Is a School Day

Coaching development and skill building don't end when you finish your training or even when you earn your credential. One of the gifts of being a coach is that we keep learning. Every new thinker, every new conversation, is part of that learning.

Cultural fluency tells us to keep growing in how we connect with people, asking us to stay open, flexible, and curious about perspectives and identities that are different from our own. Supervision asks us to keep growing in how we show up in our work, noticing our reactions and blind spots so we can hold a clean container for the people we coach. Mentor coaching asks us to keep growing in our craft, sharpening our ability to listen and ask questions that skew toward useful, thought-provoking, and partnered.

As you embark on or continue your coaching journey, there will be so many amazing opportunities for you to explore your areas of interest: Team Coaching, Somatic Coaching, LEGO Serious Play, Coaching with Metaphors, Leadership Coaching, and beyond. Each training you attend represents a piece of your lifelong learning. None of us arrive at a place where we are "done" as a coach; we get to a mile marker only to see the next one on the horizon. That's the beauty of it. We're invited to stay curious, our minds alive, as we stretch ourselves and continue to develop the way we listen and partner with every thinker we meet.

Welcome to the amazing world of coaching! May you go out and do good things and support people to become their best selves.

Thank you for choosing to be a part of making the world a better place.

Happy Coaching!

A BIG THANK YOU!

> A day without a friend is like a pot without
> a single drop of honey left inside.
>
> —A.A. Milne

No one writes a book alone. In fact, even the idea may come out of conversations and playing with ideas. I begin my thanks with Jake Mannino and Rob Brunhild for their enthusiastic support of turning the program design into a book. It wasn't where my head was when we first started building NEXGEN Executive Coaching Academy, but in hindsight, genius. Thank you for spurring me on.

I am thankful to Michael deHart, Michele Logan, Ken McKellar, Graham Segroves, Betsy Salkind, Loren Sanders, Richa Chadha, Amy Warshawsky, and many others. Thank you for being my initial readers. Your feedback, questions, and ideas helped me sharpen what I was trying to say and, just as importantly, notice what I was leaving unsaid. I'm grateful for your time, your candor, and your willingness to think alongside me while this book was still taking shape.

I have been fortunate to be in the company of incredible mentors, teachers, supervision partners, and peers, all of whom have sparked insights and supported me in my continuing developmental journey. Gideon Culman, Fran Fisher, Carly Anderson, Lisa Pachence, and Matthew Cintron-Quinones each hold a special spot in my heart.

I have also had the privilege of interviewing so many thought leaders and masterful coaches on *the Coaching Studio* podcast. Each of you has given me new insights and plenty to play with in my own thinking. Thank you for sharing yourselves so thoroughly.

Sticky Outcomes!

After the readers and the feedback comes the editing. I want to thank the Kirkus Editing team for your thoughtful support and skillful editing. Thank you for helping me notice duplication and grammar errors, and for helping me bring more clarity and precision to the structure, the language, and the overall reading experience. Your suggestions were received with appreciation.

And to all the thinkers I have had the privilege of working with, I owe you a deep debt of gratitude. Thank you for trusting me with your stories and for generously giving me permission to record our coaching sessions and allowing me to include those demonstrations to illustrate the ideas in these pages. I am amazed at how much I learn from you again and again. Your willingness to be seen in the learning process made this book far more useful than it could have been otherwise.

A Deep Bow to Each of You!

REFERENCES

Preface

deHart, Lyssa. Interview with Peter Hawkins. *The Coaching Studio Podcast*, January 5, 2026. Podcast.

Ritchie, Anne Thackeray. *Mrs. Dymond*. Smith, Elder, & Co., 1885.

Chapter 1

Cameron, Julia. The Artist's Way: A Spiritual Path to Higher Creativity. Tarcher/Putnam, 1992.

International Coaching Federation. ICF Core Competencies. International Coaching Federation, 2025. www.coachingfederation.org.

Proust, Marcel. *The Prisoner: In Search of Lost Time,* Volume 5. Penguin Classics Deluxe Edition. National Geographic Books, 2019.

Reynolds, Marcia. Coach the Person, Not the Problem: A Guide to Using Reflective Inquiry. Berrett-Koehler Publishers, 2020.

Whitmore, John. Coaching for Performance: growing People, Performance, and Purpose. Nicholas Brealey, 1992.

Chapter 2

Anderson, Carly. "Helicopter Coaching Views." 2019. https://carly-anderson.com/helicopter-coaching-views.

Fisher, Fran. "13 Quick Tips to Go Deeper with Your Coaching!" 2021. https://www.thecoachingtoolscompany.com/13-quick-tips-to-deepen-your-coaching-fran-fisher-mcc.

Greene, Robert. *Mastery.* National Geographic Books, 2012.

International Coaching Federation. *ICF Core Competencies*. International Coaching Federation, 2025. https://www.coachingfederation.org.

Chapter 3

Whitmore, Sir John. *Coaching for Performance: The Principles and Practice of Coaching and Leadership*. Medical Entomology and Zoology, 2017.

Chapter 4

Dewey, John. *How We Think*. D.C. Heath & Co. 1910.

Doidge, Norman. *The Brain That Changes Itself: Stories of Personal Triumph from the Frontiers of Brain Science*. Viking, 2007.

Schacter, Daniel L. *The Seven Sins of Memory: How the Mind Forgets and Remembers*. Houghton Mifflin, 2001.

Chapter 5

Berne, Eric. *Games People Play: The Basic Handbook of Transactional Analysis*. Tantor ebooks, 2011. Originally published 1964.

Brown, Paul, Kitty Chisholm, and Tara Swart. *Neuroscience for Leadership: Harnessing the Brain Gain Advantage*. Springer, 2015.

deHart, Lyssa. Interview with Richard E. Boyatzis. *The Coaching Studio Podcast*, August 29, 2024. Podcast.

Dictionary.com. "Meanings & Definitions of English Words." *Dictionary.com*. 2025. https://dictionary.com.

Fredrickson, Barbara L. "The Broaden-and-Build Theory of Positive Emotions." Philosophical Transactions of the Royal Society B: Biological Sciences 359, no. 1449 (2004): 1367–78. https://doi.org/10.1098/rstb.2004.1512.

Kline, Nancy. *Time to Think: Listening to Ignite the Human Mind*. Cassell Illustrated, 2021. Originally published 1999.

Kauffman, Carol, and Katherine Tulpa. "Interview with Nancy Kline. An Act of Creation: Coaching in a Thinking Environment?" *Coaching: An International Journal of Theory, Research and Practice* 3, no. 2 (2010): 99–108. https://doi.org/10.1080/17521882.2010.502665.

Rogers, Carl R. *Client-Centered Therapy: Its Current Practice, Implications and Theory*. 2000. Originally published 1951.

Chapter 6

Adler, Alfred. *The Practice and Theory of Individual Psychology*.

References

Harcourt Brace, 1927.

Bachkirova, Tatiana, and Simon Borrington. "The Limits and Possibilities of a Person-Centered Approach in Coaching Through the Lens of Adult Development Theories." *Philosophy of Coaching: An International Journal* 3, no. 1 (2018): 6–22. https://doi.org/10.22316/poc/03.1.02.

Beck, Aaron T. *Cognitive Therapy and the Emotional Disorders*. International Universities Press, 1976.

Deci, Edward L., and Richard M. Ryan. *Self-Determination and Intrinsic Motivation in Human Behavior*. Plenum, 1985.

Development Dimensions International. "DDI Data Reveals Delegation Is Top Factor in Preventing Burnout." 2025. https://www.ddi.com/about/media/burnout.

Ellis, Albert. *Reason and Emotion in Psychotherapy*. Lyle Stuart, 1962.

International Coaching Federation. *ICF Core Competencies*. International Coaching Federation, 2025. https://www.coachingfederation.org.

Miller, William R., and Stephen Rollnick. *Motivational Interviewing: Helping People Change*. Guilford Press, 2013. Originally published 1991.

MIT Sloan Management Review. "Why Delegation Is a Strength, Not a Weakness." *MIT Sloan Management Review*, 2024.

Oviawe, Edosa Gaxkin. "Delegation: Benefits, Limitations & Why Managers Find It Difficult to Delegate." 2015.

Rogers, Carl R. *Client-Centered Therapy: Its Current Practice, Implications and Theory*. Houghton Mifflin, 1951.

Rotter, Julian B. "Generalized Expectancies for Internal versus External Control of Reinforcement." *Psychological Monographs* 80, no. 1 (1966): 1–28.

Socrates. Quoted in Plato. *Apology*. In *Plato: Complete Works*, edited by John M. Cooper, 17–36. Hackett, 1997.

Chapter 7

International Coaching Federation. *ICF Core Competencies*. International Coaching Federation, 2025. https://www.coachingfederation.org.

Rogers, Carl R. *A Way of Being*. Houghton Mifflin, 1980.

Siegel, Daniel J. *The Developing Mind: How Relationships and the Brain Interact to Shape Who We Are*. Guilford Press, 1999.

Siegel, Daniel J. *The Mindful Therapist: A Clinician's Guide to Mindsight and Neural Integration*. W. W. Norton, 2010.

Chapter 8

Bachkirova, Tatiana, Carmel Murphy, and Catherine Lawton Smith. "Cognitive-Developmental Approaches to Coaching." In *The SAGE Handbook of Coaching*, edited by Tatiana Bachkirova, Gordon Spence, and David Drake, 275–93. SAGE Publications, 2020.

Bachkirova, Tatiana. *Developmental Coaching: Working with the Self*. McGraw-Hill Education, 2011.

deHart, Lyssa. Interview with Jille Bartolome. *The Coaching Studio Podcast*, October 30, 2025. Podcast.

deHart, Lyssa. Interview with Richard E. Boyatzis. *The Coaching Studio Podcast*, August 29, 2024. Podcast.

Cook-Greuter, Susanne R. *Ego Development: Nine Levels of Increasing Embrace*. Cook-Greuter & Associates, 2005.

Jackson, Peter, and Tatiana Bachkirova. "Do We Really Know What We're Trying to Achieve? An Investigation into the Real Content of Coaching Conversations." *International Journal of Organizational Theory and Behavior* (2025). https://doi.org/10.1108/IJOTB-03-2025-0073.

Kegan, Robert. *The Evolving Self: Problem and Process in Human Development*. Harvard University Press, 1982.

Kegan, Robert. *In Over Our Heads: The Mental Demands of Modern Life*. Harvard University Press, 1994.

References

Loevinger, Jane. *Ego Development: Conceptions and Theories.* Jossey-Bass, 1976.

Ware, Bronnie. *The Top Five Regrets of the Dying: A Life Transformed by the Dearly Departing.* Hay House, 2012.

Chapter 9

Graham, Martha. "I Am a Dancer." In *The Routledge Dance Studies Reader*, edited by Alexandra Carter. Routledge, 1998.

International Coaching Federation. *ICF Core Competencies.* International Coaching Federation, 2025. https://www.coachingfederation.org.

International Coaching Federation. *PCC Markers.* International Coaching Federation, 2020. https://www.coachingfederation.org.

Chapter 10

Boyatzis, Richard E., Kylie Rochford, and Anthony I. Jack. "Anticipating Intentional Change: A Holistic Perspective on Coaching and Training." *Journal of Management Development* 33, no. 2 (2014): 94–100. https://doi.org/10.1108/JMD-05-2013-0064.

Boyatzis, Richard E., and Anthony I. Jack. "The Neuroscience of Coaching." In *Coaching Psychology: An International Perspective*, edited by Siobhain O'Broin and Stephen Palmer, 31–48. Routledge, 2018.

Covey, Stephen R. *The 7 Habits of Highly Effective People.* Free Press, 1989.

deHart, Lyssa. Interview with Haesun Moon. *The Coaching Studio Podcast*, January 22, 2026. Podcast.

Felleman, Daniel J., and David C. Van Essen. "Distributed Hierarchical Processing in the Primate Cerebral Cortex." *Cerebral Cortex* 1, no. 1 (1991): 1–47. https://doi.org/10.1093/cercor/1.1.1.

Gerwing, Jennifer, Janet Beavin Bavelas, and Sarah Healing. "Listener Responses as Coordinated Action in Dialogue." *Journal of Pragmatics* 43, no. 9 (2011): 2303–2314.

Grady, Cheryl L., Lynn Hasher, and Elaine T. Rybash. "Aging and Memory for Self-Generated Associations." *Psychology and Aging* 8, no. 4 (1998): 481–88. https://doi.org/10.1037/0882-7974.8.4.481.

International Coaching Federation. *ICF Core Competencies*. International Coaching Federation, 2025. https://www.coachingfederation.org.

International Coaching Federation. *PCC Markers*. International Coaching Federation, 2020. https://www.coachingfederation.org.

Schultz, Wolfram. "Dopamine Neurons and Their Role in Reward Mechanisms." *Current Opinion in Neurobiology* 7, no. 2 (1997): 191–97. https://doi.org/10.1016/S0959-4388(97)80007-4.

Wokke, Martijn E., Yamil Vidal, Lisa Genzel, and Floris P. De Lange. "Memory-Based Predictions Prime the Visual System." *Current Biology* 35, no. 2 (2025): 123–34. https://doi.org/10.1016/j.cub.2024.12.012.

Zhou, Ming, Rui Wang, and Huan Luo. "Semantic Priming in Human Cortex: Evidence from MEG." *Cerebral Cortex* 35, no. 4 (2025): 777–90. https://doi.org/10.1093/cercor/bhae012.

Chapter 11

Disraeli, Benjamin. *Lothair*. D. Appleton, 1881.

Fisher, Fran. *The Art of Coaching: A Handbook of Tips and Tools*. Createspace Independent Publishing, 2012.

Karpman, Stephen B. *A Game Free Life: The Definitive Book on the Drama Triangle and the Compassion Triangle by the Originator and Author*. 2014.

Moon, Haesun. *Efficacy of Training in Solution-Focused Coaching: Process Study of Learners' Progress in Response Choices*. Phd diss., University of Toronto, 2022.

Russell, Bertrand. "Nobel Prize Acceptance Speech." *Nobelprize.org*. 1950. https://www.nobelprize.org/prizes/literature/1950/russell/lecture.

Schmidbauer, Wolfgang. *The Helping Syndrome: When Being Good Is*

References

Not Enough. Continuum, 1977.

Chapter 12

Brown, Paul, Kitty Chisholm, and Tara Swart. *Neuroscience for Leadership: Harnessing the Brain Gain Advantage*. Springer, 2015.

Boyatzis, Richard E. *The Science of Change: Discovering Sustained, Desired Change from Individuals to Organizations and Communities*. Oxford University Press, 2024.

Boyatzis, Richard E., and Anthony I. Jack. "The Neuroscience of Coaching." *Consulting Psychology Journal: Practice and Research* 70, no. 1 (2018): 11–27.

Deci, Edward L., and Richard M. Ryan. *Intrinsic Motivation and Self-Determination in Human Behavior*. Plenum, 1985.

Dictionary.com. "Meanings & Definitions of English Words." 2025. https://dictionary.com.

Doidge, Norman. *The Brain That Changes Itself: Stories of Personal Triumph from the Frontiers of Brain Science*. Viking, 2007.

Gupta, Shweta, Erik de Haan, Christiane Behrendt, and Paul Bertschi-Michel. "The Value of the Coaching Relationship." *Frontiers in Psychology* 12 (2021): 687137. https://doi.org/10.3389/fpsyg.2021.687137.

Miller, William R., and Stephen Rollnick. *Motivational Interviewing: Helping People Change*. 3rd ed. Guilford Press, 2013.

Norman, Clare. Remarks to MCC Incubator cohort, April 16, 2025.

Passmore, Jonathan, Claudia Day, and Qing Wang. 2023. "Hands Up for Homework: Exploring Inter-Sessional Activities in Coaching." *Journal of Work Applied Management*. https://doi.org/10.1108/JWAM-04-2023-0026.

Rogers, Carl R. *On Becoming a Person: A Therapist's View of Psychotherapy*. Houghton Mifflin, 1961.

Ryan, Richard M., and Edward L. Deci. *Self-Determination Theory: Basic Psychological Needs in Motivation, Development, and Wellness*.

Sticky Outcomes!

Guilford Press, 2000.

Chapter 13

Bradshaw, John. *Healing the Shame That Binds You*. Health Communications, 1988.

Boyatzis, Richard E., and Anthony Jack. "The Neuroscience of Coaching." In *HBR Guide to Coaching Employees*. Harvard Business Review Press, 2018.

Brown, Brené. *Daring Greatly: How the Courage to Be Vulnerable Transforms the Way We Live, Love, Parent, and Lead*. Gotham Books, 2012.

Drake, David B. *Narrative Coaching: The Definitive Guide to Bringing New Stories to Life*. CNC Press, 2018.

Edmondson, Amy C. *The Fearless Organization: Creating Psychological Safety in the Workplace for Learning, Innovation, and Growth*. Wiley & Sons, 2018.

International Coaching Federation. *ICF Core Competencies*. International Coaching Federation, 2025. https://www.coachingfederation.org.

International Coaching Federation. *PCC Markers*. International Coaching Federation, 2020. https://www.coachingfederation.org.

deHart, Lyssa. Interview with Carol Kauffman. *The Coaching Studio Podcast*, September 4, 2025. Podcast.

Marcos, Daniel. "Steve Ballmer or Satya Nadella? Leadership Lessons Every Entrepreneur Can Learn From Microsoft." *Entrepreneur*, January 17, 2025. https://www.entrepreneur.com/leadership/leadership-lessons-every-entrepreneur-can-learn-from/484649.

Miller, William R., and Stephen Rollnick. *Motivational Interviewing: Helping People Change*. 3rd ed. Guilford Press, 2013.

Peck, M. Scott. The Road Less Traveled: A New Psychology of Love, Traditional Values and Spiritual Growth. Simon & Schuster, 1978.

Van der Kolk, Bessel. *The Body Keeps the Score: Brain, Mind, and

Body in the Healing of Trauma. Penguin, 2014.

Chapter 14

American Psychological Association. *Multitasking: Switching Costs*. American Psychological Association, 2006.

Bachkirova, Tatiana, and Simon Borrington. "The Limits and Possibilities of a Person-Centered Approach in Coaching Through the Lens of Adult Development Theories." *Philosophy of Coaching: An International Journal* 3, no. 1 (2018): 6–22.

Covey, Stephen R. *The 7 Habits of Highly Effective People*. Free Press, 1989.

International Coaching Federation. *ICF Core Competencies*. International Coaching Federation, 2025. https://www.coachingfederation.org.

Levitin, Daniel J. *The Organized Mind: Thinking Straight in the Age of Information Overload*. Dutton, 2014.

Rogers, Carl. *Client-Centered Therapy*. Houghton Mifflin, 1951.

Silsbee, Doug. *Presence-Based Coaching: Cultivating Self-Generative Leaders Through Mind, Body, and Heart*. Jossey-Bass, 2008.

Weil, Simone. Gravity and Grace. G. P. Putnam's Sons, 1952.

Chapter 15

Bartlett, Stephen. Interview by Jimmy Fallon. *The Tonight Show Starring Jimmy Fallon*, September 2025.

Felleman, Daniel J., and David C. Van Essen. "Distributed Hierarchical Processing in the Primate Cerebral Cortex." *Cerebral Cortex* 1, no. 1 (1991): 1–47.

Friston, K. "The Free Energy Principle: A Unified Brain Theory?" *Nature Reviews Neuroscience* 11, no. 2 (2010): 127–38.

Ford, Carin T. *Helen Keller: Lighting the Way for the Blind and Deaf*. Enslow Publishing, 2001.

Friston, K. "Does Predictive Coding Have a Future?" *Nature Neuro-*

science 21, no. 8 (2018): 1019–21.

Gibson, Edward. "The Interaction of Top-Down and Bottom-Up Processes in Sentence Comprehension." *Journal of Memory and Language* 54, no. 4 (2006): 595–623. https://doi.org/10.1016/j.jml.2005.12.002.

Grady, Cheryl L., et al. "Age-Related Changes in Cortical Blood Flow Activation During Visual Processing of Faces and Location." *Journal of Neuroscience* 18, no. 2 (1998): 581–95.

Kahneman, Daniel. *Thinking, Fast and Slow*. Farrar, Straus and Giroux, 2011.

Levinson, Stephen C., and Francisco Torreira. "Timing in Turn-Taking and Its Implications for Processing Models of Language." *Philosophical Transactions of the Royal Society B: Biological Sciences* 370, no. 1661 (2015): 20140170. https://doi.org/10.1098/rstb.2014.0170.

Schacter, Daniel L. *The Seven Sins of Memory: How the Mind Forgets and Remembers*. Houghton Mifflin, 2001.

van Nieuwerburgh, Christian, and Robert Biswas-Diener. *Radical Listening*. Berrett-Koehler, 2025.

Yon, Daniel. *A Trick of the Mind: How the Brain Invents Your Reality*. Cornerstone, 2025.

Chapter 16

Barrett, Lisa Feldman. *How Emotions Are Made: The Secret Life of the Brain*. Houghton Mifflin Harcourt, 2017.

Brown, Sherrie, and Douglas Brown. *Neuropsychology for Coaches: Understanding the Basics*. Mcgraw-Hill Education, 2012.

Covey, Stephen R. *The 7 Habits of Highly Effective People: Powerful Lessons in Personal Change*. Free Press, 1989.

Damasio, Antonio. *Descartes' Error: Emotion, Reason, and the Human Brain*. G. P. Putnam's Sons, 1994.

Doidge, Norman. *The Brain That Changes Itself: Stories of Personal

References

Triumph from the Frontiers of Brain Science. Viking, 2007.

Einstein, Albert. Attributed quotation; original source not identified.

Frankl, Viktor E. *Man's Search for Meaning.* Beacon Press, 2006. Originally published 1946.

Gershon, Michael D. *The Second Brain: A Groundbreaking New Understanding of Nervous Disorders of the Stomach and Intestine.* Harpercollins, 1998.

Hebb, D. O. *The Organization of Behavior: A Neuropsychological Theory.* Wiley, 1949.

International Coaching Federation. *ICF Core Competencies.* International Coaching Federation, 2025. https://www.coachingfederation.org.

Porges, Stephen W. *The Polyvagal Theory: Neurophysiological Foundations of Emotions, Attachment, Communication, and Self-Regulation.* W. W. Norton, 2011.

Soosalu, Grant, and Marvin Oka. *Mbraining: Using Your Multiple Brains to Do Cool Stuff.* Neuropower Press, 2012.

Chapter 17

Boyatzis, Richard E., Melvin L. Smith, and Ellen Van Oosten. *Helping People Change: Coaching with Compassion for Lifelong Learning and Growth.* Harvard Business Press, 2019.

Cowan, Nelson. "The Magical Mystery Four: How Is Working Memory Capacity Limited, and Why?" *Current Directions in Psychological Science* 19, no. 1 (2010): 51–57. https://doi.org/10.1177/0963721409359277.

International Coaching Federation. *2025 ICF Core Competencies.* International Coaching Federation, 2025. www.coachingfederation.org.

Kline, Nancy. *Time to Think: Listening to Ignite the Human Mind.* 2nd ed. Cassell Illustrated, 1999.

Oz, Amos. *A Tale of Love and Darkness.* Mariner Books, 2004.

Sweller, John. "Cognitive Load During Problem Solving: Effects on Learning." *Cognitive Science* 12, no. 2 (1988): 257–85. https://doi.org/10.1207/s15516709cog1202_4.

Tomasello, Michael. *Why We Cooperate*. MIT Press, 2009.

Wiliam, Dylan. *Embedded Formative Assessment*. Solution Tree Press, 2011.

Chapter 18

Barrett, Lisa Feldman. *How Emotions Are Made: The Secret Life of the Brain*. Houghton Mifflin Harcourt, 2017.

Bhatia, R., S. Jain, and A. Gupta. "Emotional Intelligence as a Mediator Between Organizational Politics and Employee Outcomes." *International Journal of Organizational Psychology* 13, no. 2 (2025): 182820.

Boyatzis, Richard E., Daniel Goleman, and Hay Group. *Clustering Competence in Emotional Intelligence: Insights from the Emotional Competence Inventory (ECI)*. Hay/McBer Group, 2000.

Feltman, Rachel. "Unpacking the Brain's Role in Inventing Your Perception," featuring Daniel Yon. *Science Quickly*, Scientific American, September 12, 2025. Podcast.

Gallese, Vittorio, Luciano Fadiga, Leonardo Fogassi, and Giacomo Rizzolatti. "Action Recognition in the Premotor Cortex." *Brain* 119, no. 2 (1996): 593–609. https://doi.org/10.1093/brain/119.2.593.

Goleman, Daniel. *Emotional Intelligence: Why It Can Matter More than IQ*. Bantam, 1995.

Goleman, Daniel. *Working with Emotional Intelligence*. Bantam, 1998.

Goleman, Daniel, Richard Boyatzis, and Annie McKee. *Primal Leadership: Unleashing the Power of Emotional Intelligence*. 10th anniversary ed. Harvard Business Review Press, 2013.

Hudson, Nathan W., R. Chris Fraley, Claudia C. Brumbaugh, and Amanda M. Vicary. "Coregulation in Romantic Partners' Attachment Styles: A Longitudinal Investigation." *Personality and Social Psychology Bulletin* 40, no. 7 (2014): 845–57. https://doi.

References

org/10.1177/0146167214528989.

Iacoboni, Marco, Roger P. Woods, Mirella Brass, Harold Bekkering, John C. Mazziotta, and Giacomo Rizzolatti. "Cortical Mechanisms of Human Imitation." *Science* 286, no. 5449 (1999): 2526–28. https://doi.org/10.1126/science.286.5449.2526.

International Coaching Federation. *ICF Code of Ethics*. International Coaching Federation, 2025. https://www.coachingfederation.org.

Jordan, Peter J., and Ashlea C. Troth. "Emotional Intelligence and Conflict Resolution: Implications for Human Resource Development." *Advances in Developing Human Resources* 4, no. 1 (2002): 62–79.

Mayer, John D., and Peter Salovey. "Emotional Intelligence." *Imagination, Cognition and Personality* 9, no. 3 (1990): 185–211.

Mclain, Cody. "Hallucinating Reality: Brain's Greatest Trick with Dr. Yon." *Unlock Your Full Potential | Mindhack Podcast*, Mindhack, August 18, 2025. Podcast.

Porges, Stephen W. *The Polyvagal Theory: Neurophysiological Foundations of Emotions, Attachment, Communication, and Self-Regulation*. W. W. Norton, 2011.

Porges, Stephen W. *The Pocket Guide to the Polyvagal Theory: The Transformative Power of Feeling Safe*. National Geographic Books, 2017.

Rizzolatti, Giacomo, Luciano Fadiga, Vittorio Gallese, and Leonardo Fogassi. "Premotor Cortex and the Recognition of Motor Actions." *Cognitive Brain Research* 3, no. 2 (1996): 131–41. https://doi.org/10.1016/0926-6410(95)00038-0.

Rizzolatti, Giacomo, and Laila Craighero. "The Mirror-Neuron System." *Annual Review of Neuroscience* 27, no. 1 (2004): 169–92. https://doi.org/10.1146/annurev.neuro.27.070203.144230.

Saxbe, Darby, and Rena Repetti. "For Better or Worse? Coregulation of Couples' Cortisol Levels and Mood States." *Journal of Personality and Social Psychology* 98, no. 1 (2010): 92–103. https://doi.org/10.1037/a0016959.

Chapter 19

Aristotle. *The Rhetoric.* Translated by W. Rhys Roberts. Cambridge University Press, 2014.

Cardillo, Eileen R., Christine E. Watson, Gwenda L. Schmidt, Alexander Kranjec, and Anjan Chatterjee. "From Novel to Familiar: Tuning the Brain for Metaphors." *Neuroimage* 59, no. 4 (2012): 3212–21. https://doi.org/10.1016/j.neuroimage.2011.11.079.

deHart, Lyssa. *Light Up: The Science of Coaching with Metaphors.* Barn Swallow Publishing, 2025.

Flower, Laura J., and Liina Pylkkänen. "The Time Course of Prediction and Integration in Language: Evidence from Magnetoencephalography." *Journal of Neurolinguistics* 80 (2024): 101252. https://doi.org/10.1016/j.jneuroling.2024.101252.

Gibson, Edward. "The Interaction of Top-Down and Bottom-Up Processes in Sentence Comprehension." *Journal of Memory and Language* 54, no. 4 (2006): 595–623. https://doi.org/10.1016/j.jml.2005.12.002.

Lakoff, George, and Mark Johnson. *Metaphors We Live By.* University of Chicago Press, 1980.

Lai, Vicky Tzuyin, Tim Curran, and Lise Menn. "Comprehending Conventional and Novel Metaphors: An ERP Study." *Brain Research* 1284 (2009): 145–55. https://doi.org/10.1016/j.brainres.2009.05.088.

Matar, Samira, Joumana Dirani, Alec Marantz, and Liina Pylkkänen. "Left Posterior Temporal Cortex Is Sensitive to Syntax within Conceptually Matched Arabic Expressions." *Scientific Reports* 11, no. 1 (2021): 1–14. https://doi.org/10.1038/s41598-021-84459-0.

Mathieson, Fiona, Gary Gow, and Mick Cooper. "Metaphor Co-Construction in Therapy: Metaphor Use Brings New Meanings." *Counselling and Psychotherapy Research* 19, no. 2 (2019): 137–47. https://doi.org/10.1002/capr.12185.

Reddy, Michael J. "The Conduit Metaphor: A Case of Frame Conflict in Our Language about Language." In *Metaphor and Thought*, edited by Andrew Ortony, 284–324. Cambridge University Press, 1979.

Yon, Daniel. *A Trick of the Mind: How the Brain Invents Your Reality.*

References

Cornerstone, 2025.

Chapter 20

Brown, H. Jackson, Jr. *Life's Little Instruction Book: A Few More Suggestions, Observations, and Reminders on How to Live a Happy and Rewarding Life*. Thomas Nelson, 2000.

International Coaching Federation. *ICF Code of Ethics*. International Coaching Federation, 2025. https://www.coachingfederation.org.

Chapter 21

Borge, Victor. Attributed quotation; original source not identified.

deHart, Lyssa, host. "Interview with Jonathan Passmore." *The Coaching Studio Podcast*, February 5, 2026. Podcast.

Fredrickson, Barbara L. "The Role of Positive Emotions in Positive Psychology: The Broaden-and-Build Theory of Positive Emotions." *American Psychologist* 56, no. 3 (2001): 218–26. https://doi.org/10.1037/0003-066X.56.3.218.

Fredrickson, Barbara L. "The Broaden-and-Build Theory of Positive Emotions." *Philosophical Transactions of the Royal Society B: Biological Sciences* 359, no. 1449 (2004): 1367–78. https://doi.org/10.1098/rstb.2004.1512.

The LEGO Group. "The LEGO Group." N.d. https://www.lego.com/en-us/themes/serious-play/background.

Martin, R. A., and N. A. Kuiper. "Daily Occurrence of Laughter: Relationships with Age, Gender, and Type A Personality." *Humor* 27, no. 2 (2014): 263–83. https://doi.org/10.1515/humor-2014-0017.

Papert, Seymour. *The Children's Machine: Rethinking School in the Age of the Computer*. Basic Books, 1993.

"Taking Laughter Seriously, with Dr. Sophie Scott." *This Is Your Brain*, July 28, 2023. https://thisisyourbrain.com/2023/07/taking-laughter-seriously-with-dr-sophie-scott/.

Provine, Robert R. "Laughter." *American Scientist* 87, no. 1 (1999): 38–45. https://doi.org/10.1511/1999.1.38.

Salkind, Betsy, and Amy J. Warshawsky. *Coaching With a Twist:*

Improv for Coaches. 2025.

Chapter 22

International Coaching Federation. *ICF Mentor Coaching Competency Model.* International Coaching Federation, 2025. https://www.coachingfederation.org.

Bachkirova, Tatiana, Peter Jackson, and David Clutterbuck. *Coaching and Mentoring Supervision: Theory and Practice.* 2nd ed. McGraw-Hill Education, 2021.

deHart, Lyssa, host. Interview with Peter Hawkins. *The Coaching Studio Podcast*, January 8, 2026. Podcast.

Hawkins, Peter, and Robin Shohet. *Supervision in the Helping Professions.* McGraw-Hill Education, 2012.

hooks, bell. *Feminism Is for Everybody: Passionate Politics.* Pluto Press, 2000.

Thank You

Milne, A. A. *The Complete Tales of Winnie-The-Pooh.* National Geographic Books, 1996.

About Lyssa

Hello, I'm Lyssa deHart. I spent twenty years as a clinical social worker specializing in relationship therapy, complex trauma, PTSD, and dissociative disorders. After closing my private practice in New Mexico and relocating to the Pacific Northwest in 2013, I fully embraced coaching.

I achieved my MCC certification in 2018 and have been dedicated to this path ever since. I am the host of *the Coaching Studio* podcast and am a leadership and confidence coach, certified mentor coach, coaching supervision partner, ICF PCC assessor, and a well-regarded coaching educator.

I authored *StoryJacking: Change Your Dialogue, Transform Your Life, the Reflective Coach,* and *Light Up: The Science of Coaching with Metaphors*. My latest work, *Sticky Outcomes: at the Intersection of Coaching, Neuroscience, and Lasting Change,* reflects my deep commitment to enhancing coaching practices, emphasizing partnership, thinker agency, and the mastery of coaching skills.

With a solid understanding of ICF core competencies and neuroscience, I am passionate about empowering coaches and therapists to improve their listening and partnering abilities, enhance their presence, and create nurturing environments for client growth. My global practice serves clients across continents and numerous countries. I focus on helping professional coaches and therapists make a significant impact, infusing their work with ease and a sense of fun.

My personal experience with dyslexia led me to create an exam preparatory program, **The Credentialing Lab**, for both the ACC exam and the PCC/MCC exam. The program supports coaches in internalizing the ICF competencies and Code of Ethics, thereby enhancing their chances of success on the credentialing exam.

I offer courses on **Coaching with the Power of Metaphors, Group Mentor Coaching, the Credentialing Lab,** and **the MCC Incubator** a **Level 3 program.**

This book was born from the creation of **NEXGEN Executive Coaching Academy,** a coaching school designed to develop the next generation of coaches. This program is accredited by the International Coaching Federation for **Levels 1 and 2.**

Thank you for exploring this book. I hope it provides valuable insights for your work. I have a request: Your feedback is incredibly important; please consider sharing your thoughts with a review on Amazon.com or GoodReads. Your support is greatly appreciated. **Follow the QR code to leave a review :)**

Let's connect:

Website: LyssadeHart.com & NEXGENcoaches.com
YouTube: @LyssadeHart
LinkedIn: https://www.linkedin.com/in/lyssadehart

Final Notes

What has been most useful and/or valuable to you as you have gone through this book?

Before you put this book away, what are a couple of coaching skills you want to play with in your coaching? Write them down and create an intention for yourself.

_____
_____
_____
_____
_____
_____
_____
_____
_____
_____
_____
_____
_____
_____
_____

Bravo and Happy Coaching!

www.ingramcontent.com/pod-product-compliance
Lightning Source LLC
LaVergne TN
LVHW012034070526
838202LV00056B/5500